ANUBIS SOLUTIONS INC.
1420 Harbor Bay Pkway
Suite 195
Alameda, CA 94502
Tel. (510) 749-8800
http://www.anubisinc.com

REVISED EDITION

THE HANDBOOK OF 401(k) PLAN MANAGEMENT

REVISED EDITION

THE HANDBOOK OF 401(k) PLAN MANAGEMENT

TOWERS PERRIN

IRWIN
Professional Publishing®
Chicago • London • Singapore

Library of Congress Cataloging-in-Publication Data

The handbook of 401(k) plan management / Towers Perrin, editor. —
Rev. ed.
   p. cm.
Includes bibliographical references and index.
ISBN 0-7863-1117-7
   1. 401(k) plans—Management. 2. Compensation management—United
States. 3. Employee fringe benefits—United States—Management.
4. Employee stock options—United States—Management. 5. Employee
fringe benefits—Taxation—United States. I. Towers Perrin.
HF5549.5.C67H35 1997
658.3'25—dc20   96–36233

Printed in the United States of America
1 2 3 4 5 6 7 8 9 0 DO 3 2 1 0 9 8 7 6

PREFACE

During the last 20 years, Section 401(k) plans have become a major factor in employee benefit planning. By any measure—number of plans, number of employees covered, or asset accumulations—the growth of these plans since the early 1980s has been remarkable.

Most employers established their 401(k) plans without specific objectives and employee needs in mind, viewing them simply as a source of additional funds for general benefit purposes. More and more plan sponsors are beginning to recognize the growing value of these plans and the role they can play in meeting specific employee needs—providing for postretirement inflation or long-term care protection, for example. Whatever purpose they serve, it is clear that 401(k) plans have become quite important to both employers and employees.

As a result, it is equally important that benefit professionals understand the complex tax and legal environment in which 401(k) plans operate, and how these plans can be designed and administered to operate as efficiently as possible in this environment. This book is intended to aid practitioners in gaining that understanding. The neophyte will find a comprehensive treatment of all aspects of 401(k) plans—design, the general tax and legal requirements that apply to these plans, and administrative and investment considerations. There is also much for the experienced practitioner, including in-depth, annotated coverage of the tax law and regulations.

Part One of the text includes introductory and background material on such matters as the history and development of 401(k) plans, their basic characteristics, and their relative advantages and disadvantages. It also includes a discussion of the changing employee benefit environment and the emerging role of 401(k) plans.

Tax and legal requirements are covered in Part Two. Because Section 401(k) of the Internal Revenue Code simply authorizes a profit-sharing or stock bonus plan to offer participants a choice between current or deferred compensation, Part Two begins with a discussion of the general tax law requirements that apply to these plans. It then covers the specific tax law requirements that apply to the cash or deferred arrangement itself—the 401(k) feature. Part Two also covers employee stock ownership plans (ESOPs) and legal provisions governing the deductibility of contributions, the taxation of distributions, and so forth. It concludes with a discussion of non-tax legal requirements—age and sex discrimination, Securities and Exchange Commission requirements, and labor law provisions on disclosure and fiduciary obligations.

Part Three focuses on the design and operational issues that affect 401(k) plans. Topics include employee and employer contributions, provisions on vesting, retirement age, distributions at termination of employment, in-service withdrawals and loans, and such miscellaneous plan features as service counting, eligibility requirements, committee and trustee provisions. Part Three also covers plan investment provisions, administrative issues, and effective employee communications.

Appendix I is an historic table of tax law limits on contributions and benefits, on elective deferrals, and on the pay that can be taken into account for plan purposes. Appendix II is a specimen plan document.

Many individuals at Towers Perrin have contributed to this effort. We would particularly like to acknowledge Everett T. Allen Jr., Robert Ayache, Michael Dickerman, Jim Klein, Elinor Merl, Jeanne Murphy, Sharon Sherman, Frances Sieller, and Carol Steiger.

We are also indebted to the authors of the Seventh Edition of *Pension Planning*, Everett T. Allen Jr., Joseph J. Melone, Jerry S. Rosenbloom, and Jack L. VanDerhei, and to Richard D. Irwin, Inc., for permission to use material that appears in their book.

Towers Perrin

CONTENTS

Chapter 4

CODAs: Additional Tax Law Requirements   75

Chapter 5

ESOPs and KSOPs   111

Chapter 6

Other Tax Law Provisions   123

Chapter 10

Plan Design—Miscellaneous Plan Provisions   219

Chapter 11

Investing Plan Assets—Basic Principles 231

Chapter 12

Investing Plan Assets—Plan Provisions And Operation 247

Chapter 13

Plan Administration 263

REVISED EDITION

THE HANDBOOK OF 401(k) PLAN MANAGEMENT

PART ONE

Introduction

CHAPTER 1

History and Development

Approximately 75 percent of all new tax-qualified retirement plans established since the late 1970s have been defined contribution plans,[1] and most of these plans include what is known as a cash or deferred arrangement (CODA).

The Internal Revenue Service (IRS) recognized CODAs as acceptable ways for employers to allow employees to choose between receiving current compensation as taxable cash or deferring it into the plan on a pretax basis, as early as the 1950s. It questioned the tax status of these plans during the 1970s, however, and it was not until the Revenue Act of 1978 that CODAs were again formally sanctioned under the tax law. Once the IRS issued clarifying regulations, these plans began to proliferate. In 1996, for example, 209 employers in a group of 225 large companies reported that they sponsored CODAs; only seven of these same employers sponsored CODAs in 1982.[2]

---

1. John A. Turner and Daniel Beller, eds., *Trends in Pensions* (Washington, D.C.: U.S. Department of Labor, 1989). The Internal Revenue Service reports that 86 percent of the new plans for which it issued determination letters in fiscal 1990 were defined contribution plans. *Spenser's Research Reports on Employee Benefits,* January 18, 1991.
2. The number of companies in this group sponsoring defined benefit plans dropped to 203 in 1996 from 221 in 1982 Source: Towers Perrin Employee Benefit Information Center (EBIC).

This introductory chapter covers the legislative history of CODAs and some of the general tax concepts that apply to these plans, as well as their overall characteristics, advantages and disadvantages. Chapter 2 discusses the emerging role of these plans in employee benefit programs.

LEGISLATIVE HISTORY

CODAs were originally permitted only in true profit-sharing arrangements where employees were given an annual choice between receiving an employer contribution in cash or having it deferred under the terms of the plan. During the 1960s, the IRS began approving salary reduction plans (including defined benefit pension plans) that permitted employees to defer pretax salary dollars.[3]

The IRS changed course in December of 1972, issuing proposed regulations stating that any compensation an employee had the option of receiving in cash would be subject to current taxation even if the employee deferred it as a contribution to the employer's qualified plan. Primarily directed at salary reduction plans, the proposed regulations also applied to profit-sharing arrangements that gave employees the option of receiving their allocation in cash.

Deliberations over the Employee Retirement Income Security Act of 1974 (ERISA) focused congressional attention on the CODA concept as well. In enacting ERISA, Congress froze the existing tax status of CODAs that were in effect on June 27, 1974, until the end of 1976. Contributions to plans established after that date were to be treated as employee contributions and, as a result, were currently taxable. Congress extended the moratorium twice, pushing the deadline to the end of 1979.

The Revenue Act of 1978 addressed CODAs by adding Section 401(k) to the Internal Revenue Code (IRC), effective for plan years beginning after December 31, 1979. The status of salary reduction plans remained uncertain until the IRS issued regulations

---

3. To satisfy nondiscrimination requirements, more than half of the total benefit dollars deferred into such plans had to come from the lowest-paid two thirds of all eligible employees.

interpreting Section 401(k) in late 1981, making it clear that CODAs could be used for salary reduction plans as well as for conventional cash option profit-sharing plans. Unlike the situation that existed before 1972, these regulations did not permit the use of salary reduction in pension arrangements.

The Tax Reform Act of 1984 made some subtle modifications to Section 401(k). Among other things, it made it clear that CODAs cannot be integrated with social security.[4]

The Tax Reform Act of 1986 (TRA '86) made much more substantial changes. In addition to imposing a dollar limit on salary reductions (elective deferrals), this legislation created a new definition of highly compensated employees, made the nondiscrimination requirements that apply to CODAs more stringent, applied new discrimination requirements to matching employer and after-tax employee contributions, imposed a new penalty tax on early distributions, and reduced employer flexibility in setting plan eligibility requirements.[5]

The most recent legislative changes affecting CODAs are found in the pension simplification provisions of the Small Business Job Protection Act of 1996. Among other things, this legislation:

1. Simplified nondiscrimination testing for CODAs.
2. Provided safe harbors for CODAs that provide minimum levels of employer contributions.
3. Extended the availability of CODAs to tax-exempt organizations (but not to governments).
4. Repealed five-year averaging as it applies to lump sum distributions.
5. Instituted a new and simpler definition of highly compensated employee.
6. Eliminated the Section 415 combined plan limitation on contributions and benefits for highly paid employees.

---

4. It also extended cash or deferred tax treatment to pre-ERISA money purchase pension plans, although it limited contributions to the levels existing on June 27, 1974.
5. TRA '86 also prohibited tax-exempt organizations and state and local governments from sponsoring CODAs unless the plans were adopted before July 2, and it prohibited state and local governments from sponsoring CODAs unless they were adopted before May 6, 1986.

Overall, these changes should ease the administrative and compliance problems that many employers have had in operating their CODAs, and should encourage the further growth of these plans.

OVERALL TAX LAW CONCEPTS

An extensive discussion of the specific tax law provisions governing CODAs appears in Part Two; a brief overview of the subject follows.

A qualified plan is a plan that is eligible for favorable tax treatment under the IRC. The tax advantages associated with qualified plans are significant: contributions (within prescribed limits) are currently tax-deductible by the employer even though they are not immediately taxable to employees, and investment income on plan assets is not taxed until it is distributed as a benefit. In addition, certain lump sum distributions made before the year 2000 and certain lump sum distributions made to individuals who were born before January 1, 1936, may receive favorable tax treatment.

In general, the law recognizes three major types of plans for qualification purposes: pension, profit-sharing, and stock bonus plans. It does not recognize CODAs or Section 401(k) plans as separate and distinct types of plans unless the CODA consists only of elective contributions made by the employer.

A *pension* plan can be either a defined benefit plan, which promises a specific benefit, or a defined contribution plan, which specifies the amount the employer will contribute. Most pension plans are defined benefit plans, although there are defined contribution pension plans known as money purchase plans. *Profit-sharing* plans, as the name implies, are defined contribution plans where the employer's contribution is determined with reference to profits (though this is not required), and may be made on a discretionary basis. *Stock bonus* plans are similar to profit-sharing plans but are designed to invest primarily in employer securities.

Because a thrift or savings plan (with or without a CODA) is not recognized, as such, for qualification purposes, it is usually established as a profit-sharing plan.[6] Section 401(k) of the Internal

---

6. Occasionally, a savings plan will be established as a money purchase pension plan, but this is unusual because a pension plan cannot include some of the key features of the typical savings plan (e.g., in-service withdrawals).

Revenue Code allows a cash or deferred arrangement to be made part of a profit-sharing or stock bonus plan.[7]

Thus, as a threshold matter, a plan that includes a CODA must meet the overall tax law requirements that generally apply to qualified profit-sharing or stock bonus plans. The CODA portion of the plan must also meet additional requirements imposed by Section 401(k).[8]

The provisions of Section 401(k) cover two different kinds of arrangements. The first and most common permits employees to contribute pretax salary dollars to the plan; these salary reduction arrangements are what most people are referring to when they talk about "401(k) plans." The second and less common arrangement is the cash option profit-sharing plan, where the employer makes a contribution and gives the employee the option of taking it in cash (and paying taxes) or deferring it into the plan on a pretax basis. In either case—and for many tax law purposes—the amount an employee elects to defer is treated, when paid to the plan, as an employer contribution.

Pretax dollars deferred by or on behalf of employees are subject to specific requirements and limits under Section 401(k). First and foremost, they must be nonforfeitable at all times (i.e., they must be fully vested in the employees). Second, they are subject to significant in-service withdrawal restrictions, and can generally be distributed only when employees reach age 59 $\frac{1}{2}$, separate from service, become disabled, or die. There are some limited hardship exceptions to these rules, however, and employees may have some access to these funds through plan loan arrangements.

Another key requirement is that unless the plan meets certain safe harbor provisions of the law (which are not effective for plan years beginning prior to December 31, 1998), the pretax contributions or elective deferrals made by highly compensated employees cannot, on average, exceed those made by other employees by more than a stipulated margin. If the safe harbors are not met, employers must conduct what is known as the actual deferral

---

7. With the exception of pre-ERISA money purchase plans (and defined contribution pension plans of rural electric cooperatives), a CODA may not be attached to a pension plan—defined benefit or defined contribution.

8. For convenience, and in recognition of common usage, the terms *CODA* and *CODA plan* will generally be used in this text to refer to any plan that includes a CODA and not only to the CODA portion itself.

percentage (ADP) test each year to ensure compliance with this rule. A similar test, known as the actual contribution percentage (ACP) test, applies each year to employee aftertax and employer matching contributions that do not meet safe harbor requirements. Further, an employee's elective deferrals in any calendar year cannot exceed a stipulated dollar amount. This amount, originally set at $7,000 and indexed to increase with changes in the consumer price index (CPI), was $9,500 for 1996.[9]

The tax law provisions that apply to CODAs implement the government's policy of encouraging employees to save under tax-favored circumstances and discouraging the use of these savings for purposes other than retirement. The government also wants to make sure that the tax advantages of CODAs accrue primarily to rank-and-file employees; significant limits apply in terms of the advantages created for highly compensated employees.

TYPICAL PLAN FEATURES

Except for the fact that cash option profit-sharing plans allow an employee to choose between current cash or a deferred contribution, these plans share many of the characteristics of traditional profit-sharing plans; significant features of savings plan CODAs include the following:

- Employee participation in a CODA is generally voluntary; to participate, an employee must agree to make contributions.
- An employee usually has the option of determining how much to contribute within minimums and maximums specified in the plan.
- As noted, employee contributions are usually made in the form of salary reductions—that is, on a pretax basis. Some plans also permit aftertax employee contributions as an alternative or in addition to pretax contributions.

---

9. This is one of several dollar limits set forth in the IRC; others, including a limit on the total amount that can be added to an employee's account each year, will be discussed later in this book. Most of these limits are "indexed," increasing with upward movement in the consumer price index. Appendix I shows various dollar limits in effect between 1987 and 1996.

- Employers usually match all or some part of the contributions employees make up to a specified level.
- Both employer and employee contributions are usually made to a trust fund (although they can be made directly to an insurance company under some arrangements).
- Plans establish and maintain individual accounts for each employee.
- Employees can typically choose to invest their contributions (and sometimes employer contributions) in one or more investment funds. In some plans, employer contributions are automatically invested in securities of the employer, while the employee chooses how to invest his or her own contributions.
- An employee's account is generally payable to (or on behalf of) the employee on retirement, death, disability, or termination of employment. Benefits distributed on termination of employment are limited to vested amounts.
- Many CODAs permit an employee to withdraw the value of vested employer contributions, as well as the value of the employee's own aftertax contributions, during active employment. Many CODAs also permit an employee to withdraw elective (pretax) contributions and earnings thereon to the extent permitted by law.
- A plan may allow an employee to take loans from the plan (using his or her account balance as collateral) up to the limits permitted under labor and tax laws.

ADVANTAGES AND DISADVANTAGES

From an employer's viewpoint, CODAs have the advantages normally associated with any employee benefit plan—that is, they play a role in attracting and retaining employees and in improving employee morale. Because they are defined contribution plans, they have these advantages as well:

- They can provide significant funding flexibility through the use of discretionary contribution formulas.
- They provide a tax-effective way for employees to contribute to the cost of their benefits.

- They provide significant opportunities to control the impact of inflation.
- They are easy for employees to understand and appreciate.
- They can readily accommodate different work situations that have emerged with demographic change (e.g., part-time employment, continued employment after normal retirement age, job changes, phased retirement arrangements, broken periods of employment).
- They arguably permit a more equitable allocation of employer contributions—one that is not sensitive to an employee's age.
- They are not subject to the plan termination provisions of Title IV of ERISA.
- They do not require actuarial valuations for accounting, minimum/maximum funding, and Pension Benefit Guaranty Corporation (PBGC) premium determination purposes.

In addition, the nondiscrimination requirements of Section 401(a)(4) of the IRC have proven significantly less burdensome for defined contribution plans than for defined benefit plans.

Among the advantages cited above, the fact that defined contribution plans are not subject to the plan termination provisions of Title IV of ERISA has been particularly influential in increasing the prevalence of these plans. Changes in accounting policies have also fueled their growth, as have changes in the economic climate that have underscored the importance of controlling employee benefit costs.

Defined contribution plans also give employers the opportunity to align employee interests more closely with those of the corporation—by tying the company's contributions to profits, by investing plan funds in employer securities, or both. No more than 10 percent of the assets of a defined benefit plan can be invested in securities of the employer, but this limitation does not apply to most defined contribution plans, and the ability to invest defined contribution plan funds in employer stock has proven particularly attractive—for example, as a way to create a large block of friendly shareholders to help ward off takeover attempts. Employee stock ownership plans (ESOPs) have also been granted a number of specific tax benefits over the years.[10]

The cash-or-deferred feature itself can also support specific employer objectives. The addition of a CODA to a plan that formerly permitted employees to contribute on an aftertax basis only will typically increase employee participation in the plan, for example. Some employers may find that conversion of a conventional savings plan to a CODA minimizes pressures for additional cash compensation by increasing take-home pay for participating employees. The addition of a CODA to a profit-sharing plan will also give employees the flexibility to meet changing needs by deciding, on a year-to-year basis, whether to take all of their salary or profit sharing in cash or to defer some of this money under the CODA.

The first and foremost advantage of a CODA for employees is that it permits them to accumulate investment income on a pretax basis. (While this is true of all defined contribution plans, it is a particularly visible characteristic in a CODA, because pretax investment income also accumulates on the amounts employees would otherwise have paid in taxes.) As with other defined contribution plans, distributions from a CODA may also receive favorable tax treatment. Installment distributions during retirement may be taxed at a lower effective rate than would have been applicable during the employee's working years, for example. The impact of these tax advantages is illustrated in Exhibit 1–1, which compares the results of investing like amounts in a bank account, a traditional savings plan, and a 401(k) plan over three different periods of time.

From an employer's perspective, CODAs also have some disadvantages. They are more complicated to administer and communicate than conventional savings plans, and, as noted earlier, they cannot be integrated with social security. Further, nondiscrimination strictures limit the value of these plans for highly compensated employees, which means employers must find other ways to provide benefits for this group. Employers may also face employee relations problems when a plan fails to meet the nondiscrimination tests, because the cure for such failures may involve the return of contributions. Finally, employers must also recognize the fiduciary

---

10. See Chapter 5.

E X H I B I T   1–1

Fund Accumulation on Fixed Dollar Deposit at 8 Percent
Interest

	Account Type		
Fixed Deposit*	**Bank** **$670/Year**	**401(a)** **$670/Year**	**401(k)** **$1,000/Year**
35 Year Accumulation			
Lump sum	$68,721	$124,688	$186,102
Aftertax proceeds	68,721	91,279	124,688
25 Year Accumulation			
Lump sum	$35,413	$52,899	$78,954
Aftertax proceeds	35.413	40,970	52,899
15 Year Accumulation			
Lump sum	$15,652	$19,647	$29,324
Aftertax proceeds	15,652	16,480	19,647

*Deposit of $670/year in a bank account or 401(a) qualified plan is equivalent to a $1,000 deposit in a 401(k) account assuming 33 percent income tax rate (28 percent federal plus 5 percent state and local).

implications relating to the investment of plan assets where
employees are at risk with respect to investment results. Savings
plan CODAs have fewer disadvantages for employees, except for
the fact that they are making the greatest portion of plan contributions. In fact, the only significant disadvantage is that elective
deferrals are subject to in-service withdrawal restrictions. This can
be important for some employees—particularly at lower income
levels—and could be a barrier to participation in the plan.

In deciding whether to adopt a CODA or other defined contribution plan, and what specific design features to incorporate, an
employer must weigh the advantages and disadvantages discussed above in the context of environmental considerations, organizational objectives, and employee needs. These issues—and the
emerging role of the defined contribution plan—are the subject of
the next chapter.

The Emerging Role of Defined Contribution Plans and CODAs

Employee benefits represent a significant benefit cost for most employers. Given this cost, the importance of these benefits to workers and their families and a complex regulatory environment, it is essential that employers take care in designing their plans to support company goals and objectives.

A number of factors shape plan design. This chapter begins with a brief discussion of environmental influences and overall employer objectives; it then turns to recent developments that are shaping the evolution of the defined contribution plan and its role in the overall benefit program.

OVERALL INFLUENCES

In deciding whether to adopt a CODA or other defined contribution plan, and what specific design features to incorporate, an employer must weigh the advantages and disadvantages of these plans in the context of organizational needs and overall objectives.[1] Many factors influence the choices an employer makes, including:

---

1. For a more comprehensive discussion of overall employer objectives in designing employee benefit plans, see Everett T. Allen, Jr., Joseph J. Melone, Jerry S. Rosenbloom, and Jack L. VanDerhei, *Pension Planning*, 7th ed. (Homewood, Ill.: Irwin, 1992).

- **Environmental considerations:** the industry in which the employer operates; its legal status; the diversity of its operations; its profitability patterns and capital needs; the demographics of its work force, and whether or not benefits are subject to collective bargaining.

- **Employer attitudes and philosophies:** its views on total compensation, on employee cost sharing, and on whether the company or employees should bear investment and inflation risks; its preferences with respect to retirement patterns, and its benefit strategies for highly compensated versus non-highly compensated employees.

- **Benefit and cost/expense objectives:** the type and level of benefits to be provided; the total liabilities the employer is willing to assume for each plan and for the overall benefit program; expense and cash flow patterns; employee contribution levels; funding flexibility, and inflation protection.[2]

The importance an employer attaches to the tax advantages associated with qualified plans can also influence plan design. Thus, for example, a desire to maximize tax benefits for highly compensated employees could result in contribution formulas that integrate or coordinate plan benefits with those provided by social security to the maximum extent permitted, the use of so-called target benefit plans,[3] and the use and distribution of employer stock.[4]

An employer must also consider what it wants to achieve with its benefit program. Most employers feel that some form of employee benefit program is necessary to attract and retain desirable employees, for example, not so much because benefits exert a positive influence, but because their absence could hinder

---

2. Minimizing administrative costs has also become an important objective in light of government regulations and requirements that complicate plan design and funding. But administrative costs are not the most significant element of total plan cost, and good plan design should not be sacrificed in order to hold those costs down.

3. A target benefit plan uses a defined benefit formula to establish projected retirement benefits and annual contributions for individuals. Contributions are made to individual accounts and the plan operates as a defined contribution plan. The result is larger allocations to older employees than would be the case under a typical defined contribution plan. In most situations, this will benefit key individuals.

4. Unrealized appreciation on such stock may be reported as income, for tax purposes, either when the stock is distributed or when it is actually sold—at the employee's option. See Chapter 6.

recruiting and retention efforts. While competitive standards—within an industry or community—will influence program design in this regard, some benefits are particularly attractive to both potential and existing employees. Examples include true profit-sharing plans and savings plans with an employer matching contribution—especially CODAs—as well as flexible benefits arrangements.

CODA OBJECTIVES

Both types of CODAs—the cash option profit-sharing plan and the savings plan—give employers the opportunity to meet several special objectives. While employers do not always establish a savings plan with the specific objective of encouraging *employee thrift*, for example, many feel that employees bear some responsibility for providing for their own economic security, and a savings plan is an efficient capital accumulation vehicle.

Either type of CODA can also be structured to include *employee incentives* and, as a result, to improve productivity. To achieve this objective, the employer's contribution formula can be directly tied to profitability or to the attainment of specific corporate goals. In addition, employers can increase employee identification with overall company business objectives by permitting or requiring employees to acquire an ownership interest in the firm—by making employer securities an investment option in a CODA, for example.[5]

As noted in Chapter 1, employers may also be able to increase employee participation by converting a conventional savings plan to a CODA.

A CHANGING ENVIRONMENT

In designing their defined benefit plans, employers typically attempt to fulfill specific retirement income objectives. The pension formula might be set to achieve, along with social security, an income-replacement ratio of 80 percent of a 30-year employee's final pay of $30,000, for example, with the replacement percentage

---

5. The pros and cons of offering employer securities as an investment option are discussed in Chapter 12.

dropping to perhaps 55 percent for a 30-year employee with final pay of $100,000. Few employers have been operating their defined contribution plans with such specific objectives in mind. While some plan sponsors take CODA benefits into account in determining whether income-replacement targets are being met, most view CODAs as simply *supplementing* other benefit plans and social security, and do not assign them a specific role in meeting overall program objectives. In most cases, an employee's account balance in a CODA is simply an unallocated pool of assets payable at death, retirement, disability, or termination of employment.

In recent years, however, the convergence of several factors has prompted employers to consider whether their defined contribution plans should serve a more explicit function in the total benefit program. For one thing, many of these plans have existed for some time and are now producing payouts for retirees that are more than supplemental by almost any standard. For another, new needs are being recognized for both employers and employees—needs that are not necessarily addressed by existing benefit programs.

One of the most pressing needs employers face today, for example, is finding a way to manage their postretirement health care obligations. Since 1993, employers have been required to account for their postretirement health care and life insurance expenses on an accrual basis.[6] This shift in accounting has had significant financial implications for most companies. A Towers Perrin study of 285 employers indicated that the median annual expense in 1994 for postretirement health care benefits per active employee was $1,263; median benefit payments to retirees per active employee were $669. These cost levels could increase significantly if medical benefit costs rise sharply in the future. Faced with increases of this magnitude, many employers will require their retirees to pay a larger share of these costs.

Demographic change is also having an impact on retirement needs. The longer people live, the more likely they are to need some form of long-term care. And the longer they live, the more inflation can erode their resources.

---

6. Financial Accounting Standards Board Statement of Financial Accounting Standards No. 106, *Employers' Accounting for Postretirement Benefits Other Than Pensions*, December 1990.

In an effort to avoid unnecessary or redundant benefit pay-ments, and to deploy assets as effectively as possible, employers are beginning to reexamine their defined contribution plans and the large—and largely uncommitted—pools of assets these plans are producing. Among the key issues:

- Where does the plan fit into the total retirement income program? Should it play a specific role, or should it con-tinue to be viewed as purely supplemental?
- Do plan provisions enable employees—and thus employ-ers—to maximize the value of their benefits?
- Do employees have the information they need to do their part in making the best use of the opportunities provided them?

These issues are discussed in more detail below.

MEETING SPECIFIC NEEDS

Broadly speaking, there are two approaches to providing specific benefits through a defined contribution plan. One is to make plan payouts an explicit part of benefit objectives, for example, as part of the income replacement equation, along with pension and social security benefits. To do so, employers will have to determine the contributions necessary to produce the desired results for career employees, taking such matters as pay growth, inflation, and investment returns into account. However, it is not easy to produce a specified amount of pay-related income at some future time via a defined contribution plan.

The other approach is to encourage employees to earmark plan assets for specific needs. Three examples follow.

Inflation Protection

Social security benefits are automatically indexed to increase with the CPI, affording significant inflation protection for many retirees. Most government workers (federal, state, and local) participate in pension systems that are also indexed to the CPI. But the vast majority of private employers do not automatically increase pen-sion benefits as the cost of living rises, though they may provide increases on an ad hoc basis. Further, retirees are apt to be very conservative with their investments—opting for savings accounts, certificates of deposit, and other fixed income vehicles that offer little, if any, real growth opportunity.

Thus, inflation is an important issue for most retirees. At the end of 20 years, for example, 4 percent annual inflation will have reduced the purchasing power of a retiree's $25,000 annual pension to $11,410. Put another way, this retiree would need a capital sum of $98,980 at retirement, invested at 8 percent, to increase the pension by 4 percent a year and maintain purchasing power in the face of inflation.

The typical CODA provides for a 50 percent employer matching contribution on employee contributions of up to 6 percent of pay, or a maximum annual contribution of 9 percent of pay. As illustrated in Exhibit 2–1, the maximum contribution would provide postretirement inflation protection (the 4 percent annual increase noted above) at all entry ages shown. The figures assume 6 percent annual pay increases, retirement at age 65, and a defined benefit pension of 40 percent of final pay.

Employees may not be aware of the impact inflation will have on their financial resources during retirement; thus, encouraging them to allocate a portion of their assets for this purpose may simply be a matter of communicating both needs and potential resources for meeting these needs. (Plan design features can also support this objective, as discussed in more detail below.)

There is also a more formal way for employees to use defined contribution assets to provide inflation protection. As a result of a

E X H I B I T 2–1

Annual Savings Required to Provide Annual 4 Percent COLA on Pension

	Annual Required Savings (Percent of Pay)	
Entry Age	At 8 Percent Interest	At 10 Percent Interest
30	3.2%	1.8%
40	5.0	3.0
50	9.0	6.2

provision (Section 415(k)) added to the IRC by TRA '86, a defined benefit plan can permit participants to purchase inflation protection in the form of cost-of-living adjustments to the pension benefit. An employee can purchase this qualified cost-of-living arrangement (QCOLA) by transferring defined contribution funds attributable to employer contributions (including employee elective deferrals under a CODA) to the defined benefit plan.

A QCOLA offers several advantages. For example, the employee need not worry about outliving the inflation protection. More important, the QCOLA can be an attractive investment opportunity. Retirees tend to be risk averse, favoring fixed income, lower return investments. Plan sponsors, who have an infinite investment horizon, can afford to take reasonable risk to achieve higher rates of return over time. Thus, the amount the employee is charged for the QCOLA can usually reflect a higher rate of return than might be available to the employee under conventional fixed income alternatives.[7]

QCOLAs enable plan sponsors to focus employee attention on postretirement needs and the value of defined contribution plan assets in meeting these needs. They also offer an attractive (and relatively safe) investment opportunity for employees, at no cost to the employer. QCOLAs are described in more detail in Chapter 9.

Long-Term Care

An estimated 40 percent to 50 percent of all Americans over age 65 will enter a long-term care facility at some time in their lives. The cost of this care can be as much as $40,000 or more a year, and interest in some form of financial protection against this contingency is growing rapidly (See Chapter 6).[8]

Some employers offer optional group long-term care coverage to their employees. Few subsidize this benefit, however, largely

---

7. Another advantage, for some employees, is that they would still have the option of taking a lump sum distribution of the remaining defined contribution plan assets and be entitled to favorable tax treatment. This would apply to qualifying lump sum distributions received before 2000 and to qualifying lump sum distributions to employees who were born before January 1, 1936.
8. While Medicaid will pay some long-term care expenses, almost all personal assets must be exhausted before coverage is available. (A spouse who remains at home is permitted to keep some additional assets, however.)

because the cost is prohibitive. Further, currently available insurance products—whether group or individual—vary widely in such important areas as eligibility standards, premiums, underwriting policies, and covered services. Premiums, for example, are typically not guaranteed and can be increased at some future time. And the typical policy is written on a term insurance basis. Thus, if the insured stops paying premiums, the policy may have no cash value, there may be no return of premiums paid, and there may be no paid-up benefits.

Employers are also exploring other options, such as an accelerated death benefit rider on postretirement life insurance coverage that will provide living benefits for employees confined to a nursing home.

Educating employees about the role the defined contribution plan can play in financing long-term care is another possibility. Employees who are not contributing to the plan at the permitted maximum levels might choose to increase their savings plan contributions in anticipation of future long-term care needs, for example. By projecting account balances forward based on various pay and contribution levels, and comparing those balances to projected long-term care costs, employers can illustrate the outcome of different contribution strategies and the role defined contribution funds could play in meeting long-term care needs.

Exhibit 2–2 provides an illustration. The employee in this example is age 50, is currently earning $50,000 a year, and wants to contribute an additional 2 percent of his pay to a CODA (with a matching employer contribution of 50 percent). Assuming pay growth of 5 percent a year, the exhibit projects the account balances this employee will accumulate at age 65 (when the employee is

E X H I B I T   2–2

Projected Fund Balances

	At 65		At 80	
	8 Percent	10 Percent	8 Percent	10 Percent
Employee	$30,319	$35,252	$96,178	$147,255
Employer	15,159	17,626	48,089	73,627
Total	$45,478	$52,878	$144,267	$220,882

assumed to retire and stop contributing) and also at age 80 if the funds are left to accumulate under the CODA. (The example assumes the minimum distribution rules have been met by the distribution of other funds in the employee's account.) To emphasize the importance of maximizing investment return, projections at both an 8 percent and a 10 percent investment return are shown.

While these are pretax projections, the results are nevertheless interesting. The leveraging effect of compound interest is much greater over the longer period (to age 80 rather than age 65); further, an additional 2 percent return produces dramatically different results.

Another way of looking at the potential value of CODAs in meeting long-term care needs is to compare the projected results in Exhibit 2–2 with what the cost of long-term care might be in 30 years. Assuming that the current cost of a one-year stay in a nursing home is $40,000, and assuming that this cost increases each year by an inflation rate of 4 percent, this annual cost will be approximately $130,000 in 30 years. At age 80, the employee would have enough funds, on a before-tax basis, to cover a full one-year stay under both interest assumptions—and an even longer stay under the assumption of a 10 percent growth rate.

An important advantage of prefunding the costs of long-term care through a CODA or other supplemental plan is that the amount saved, adjusted for investment results, is always available to the employee (or the employee's beneficiaries) for any purpose, as is the remaining account balance. By contrast, the typical long-term care insurance policy has no value unless a claim is made while the policy is in force.

Postretirement Health Care

The Financial Accounting Standards Board issued its final statement on accounting for postretirement welfare benefits—known as FAS 106—in December 1990. The statement, which requires that postretirement health care and life insurance benefits be accounted for on an accrual rather than a pay-as-you-go basis, has had significant financial implications for employers who sponsor traditional health plans.

Many employers have modified their postretirement health care programs in response to FAS 106, by changing plan design, funding, or both. While a comprehensive discussion of employer options with respect to FAS 106 is beyond the scope of this text, some employers are planning to coordinate changes in their retiree health care plans with changes in their supplemental defined contribution plans. One approach makes use of the defined contribution plan to reduce or even *eliminate* postretirement health care liabilities for future retirees.

Under this approach, the employer would no longer subsidize postretirement health care coverage, phasing out the subsidy over a period of perhaps 15 years and protecting existing retirees by grandfathering their benefits. The plan would continue to make postretirement health care coverage available to future retirees, but on a retiree-pay-all basis. (Employees retiring during the phase-out period would continue to receive employer-subsidized coverage—possibly with gradual reductions in the level of employer contributions.) At the same time, the employer would increase its contribution to the supplemental savings plan by an amount that, with anticipated investment returns, could be expected to create sufficient additional capital for future retirees to purchase health care coverage.

Assume, for example, that the employer wants to provide employees who are age 65 with $1,500 for each year of service ($45,000 for a 30-year employee) to pay for this coverage. For an employee now age 50, this would require an annual contribution of about 3 percent of pay over the next 15 years (assuming pay growth at 5 percent a year and an 8 percent investment return). The employer would make this additional contribution—clearly identified as intended to help employees pay for their postretirement health care benefits—to the savings plan.

The employer could also increase its contribution by an amount equal to the current cost of postretirement health care coverage for each year of plan participation. The employee would of course bear the risk that the investment return on this contribution will at least equal future increases in the cost of health care. Assuming that it does, the employee, in effect, will receive a year's worth of employer health care contributions (at future health care cost levels) for each year of future service. Periodic adjustments would be necessary to keep the level of employer contributions in line with current health care costs, but the employer would control such increases.

Under these scenarios, the employer will sharply reduce (and perhaps eventually eliminate) its FAS 106 liability, and will convert its retiree medical expenditures into an annual tax-deductible contribution to the defined contribution plan. Further, it will impose a degree of inflation control by shifting from a defined benefit to a defined contribution commitment. As noted, however, investment risk will be transferred to the employee. Further, these methods are not as tax-efficient as providing nontaxable health care benefits. They may also be more costly to the employer since employees who terminate before retirement eligibility and with a vested interest will, in effect, take some of the pre-funding of their postretirement health care benefits with them.

MAXIMIZING PLAN VALUES

Regardless of the use to which plan assets are ultimately put, economic constraints make it imperative for employers and employees to get as much mileage as possible from the dollars they contribute to their CODAs and other defined contribution plans. In many cases, however, plan design can pose obstacles to achieving this goal.

By leaving funds in the plan as long as possible, for example, employees can maximize the value of a powerful tax shelter.[9] Yet few plans give employees this option, and many do not even offer installment or annuity distributions. Of the 596 companies that offer defined contribution plans in Towers Perrin's Employee Benefit Information Center database, for example, 100 percent make lump sum distributions available to participants, while only 55 percent offer installment distributions and 28 percent offer annuities.[10]

A modest increase in the annual investment return can also produce a sizable payoff over time in a tax-sheltered environment. But plan design often encourages employees to make conservative investment choices by offering sharply different options—an

---

9. A lump sum distribution can be rolled over into an individual retirement account (IRA), of course, but the retiree might not have the investment opportunities available under the employer's plan, and could also face additional investment management expenses that might otherwise be paid for by the employer.
10. The potential value of installment distributions in maximizing tax-sheltering opportunities is discussed in greater detail in Chapter 9.

equity fund and a guaranteed investment contract (GIC) or other fixed income fund, for example.

Even in cases where sufficient investment and distribution options are available, employees may not have the information they need to make appropriate choices.

At the most basic level, employees need to understand how much money they are likely to need during retirement, factoring in inflation, taxes, and medical expenses. They also need to know how much they can expect from social security and their employer's defined benefit, defined contribution, and postretirement health care and life insurance plans. Only then will they be in a position to make informed retirement planning decisions.

Employees who do not participate in CODAs as fully as possible might be more inclined to sacrifice current cash if they could see how the maximum contribution would improve their financial status in 20 years' time, for example. Employees who opt for conservative, low-return investment choices might make different choices if they understood the importance of diversification and the relationship between risk and reward. Finally, employees might reconsider their choice of distribution methods if they understood that the financial consequences of various options can differ.

Exhibit 2–3 illustrates the importance of employee education by comparing the financial impact of different investment and distribution choices. The graphs compare retirement income and expenses under two different scenarios for a married employee who is now 42 years old, earns $50,000, and will retire at 62.[11]

In the left-hand graph of Exhibit 2–3, the employee earns an average pre- and postretirement return of 8 percent on her defined contribution account balance and takes her distribution in the form of a level five-year annuity. In the right-hand graph, she earns an

---

11. The graphs assume life expectancies of 81 for the employee and 86 for the spouse, with the spouse entering a long-term care facility at age 83. Projected expenditures are based on Bureau of Labor Statistics data, adjusted to reflect pay levels and take inflation into account throughout the retirement years. Expenditure items include daily living expenses; income and property taxes; medical expenses, including Medicare premiums; entertainment/vacation expenses; and auto/transportation expenses. Revenue sources include social security (with an imputed value for Medicare) plus employer-sponsored defined benefit, defined contribution, postretirement health care, and life insurance plans.

E X H I B I T   2–3

Retirement Income and Expenses

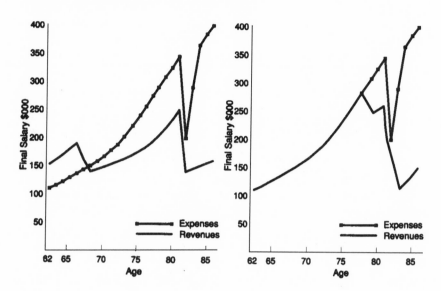

additional 1 percent annual return and draws down her account balance on an as-needed basis.[12]

As a result of these two changes, this employee achieves a much better match between retirement revenues and expenses—at no additional cost to the plan sponsor. Meaningful choices and meaningful information can clearly lead to improved rates of return and to more efficient use of plan assets.

If supplemental defined contribution plans are to play a more significant role in the overall employee benefit program, they must be managed as effectively as possible. This, in turn, requires careful attention to plan design and administration, to investment management, and to employee communication. These subjects are discussed in more detail in Part Three.

---

12. Subject to the minimum distribution requirements covered in Chapter 3.

PART TWO

Tax and Legal Requirements

The Basic Qualification Rules

Federal tax policy encourages employers to provide retirement and capital accumulation benefits to their employees. The government forgoes significant tax revenues by permitting deductions for contributions made to tax-qualified plans and by deferring taxation of investment income on plan assets. Moreover, it wants these tax expenditures to support broad social goals, and not to create special benefits for the highly paid. Thus, almost all of the tax law provisions relating to qualified plans revolve around a central theme: preventing discrimination in favor of these employees.

A CODA is usually part of an underlying profit-sharing or stock bonus plan, and the underlying plan must meet the general tax law requirements that apply to all qualified plans.[1] This chapter discusses these requirements as they apply to defined contribution plans, including CODAs. Additional qualification requirements that apply to CODAs are covered in Chapter 4. Special provisions governing employee stock ownership plans (ESOPs) are the subject of Chapter 5. Other tax law provisions (e.g., deduction limits, the taxation of distributions) are treated in Chapter 6. Nontax legal concerns (e.g., labor law, Securities and Exchange Commission requirements) are covered in Chapter 7.

---

1. IRC Section 401(k)(2).

OVERVIEW OF QUALIFICATION REQUIREMENTS

The general requirements that employer-sponsored defined contribution plans must meet to maintain tax-qualified status are set forth in Section 401(a) of the IRC. In brief:

- A plan must be created and maintained exclusively for the benefit of employees and their beneficiaries.
- It must be impossible for trust funds to be used other than for the exclusive benefit of employees or their beneficiaries prior to the satisfaction of all plan liabilities.
- A plan must not discriminate in favor of highly compensated employees in coverage.
- A plan must not discriminate in favor of highly compensated employees in contributions and benefits.
- Annual additions to an employee's account (employer and employee contributions plus forfeitures) cannot exceed stipulated amounts in any given year.
- Employee compensation in excess of a stipulated amount may not be taken into account for plan purposes.
- Age and service requirements for participation in the plan cannot be more stringent than specified minimums.
- Benefits must vest in accordance with specific rules.
- Special vesting and benefit requirements apply to top-heavy plans—those that benefit certain key employees to a significant extent.
- Qualified joint and survivor and preretirement survivor benefits must be provided under money purchase pension plans, and under other types of defined contribution plans if certain conditions are not met.
- Benefit distributions must satisfy amount and timing requirements known as the minimum distribution rules.
- There are limits on the assignment or alienation of benefits other than pursuant to qualified domestic relations orders (QDROs).
- Individual accounts must be maintained for each participant.
- A participant's account balance must be fully protected in the event of a plan merger or consolidation or transfer of plan assets.

Still other requirements apply to specific types of defined contribution plans such as profit-sharing plans and ESOPs. And additional requirements apply to CODAs and to plans that provide for matching employer contributions or aftertax employee contributions. These requirements are discussed in Chapters 4 and 5.

SOME KEY CONCEPTS

It is important to understand a few basic concepts before proceeding to a detailed discussion of the qualification rules that apply to defined contribution plans and CODAs. These include:

- Controlled groups.
- Separate lines of business.
- Highly compensated employees.
- Compensation.

Controlled Groups

The qualification rules would be meaningless if employers could circumvent them by establishing separate business entities and applying the rules separately to each entity. It would be easy, for example, to split one company into two companies—one employing all rank-and-file employees and the other employing only management personnel. The latter company could then establish a plan covering 100 percent of its employees, leaving employees of the other company with no benefits.

This will not work, however. It is a well-established rule of general tax law that two entities will be treated as a single entity for purposes of certain tax rules if the entities constitute a controlled group.[2] In the benefit area, companies in a controlled group will be treated as a single entity for purposes of applying the general qualification rules, for crediting service for eligibility and vesting purposes, and for monitoring annual contribution and benefit limits.[3]

The most common controlled group consists of a parent and subsidiary, where one entity owns at least 80 percent of the other

---

2. IRC Section 1563.
3. IRC Sections 414(b) and (c).

entity. A second type is the brother-sister controlled group, where five or fewer "persons" (individuals, estates, or trusts) own (1) at least 80 percent of the entities being examined, and (2) more than 50 percent of the entities being examined, taking into account "identical interest" only. For purposes of the more-than-50-percent test, an owner's identical interest means the lowest level of ownership he or she has in the entities being examined.

Two or more entities may also be treated as a single entity if they are deemed to be an affiliated service group.[4] Unlike the parent-subsidiary and brother-sister rules, which require a significant ownership interest, the affiliated service group rules look at a combination of very low ownership interests and services between entities. Thus, two entities that need not be aggregated under the regular controlled group rules may still be treated as a single entity. These rules apply only to service organizations and organizations performing management functions for one organization (or a group of related organizations).

The IRS is also authorized under Section 414(o) to promulgate regulations to prevent the avoidance of the qualification and other nondiscrimination requirements through the use of separate organizations, employee leasing, or other arrangements.

Separate Lines of Business

The controlled group rules can result in the aggregation of employee groups for qualification testing purposes that would otherwise be considered separate. But an employer may be able to test a plan in a controlled group separately if it can show that employees covered by the plan are in a qualified separate line of business (QSLOB).[5] These rules are designed to allow employers to structure benefit programs that meet the competitive needs of separate business operations or operating units in separate geographic locations.

The IRS has established stringent requirements that will make it very difficult for most employers to establish separate lines for testing purposes.[6] These regulations establish a five-step procedure

---

4. IRC Section 414(m).
5. IRC Section 414(r).
6. IRS Reg. 1.414(r).

that employers must follow if they want to test on a separate line basis. They must:

- Identify their lines of business.
- Establish that the lines are organized and operated separately.
- Demonstrate that the separate lines are qualified.
- Allocate each employee to a qualified separate line.
- Test plans covering employees of separate lines: first, under the nondiscriminatory classification test on a controlled group basis, and then again under the coverage and nondiscrimination rules on a QSLOB basis.

Identifying Lines of Business   An employer must identify lines of business according to the property and services provided to customers. The employer can include businesses that provide different products and services in one line; a manufacturer might designate its boat-building and ice cream businesses as one line, for example, and its timber business as another line.

Separate Lines   In order to qualify as a separate line under the final rules, each line must meet four tests. The line qualifies if it is formally *organized* as a separate unit and is a separate profit center with separate *profit and loss reporting*. The line must also have a *separate work force* and a *separate management*.

Qualified Lines   The employer must identify each line to the IRS as a separate line. Each line must also pass administrative scrutiny. A line that falls into a statutory safe harbor or one of five administrative safe harbors contained in the regulations will qualify. In addition, in certain circumstances the employer may seek an individual determination from the IRS on whether the administrative scrutiny requirement is satisfied.

Employee Allocation   The final regulations provide a number of alternatives for allocating shared employees such as headquarters personnel among different lines for testing on a QSLOB basis.

Nondiscrimination Testing   In addition to satisfying the foregoing requirements, a plan must pass the nondiscriminatory classification test on a companywide (controlled group) basis before it can be tested on a QSLOB basis. Thus, in each plan covering employees in a line of business, the ratio of the percentage of all high-paid employees to the percentage of all low-paid employees covered by that plan must meet or exceed the acceptable minimum ratio under the test, which is described in detail beginning on page 42. Except in unusual circumstances, a plan using QSLOB testing will pass the nondiscriminatory classification test on a controlled group basis if it passes using the unsafe harbor percentages of that test. If this test is passed, then the plan of each separate line of business, as it applies to employees allocated to that line, can be tested on its own—excluding employees of other lines of business—for purposes of satisfying the coverage and nondiscrimination requirements of the IRC.

Generally, a sponsor that elects to test one plan on a separate line basis must test every other plan separately using the same qualified lines of business. However, under a special rule, sponsors using separate lines may test a plan on a controlled group basis, provided the plan benefits (or, in the case of a CODA, makes eligible) at least 70 percent of all low-paid employees. For example, an employer that maintains different pension plans for different businesses in order to provide competitive benefits, but maintains a companywide CODA, may test the CODA on a controlled group basis, as long as at least 70 percent of the low-paid are eligible for the CODA, even though the employer tests its pension plans on a separate line basis.

Highly Compensated Employees (HCEs)

For years prior to 1997, the tax law contained extremely complicated provisions defining who was to be considered a highly compensated employee for purposes of various nondiscrimination requirements. These provisions were greatly simplified by the Small Business Job Protection Act of 1996. Beginning in 1997, an employee will be a highly compensated employee (HCE) if he or she (1) was a five percent owner of the employer during the current or preceding year, or (2) had compensation in the preceding year in excess of $80,000 (indexed for inflation) and (at the election of the employer) was in the top 20 percent of employees in terms of compensation for that year.

If the employer makes this election, the determination of who falls into the top 20 percent of employees is a two-step process. The first step is determining how many employees constitute 20 percent. In making this determination, employers may exclude:

- Employees who have not completed six months of service.
- Employees who normally work less than 17-1/2 hours per week.
- Employees who normally work less than six months during any year.
- Employees who have not attained age 21 by the end of the year.
- Employees who are included in a collective bargaining agreement that does not provide for participation in the plan, but only if 90 percent or more of all employees of the company are covered under such an agreement.
- Nonresident aliens with no U.S. source income.

The next step is identifying specific members of the top 20 percent. To do this, the employer must subtract excludable employees (except for union employees) from the total number of employees and multiply the resulting number by 20 percent. The excluded employees are added back in to determine which specific employees are in the top-paid group, however.

Assume, for example, that a company has 1,000 employees and 220 of them are excludable. The number of employees constituting the top 20 percent is 156 ([1,000 – 220] × .20). When all 1,000 employees (including the 220 who were excluded) are listed in descending order of pay, the first 156 constitute the top-paid group.

Some key points to keep in mind when determining who is an HCE include the following:

- The compensation on which the HCE determination is based is set forth in Section 414(q)(7), discussed below.
- The $80,000 dollar amount will be adjusted for increases in the CPI; after the new dollar amount is determined, it will be rounded down to the next lower multiple of $5,000.
- Family aggregation rules will not apply when determining who is an HCE, beginning in 1997.

- The entire controlled group or other aggregated group is examined when determining who is an HCE; the examination is not limited to the particular entity (within the larger controlled group) that sponsors the plan being tested. The regulations also state that the determinations for a particular plan are based on that plan's plan year. Thus, if an employer maintains two plans, each with a different plan year, it is possible that two different groups of HCEs will emerge— each group calculated with respect to a different plan year.

Compensation: Contributions

An employer may base plan contributions on behalf of an employee on any definition of compensation it chooses (e.g., base pay), provided the definition does not result in discrimination in favor of HCEs.

A special rule could affect the definition of compensation on which contributions may be based in some CODAs.[7] Generally, such a plan may base contributions on any definition of pay, such as regular or base pay. However, under the final 401(k) and 401(a)(4) regulations, the right to make each level of elective contributions (including the compensation on which those contributions are based) is a benefit, right, or feature that must be available to a nondiscriminatory group of employees. Thus, if a plan allows elective deferrals on base pay for one group of employees under a plan and total pay for another, each group would have to satisfy the nondiscrimination requirements with respect to benefits, rights, and features discussed below. In addition, if the plan definition of compensation has the effect of restricting access by non-highly compensated employees (NHCEs)—e.g., compensation in excess of the social security wage base—the plan's definition of compensation will be discriminatory even though the same definition is used for all employees under the plan. Similar rules govern the compensation on which aftertax employee and employer matching contributions are based.

---

7. IRS Reg. 1.401(k)-1(a)(4)(iv) and 1.401(m)-1(a)(2).

Compensation: Nondiscrimination Testing

The law is explicit as to the compensation that is to be used for various nondiscrimination testing and limitation purposes, regardless of the definition used for determining plan contributions.

Prior to the TRA '86, the sole IRC definition of compensation as it applied to qualified plans was found in Section 415(c)(3), which defines the compensation to be used in determining the annual limit on contributions and benefits that can be provided to a participant under a qualified plan. In general, 415(c)(3) compensation is W-2 compensation less income realized from the exercise of a nonqualified stock option or when restricted stock either becomes freely transferable or is no longer subject to a substantial risk of forfeiture, or from the sale of stock acquired under a qualified stock option or the disqualifying disposition of an incentive stock option. For limitation years beginning after 1997, Section 415(c)(3) compensation will include salary reductions under flexible benefit plans, amounts elected to be deferred under 457 plans and elective deferrals under CODAs, simplified employee pension arrangements, simple retirement accounts and tax-sheltered annuities.

TRA '86 added two new definitions of compensation in IRC Sections 414(q) and 414(s). Section 414(q)(7) defines the compensation that is to be used for determining who is an HCE. This is Section 415(c)(3) compensation plus salary reductions under flexible benefit plans and elective deferrals under CODAs, simplified employee pension arrangements and tax-sheltered annuities.[8] (Although these items will be included in Section 415(c)(3) compensation beginning in 1998, they were not part of the Section 415(c)(3) compensation definition at the time Section 414(q)(7) was added.) Section 414(s) specifies the compensation that is to be used for various nondiscrimination tests, permitting employers to select from among four definitions that are automatically deemed to meet Section 415(c)(3). These four safe harbors are:

- **Traditional 415 Compensation.** This is the basic 415 definition described above.

---

8. Tax-sheltered annuities are available to organizations exempt from tax under Section 501(c)(3) of the IRC (charities, hospitals, and certain educational organizations). They are authorized by Section 403(b) of the IRC and may be provided, on a tax-deferred basis, by employer contributions or by salary reductions up to specified limits.

- **Modified 415 Compensation.** This is sometimes referred to as the short list definition because it includes only some of the items included in the traditional definition. For example, deductible moving expenses are not included.
- **W-2 Wages.** The amount reported in Box 1 on Form W-2.
- **Wages Subject to Withholding.** This is compensation from which an employer must withhold federal income tax.

Exhibit 3–1 on pages 39–40 lists compensation elements and indicates whether they may be included in the safe harbor definitions.

Employers may modify the four safe harbor definitions for nondiscrimination testing purposes to include or exclude certain elements of compensation. Items that may be included for years prior to 1998 are elective deferrals under a CODA, a simplified employee pension arrangement, and a tax-sheltered annuity and salary reductions under a flexible benefits plan. Items that may be excluded are expense reimbursements or allowances, cash or non-cash fringe benefits, moving expenses, deferred compensation, and welfare benefits.

Instead of choosing from among the safe harbor definitions (with or without modifications), employers can use another or alternative definition of compensation for nondiscrimination testing purposes if it meets three criteria: (1) it must be reasonable; (2) it must not, by design, favor HCEs; and (3) it must meet an objective nondiscrimination test. To satisfy this last requirement, the ratio of the alternative definition of pay to total pay for the highly compensated group, on average, cannot exceed the same ratio for the non-highly compensated group by more than a *de minimis* amount. For this purpose, total pay must be determined using one of the four basic definitions described above, with or without the inclusion items.

NONDISCRIMINATION IN COVERAGE

The foregoing concepts lay the groundwork for a discussion of the basic qualification tests that a plan must meet if it is to achieve tax-qualified status. The first such test requires that a plan be nondiscriminatory as to coverage.[9]

---

9. IRC Section 410(b); IRS Reg. 1.410(b)-1 through 11.

414(s) Safe Harbors

Source of Income	Traditional 415	Modified 415	Wages Subject to Withholding	Box 10 of IRS Form W-2 (Taxable Compensation)
1. Base pay	Yes	Yes	Yes	Yes
2. Incentive payments (bonuses)	Yes	Yes	Yes	Yes
3. Overtime	Yes	Yes	Yes	Yes
4. Shift differential	Yes	Yes	Yes	Yes
5. Commissions	Yes	Yes	Yes	Yes
6. Holiday and vacation pay	Yes	Yes	Yes	Yes
7. Severance awards	Yes	Yes	Yes	Yes
8. Sick-pay (employer-paid)	Yes	No	Yes	Yes
9. Long-term disability benefits	Yes*	No	Yes*	Yes*
10. Pay in lieu of vacation	Yes	Yes	Yes	Yes
11. Employee FICA/FUTA paid by employer	Yes	Yes	Yes	Yes
12. Earned income from foreign sources (Code section 911)	Yes	Yes	Yes	Yes
13. Group term life coverage $50,000 (Code section 79)	Yes	Yes	No	Yes
14. Coverage under discriminatory self-insured medical plan (Code section 105(h))	Yes	No (if employer-provided)	Yes	Yes
15. Flex credits received as cash	Yes	Yes	Yes	Yes
16. Employer-provided education assistance (Code section 127)	No	No	No	No
17. Employer-provided dependent care assistance (Code section 129)	No	No	No	No
18. Services provided under group legal services plan (Code section 120)	No	No	No	No
19. Taxable business expenses, reimbursements, or allowances	Yes	Yes	Yes	Yes
20. Certain employee awards/ prizes (Code section 74(c))	No	No	No	No
21. Deductible moving expenses (Code section 217)	No	No	No	Yes[v]

E X H I B I T   3–1

414(s) Safe Harbors *(concluded)*

Source of Income	Traditional 415	Modified 415	Wages Subject to Withholding	Box 10 of IRS Form W-2 (Taxable Compensation)
22. Nondeductible moving expenses (Code section 217)	Yes	No	Yes	Yes
23. 401(k) salary deferrals**	Yes***	No	No	No
24. 403(b) salary reductions	Yes***	No	No	No
25. Unfunded ERISA excess/ supplemental executive retirement plan (SERP) distributions	Yes	Yes	Yes	Yes
26. Amount taxable from 83(b) election	Yes	No	Yes	Yes
27. Amount taxable from vesting of restricted stock	No	No	Yes	Yes
28. Amount taxable from early sale or exchange of stock under ISO	No	No	No	Yes
29. Amount includable from exercise of nonqualified stock option	No	No	Yes	Yes
30. 125 cafeteria plan salary deferrals	Yes***	No	No	No
31. Amount includable from exercise of stock appreciation rights	Yes	Yes	Yes	Yes

Notes:

(1) It is not clear whether amounts paid in respect of periods after employment has terminated are included in the Section 414 definitions. This affects items 7, 9, 10, and 25.

(2) Items 16, 17, 18, and 20 assume satisfaction of statutory requirements for exclusion from gross income.

(3) The Section 414(s) regulations mandate certain adjustments to the normal definitions of wages subject to withholding or Box 1 reporting. As a result, the entries in these columns cannot be relied on for use in determining real wages for withholding or Box 1 reporting purposes.

(4) It is not clear whether the statutory change in the definition of Section 415(c)(3) compensation will carry through to each of the alternative definitions of compensation (i.e., the modified definition, wages subject to withholding and W-2 compensation). This affects Source of Income items 23, 24, and 30.

*Unless purchased with employee contributions.

**Excess deferrals that are not distributed by the April 15 deadline and excess contributions whether recharacterized or distributed are not included in 415 compensation. Excess contributions distributed more than two and a half months after close of plan year are subject to withholding.

***For years beginning after 1997.

ᵛEmployer may elect to exclude deductible moving expenses.

A plan will be considered nondiscriminatory as to coverage if it meets one of the following two tests:

- The ratio percentage test.
- The average benefits test.

Before discussing these tests, it is important to note that while employers must, in general, test each single plan to determine whether it meets the coverage requirements, there are certain single plans that *must* be disaggregated—or treated as two or more plans—for this purpose. More specifically, the portion of a plan that covers union employees, or consists of contributions subject to Sections 401(k) or 401(m), or is an ESOP, must be tested separately from the other portion of the plan.[10]

It is also possible for employers to aggregate two or more plans and test them as a single plan to meet the coverage rules, except for the plans or portions of plans that must be disaggregated. (Thus, union plans, CODAs and ESOPs *cannot* be aggregated with other plans for coverage testing.) An employer is permitted to aggregate plans for purposes of the ratio percentage test and the nondiscriminatory classification test that is part of the average benefit test. If an employer aggregates plans for coverage testing, however, the plans must also be aggregated when testing for nondiscrimination in contributions (discussed in detail beginning on page 46). For example, if an employer aggregates two CODAs—one covering hourly employees and the other salaried employees—to pass the coverage test, these CODAs will have to be combined in testing for nondiscrimination in contributions and benefits.

The Ratio Percentage Test

To perform the ratio percentage test, the employer must divide its universe of employees into two parts: HCEs and NHCEs. In doing so, the employer may exclude certain employees—those who have not met the plan's minimum age and service requirements, certain nonresident aliens, certain terminating employees, and employees represented by a collective bargaining unit (if the employer is not testing that portion of the plan). The percentage of HCEs benefiting

---

10. IRS Reg. 1.410(b)-7.

under the plan is determined by dividing the number of HCEs benefiting by the total number of HCEs in the controlled group. An employee benefits under a defined contribution plan for a plan year only if he or she actually receives a contribution during that plan year; however, an employee who is eligible to have made elective deferrals under a CODA is considered to be benefiting even though he or she makes no elective deferrals. The same procedure is followed for the NHCEs.

The plan will pass the ratio percentage test if the percentage of NHCEs benefiting under the plan is at least 70 percent of the percentage of HCEs who so benefit.

Assume an employer has 200 hourly NHCEs, 600 salaried NHCEs, and 100 salaried HCEs, and it maintains a CODA that benefits only salaried employees. Because 100 percent of the HCEs benefit, the plan would have to benefit at least 70 percent of the NHCEs to pass the ratio percentage test. The plan does pass, since it benefits 75 percent of the NHCE group (600 of 800 NHCEs).

The Average Benefit Test

If a plan fails to pass the ratio percentage test on either a standalone or an aggregated basis, it must pass the average benefit test. This test has two parts: the classification test and the average benefit percentage test.

In order to meet the *classification* test, a plan must cover a classification of employees that is reasonable and is nondiscriminatory under an objective test. To meet the reasonable requirement, the classification must be reasonable and established under objective business criteria that identify the category of employee who benefits under the plan. The IRS would consider classifications by specified job categories and nature of compensation, for example, salaried or hourly, to be reasonable; a classification identifying covered individuals by name would be unacceptable, however.

The objective test for determining whether the classification is nondiscriminatory works like the ratio percentage test described above, but it uses different passing percentages. The regulations specify both safe and unsafe harbor percentages. A plan is in a safe harbor if the percentage of NHCEs who benefit is at least 50 percent of the percentage of HCEs who benefit. A plan is in an unsafe harbor if the percentage of NHCEs who benefit is 40 percent or less of the percentage of HCEs who benefit. A plan in a safe harbor automatically passes the classification test; a plan in an unsafe harbor automatically fails. A plan that lies somewhere in between will be subject to a facts and circumstances test.

Both the safe and unsafe harbor percentages are reduced if NHCEs make up more than 60 percent of the employer's work force, as shown in Exhibit 3-2 on page 44.

A plan that fails the classification test cannot be qualified unless it can pass the test by being aggregated with some other plan.

A plan that passes the classification test must still satisfy the *average benefit percentage* part of the average benefit test. This part of the test is satisfied if the average benefit percentage (ABP) for NHCEs, determined as described below, is at least 70 percent of the ABP for HCEs.

To perform this test, the employer must determine a benefit percentage for each employee (with limited exceptions). All qualified plans—including plans subject to testing under Sections 401(k) and (m) and ESOPs—must be tested together. Because plans (and portions of plans) that cover union employees are deemed to satisfy the coverage requirements, only nonunion employees are included in the testing group. Only employer-provided benefits are tested. Thus, when a plan or portion of a plan subject to 401(m) is included in the testing group, aftertax employee contributions are ignored in determining employee benefit percentages.

If a plan covers both union and nonunion employees and identical provisions (i.e., the benefit formula, optional forms of benefits, ancillary benefits, and other rights and features) apply to each participant in the plan, a special rule is available. In this situation, the plan will be deemed to satisfy the average benefit percentage test if the plan as a whole satisfies the ratio percentage test and the union and nonunion groups covered under the plan separately satisfy the nondiscriminatory classification test discussed above.

In simple terms, the ABP test works as follows. The employer determines an annual contribution or accrual rate for each employee under each plan, representing total contributions made and/or accruals credited on behalf of the employee for the year, and divides that rate by the employee's compensation to determine a percentage. If a plan can be integrated with social security, this percentage may then be increased by an amount representing

EXHIBIT 3-2

Safe/Unsafe Harbor Percentages

Low-Paid Concentration Percentage	Safe Harbor Percentage	Unsafe Harbor Percentage
0-60%	50.00%	40.00%
61	49.25	39.25
62	48.50	38.50
63	47.75	37.75
64	47.00	37.00
65	46.25	36.25
66	45.50	35.50
67	44.75	34.75
68	44.00	34.00
69	43.25	33.25
70	42.50	32.50
71	41.75	31.75
72	41.00	31.00
73	40.25	30.25
74	39.50	29.50
75	38.75	28.75
76	38.00	28.00
77	37.25	27.25
78	36.50	26.50
79	35.75	25.75
80	35.00	25.00
81	34.25	24.25
82	33.50	23.50
83	32.75	22.75
84	32.00	22.00
85	31.25	21.25
86	30.50	20.50
87	29.75	20.00
88	29.00	20.00
89	28.25	20.00
90	27.50	20.00
91	26.75	20.00
92	26.00	20.00
93	25.25	20.00
94	24.50	20.00
95	23.75	20.00
96	23.00	20.00
97	22.25	20.00
98	21.50	20.00
99	20.75	20.00

the employer-provided portion of social security. The resulting percentage is added to the percentage for plans that cannot be integrated (e.g., CODAs and ESOPs) and the result is the benefit percentage for each employee. These percentages are then averaged for both HCEs and NHCEs to determine whether the average benefit percentage for NHCEs is at least 70 percent of the ABP for HCEs.

The ABP may be calculated on a contribution or benefits basis. The employer may also determine ABPs separately for all defined benefit and defined contribution plans, provided certain conditions are met.

A plan must generally satisfy the coverage requirements on each day of the plan year, looking at employees on each particular day. Under a quarterly testing option, a plan will be deemed to satisfy the coverage requirements for a plan year if the coverage requirements are met on one day of each quarter, looking at employees on the day being tested. Under an annual testing option, a plan may satisfy the coverage requirements on the last day of the plan year; all individuals who are or were employees at any time during the plan year must be taken into account under this option, however. Employers *must* use the annual testing option when testing a plan subject to Sections 401(k) or 401(m) and when performing the average benefit percentage test.[11]

NHCEs are not affected when a plan fails to meet the coverage requirements, but HCEs will be taxed on the present value of vested employer-derived benefits and on income on any contributions to the extent such amounts have not been previously taxed. Employers can retroactively correct their plans to cure coverage problems; retroactive corrections are also permitted to meet the contribution nondiscrimination requirements discussed below. Such corrections must be made within nine and a half months after the close of the plan year (e.g., October 15 in the case of a calendar year plan). Thus, for example, an employer may amend its plan retroactively to grant allocations to employees who had not been

---

11. The IRS allows employers to perform the coverage tests on a "snapshot" group of employees present on any day of a plan year. The group would need to be representative of the employee population during the entire plan year, although variations attributable to extraordinary events such as a merger could be ignored. In addition, barring significant changes in plan provisions, in the work force or in compensation practices, employers would be required to perform the tests only once every three years.

covered under the plan. But an employer may *not* retroactively amend plans subject to Sections 401(k) or 401(m) so as to extend eligibility to satisfy the coverage requirements.

The foregoing discussion of coverage testing under Section 410(b) is not exhaustive, but it should convey some of the complexities involved in the qualification process. It also indicates the extent to which the IRS is quantifying nondiscrimination testing, rather than relying on subjective or qualitative judgments as it has in the past.

NONDISCRIMINATION IN CONTRIBUTIONS

A plan cannot be tax-qualified if it provides for contributions or benefits in amounts that discriminate in favor of HCEs.[12] Further, every optional form of benefit, subsidy, or other right or feature under the plan must be available to a nondiscriminatory group of employees.

Amount Testing

The portion of a plan that consists of a CODA is considered to be nondiscriminatory with respect to contribution amounts if it satisfies the actual deferral percentage (ADP) test under Section 401(k) of the IRC. In addition, the portion of a plan that represents after-tax employee contributions and employer matching contributions not used in the ADP test is considered to be nondiscriminatory if it satisfies the actual contribution percentage (ACP) test of Section 401(m). Beginning in 1999, nondiscrimination testing will not be required for elective contributions and matching contributions that meet safe harbor provisions of the law. (The ADP and ACP tests,

---

12. IRC Section 401(a)(4); IRS Reg. 1.401(a)(4)-1 through 13. The nondiscrimination requirements are extremely complicated. This discussion focuses on application of the requirements to defined contribution plans, and plans subject to Sections 401(k) and 401(m) in particular, on a stand-alone basis. For a detailed discussion of the nondiscrimination requirements for defined benefit plans and plans that must be aggregated with other plans to meet the requirements, see James G. Durfee, Russell E. Hall, Christian L. Lindgren, Frances G. Sieller, Douglas J. Tormey, and John F. Woyke, *A Guide to the Final Nondiscrimination Regulations* (New York: Research Institute of America, January 1994).

and these safe harbors, are described in detail in Chapter 4.) As noted earlier, a plan that fails to satisfy the nondiscrimination requirements can be corrected on a retroactive basis. This is not the case for a plan that fails the ADP or ACP test; failure of these tests can only be cured by following the special rules covered in Chapter 4.

Defined contribution plans other than CODAs will be deemed to provide nondiscriminatory contributions if they meet one of two design-based safe harbors (or the general test described below) set forth in final regulations issued by the IRS.

The first defined contribution plan safe harbor is for plans with a uniform contribution formula—that is, where contributions equal the same percentage of compensation or the same dollar amount for every employee covered by the plan. In addition, key provisions such as the vesting schedule and definition of years of service must apply uniformly to all participants. If the plan integrates with social security benefits by providing a higher contribution percentage for pay above a specified level than for pay below that level, the plan will be deemed to satisfy this safe harbor if the formula meets the "permitted disparity" requirements of Section 401(l).[13]

The second safe harbor applies to nonintegrated uniform points plans, other than ESOPs, that allocate contributions based on a formula weighted for age and/or service and units of compensation that do not exceed $200. This is not a true safe harbor because some additional testing is required: the average of the allocation rates for HCEs in the plan cannot exceed the average of the allocation rates for the NHCEs in the plan.

Most defined contribution plans will meet the uniform contribution safe harbor. While many plans that base allocations on an age- or service-weighted formula will not meet the second safe harbor, such plans may still be considered nondiscriminatory under a general test that permits employers to restructure a plan into component plans. A plan will pass this test if each rate group under the plan satisfies the coverage requirements (e.g., the ratio percentage test discussed above). An employer may establish rate

---

13. Requirements for integrating plans with social security benefits are discussed on page 50.

groups on either a contribution or benefits basis. Generally, testing a defined contribution plan with an age- and service-weighted formula on a benefits basis will be most advantageous. To test its plan on a benefits basis, the employer converts contributions and forfeitures allocated to each participant's account for a particular year into current accruals. It then groups these accrual rates into ranges and treats all accrual rates within a range as equal. A range of 0.5 percent, or a range from 95 percent to 105 percent of a midpoint would be acceptable; to illustrate, accrual rates of from 2-1/2 percent to 3 percent of pay could be treated as being identical, as could accrual rates of between 9-1/2 percent and 10-1/2 percent of pay. The employer then establishes a rate group for every HCE in the plan and all other employees (both HCEs and NHCEs) in the plan who have an accrual rate at least equal to that of the HCE. If each rate group in a plan satisfies the coverage requirements as if it were a stand-alone plan, the plan as a whole will satisfy the nondiscrimination requirements.

The final regulations also permit an employer to restructure a plan into component plans on the basis of employee groups. The employer can use any criteria to select employee groups for this purpose, and groups can change from year to year. Examples of employee groups that can be used as a basis for restructuring include employees who work at the same work site, are in the same job classification, have the same form of compensation (hourly versus salaried), are in the same division or subsidiary or the same unit acquired in a merger or acquisition, have the same number of years of service, or are covered under the same benefit or contribution formula. Another attribute or classification may be used, but it might not be considered reasonable under the classification test discussed above.

Assume a profit-sharing plan covers employees at Division A and Division B, providing Division A employees with a 10 percent of pay contribution and employees of Division B with a 15 percent contribution. This plan will not meet the uniform formula safe harbor. If the employer restructures the plan based on employee groups, each component plan (one consisting of Division A employees and the other of Division B employees) would meet the uniform formula safe harbor and would be considered nondiscriminatory provided each component plan satisfied the coverage requirements.

Benefits, Rights, and Features

Optional forms of benefits, ancillary benefits, and all other benefits, rights, and features must also be available to employees on a nondiscriminatory basis. To satisfy this requirement, these plan features must be *currently available* to a group of employees that satisfies the nondiscriminatory classification test of Section 410(b), but they need not satisfy the average benefit test. Benefits, rights, and features must also be *effectively available* to a group of employees that does not substantially favor HCEs, based on all the facts and circumstances. This provision is intended to prevent abusive situations where only HCEs meet the criteria for a benefit, right, or feature.

In general, a determination as to whether a benefit, right, or feature is currently available to an employee is based on current facts and circumstances (e.g., current compensation or current position). Thus, if a benefit, right, or feature is subject to an eligibility condition, only those who have satisfied that condition would be considered to benefit. Certain special rules apply, however. For example, age and service conditions may generally be disregarded with respect to an optional form of benefit (but not ancillary benefits) unless the conditions must be satisfied within a limited period of time. Certain other conditions (e.g., death, disability, hardship, default on a plan loan, or election of a benefit form) may also be ignored.

An employer can also permissively aggregate two or more benefits, rights, or features to satisfy the nondiscrimination rules. To do so, one of the benefits, rights, or features must be of equal or greater value; and the more valuable benefit, right, or feature must satisfy the current and effective availability tests on a stand-alone basis.

A special rule is also available where an employer engages in an acquisition of stock or assets or merges with another company. In these situations, if a benefit, right, or feature satisfies 401(a)(4) immediately before and after the transaction, the benefit, right, or feature will be deemed to satisfy 401(a)(4) for all plan years after the year of the transaction. Thus, if an employer acquires a subsidiary that sponsors a CODA with a loan feature, and the new parent's CODA does not have such a feature, the loan feature in the subsidiary's CODA will be nondiscriminatory in all subsequent plan years if it met the nondiscrimination requirements on the day before and the day after the transaction.

Optional Forms of Benefits These are the distribution options under the plan, such as lump sums, installment payouts, or distributions in the form of stock. Any difference in the terms of an option will create a different optional form, and each form must meet the nondiscrimination standard. Thus, if a plan offers 10-year and 15-year installment options, each installment option would have to meet the nondiscrimination standard.

Ancillary Benefits In the case of a defined contribution plan, ancillary benefits include any life and health insurance provided under the plan, as well as any death benefits. Again, any such benefit available to different employees on terms that are not substantially identical must be tested as two or more benefits.

Rights and Features Rights and features include other plan features that are not considered optional forms of benefits or ancillary benefits. Examples include the right to make each level of aftertax employee and elective deferrals (including the compensation on which such contributions are based), plan loan provisions, the right to direct investments, or the right to a particular form of investment. Each would have to be currently available and effectively available on a nondiscriminatory basis.

THE INTEGRATION RULES

Social security benefits replace a higher percentage of preretirement pay for lower-paid individuals than for the higher-paid, as Exhibit 3–3 illustrates.

In recognition of the way social security is structured, the tax law in effect allows a limited form of discrimination; it permits employers to provide additional contributions or benefits for higher-paid employees under a qualified plan[14] to compensate for the fact that the relative value of social security decreases as pay goes up. Thus, a defined contribution plan can have two

---

14. IRC Sections 401(a)(4) and 401(l); IRS Reg. 1.401(a)(4)-12(b)(2)(ii) and 1.401(l)-1 through 6.

E X H I B I T   3–3

Social Security Income Replacement

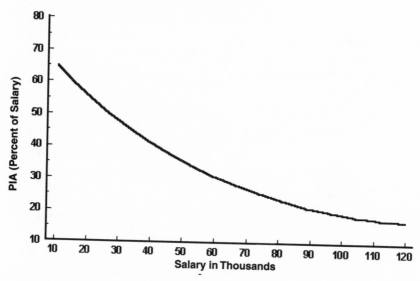

contribution levels—one for pay up to a specified amount, and another higher contribution for pay in excess of that amount. If the plan is to meet the qualification requirements, the difference between the two contribution levels cannot exceed a certain amount—called the permitted disparity. A plan that uses this type of contribution formula is said to be integrated or coordinated with social security benefits.

Before reviewing the integration requirements in more detail, the following points should be noted:

- An ESOP cannot be integrated with social security benefits.[15]

- The CODA portion of a plan cannot be integrated with social security benefits (see Chapter 4).

- Total integration is available only once. If an employer maintains a defined benefit pension plan that takes social security benefits into account to the fullest extent permitted

---

15. IRS Reg. 54.4975-11(a)(7)(ii).

by law, for example, it has no more capacity to integrate a defined contribution plan covering the same employees.

- A plan that does not meet the integration rules set out in IRC Section 401(l), which are discussed below, may still achieve qualified status if it can meet the general nondiscrimination tests of Section 401(a)(4); in a sense, the integration rules of Section 401(l) are safe harbors for compliance purposes.

The point at which the contribution percentage changes in a defined contribution plan that is coordinated with social security is called the plan's integration level. If a plan calls for a contribution of 3 percent on pay up to $20,000 and 5 percent on pay in excess of that amount, the plan's integration level is $20,000. The law permits a plan to use an integration level in any plan year of any amount up to the social security taxable wage base at the beginning of that year, for example, $62,700 for 1996.

When a plan's integration level equals the social security taxable wage base, the contribution percentage for pay above this amount may *exceed* the contribution percentage for pay below this amount by the lesser of: (1) 5.7 percent[16] and (2) the percentage applicable to pay below the wage base. In other words, when the contribution percentage applicable to pay below the integration level is equal to or less than 5.7 percent, the contribution percentage for pay above the integration level cannot be more than twice the lower contribution percentage; if the lower contribution percentage is 4 percent, for example, the higher percentage cannot exceed 8 percent. Similarly, if the lower contribution percentage is greater than 5.7 percent, then the higher percentage cannot be more than the lower percentage plus 5.7 percent; if the lower contribution percentage is 6 percent, for example, the higher percentage cannot exceed 11.7 percent (.06 plus .057). These integration limits are illustrated in Exhibit 3–4 on page 53.

The permitted disparity limits discussed above are available only if the plan's integration level is set either at the social security taxable wage base or at or below an amount equal to 20 percent of that wage base (or $12,540 for 1996). If the integration level falls

---

16. The portion of the social security tax for old-age benefits will be used for this limitation if it ever exceeds 5.7 percent; this is not likely to occur in the foreseeable future, however.

E X H I B I T   3–4

Defined Contribution Plan Integration Limits

Integration Level of Social Security Taxable Wage Base	
If Lower Contribution Percentage Is:	Upper Contribution Percentage Cannot Exceed:
1.0%	2.0%
2.0	4.0
3.0	6.0
4.0	8.0
5.0	10.0
5.7	11.4
6.0	11.7
7.0	12.7
8.0	13.7

between these two amounts, the 5.7 percent standard in the permitted disparity rules is reduced. If the plan's integration level is more than 80 percent of the social security taxable wage base, it is reduced to 5.4 percent; if the integration level falls between 20 percent and 80 percent of the wage base, it is reduced to 4.3 percent.

If a plan uses an integration level of $20,000 in 1996, for example, the permitted disparity rules operate as follows:

- If the lower contribution percentage is equal to or less than 4.3 percent, the higher contribution percentage can still be as much as twice the lower percentage.

- If the lower contribution percentage is greater than 4.3 percent, the higher contribution percentage can be as much as the lower percentage plus 4.3 percent.

INDIVIDUAL LIMITS

To achieve tax-qualified status, a defined contribution plan must observe two statutory limits on contributions. The first is a limit on the annual additions that may be made each year to an employee's account.[17] The second is a limit on the amount of an employee's

---

17. IRC Section 415(c); IRS Reg. 1.415-6.

compensation that may be taken into account in determining contributions made on the employee's behalf.[18]

Annual Additions Limit

Section 415 of the IRC imposes a limit on the total employer and employee contributions that may be added to an employee's account each year under a defined contribution plan. Any forfeitures that might be reallocated to an employee's account when other employees terminate without full vesting are also included under this limit. It should be noted that these limits are applied on a controlled group basis; for this purpose, however, the controlled group concept is applied to a parent/subsidiary group on the basis of more than 50 percent ownership or control, rather than 80 percent.

The basic limit is as follows: the amount added to an employee's account each year cannot exceed the smaller of: (1) 25 percent of the employee's compensation, and (2) $30,000. This $30,000 dollar amount will increase with changes in the CPI. The current indexing mechanism applies the percentage increase in the CPI and then rounds the result to the next lowest multiple of $5,000. Prior to 1995, the defined contribution limit was scheduled to be one fourth of the dollar limit for defined benefit plans, and both limits were to move in tandem with changes in the CPI. This is no longer the case, and both dollar limits will now move independently.

For limitation years beginning prior to 1998, an employee's elective (pretax) deferrals to a 401(k) plan, simplified employee pension and a tax-sheltered annuity, and salary reduction contributions to a flexible benefits plan, will lower the annual additions limit. If an employee with gross compensation of $60,000 defers $6,000 to a 401(k) plan, for example, her annual addition limit will be the lesser of $30,000 or 25 percent of $54,000. The limit is thus $13,500, or $1,500 less than the limit that would have applied without the deferral. For limitation years beginning after 1997, however, these deferrals or salary reduction contributions will not

---

18. IRC Section 401(a)(17); IRS Reg. 1.401(a)(17)-1.

reduce an employee's compensation for purposes of determining the Section 415 annual additions limit.

The percentage limit applies to compensation, as defined in Section 415(c)(3),[19] in a limitation year—the calendar year unless the employer elects otherwise. An election to use other than the calendar year must be made by all members of a controlled group that maintain a plan. The plan year and the limitation year will typically be the same 12-month period.

This limit on annual additions should not be confused with the tax deduction limits that apply to *sponsors* of defined contribution plans (see Chapter 6). The annual addition limit applies individually to each participant.

Plans have previously been permitted to return aftertax employee contributions that exceeded the 415 annual addition limit because of the allocation of forfeitures, a reasonable error in estimating a participant's compensation or other limited circumstances justifying relief.[20] Now the regulations also allow a plan to refund elective deferrals to correct a reasonable error in determining the amount of elective deferrals that may be made to the plan. Treasury officials have indicated orally that this provision contemplates a refund of elective deferrals to correct a reasonable error in determining the 25 percent of compensation limit, but that elective deferrals generally cannot be returned if the dollar limit on annual additions is exceeded.

Refunded elective deferrals, as well as refunded employee aftertax contributions, are disregarded for purposes of the ADP and ACP tests.[21] In addition, refunded elective deferrals do not count toward the dollar cap on elective deferrals.

A plan must also provide for the return of income on refunded elective deferrals and aftertax employee contributions. If such income is not refunded, it will be treated as an additional employee contribution, if attributable to aftertax employee contributions, or as an additional employer contribution, if attributable

---

19. See page 37.
20. IRS Reg. 1.415-6(b)(6).
21. IRS Reg. 1.415-6(b)(6)(iv).Note, however, that this is generally not the case for elective deferrals that are refunded due to the elective deferral limit; in this situation, the refunded elective deferrals are taken into account for the ADP test.

to an elective deferral. In either case, it counts as an annual addition for the year in which the contribution was made.

As noted, Section 415 also limits the benefits payable from a defined benefit plan.[22] This limit is generally the lesser of: (1) 100 percent of high three-year average pay, and (2) a specified dollar amount. This dollar amount was set at $90,000 by TRA '86, and increases with changes in the CPI ($120,000 for 1996).[23] As is the case with the defined contribution limit, the dollar amount, after adjustment for CPI changes, is rounded down to the next lower multiple of $5,000. If an employer maintains both a defined benefit and a defined contribution plan, a special combined plan limit applies for years through 1999. The pension simplification provisions of the Small Business Job Protection Act of 1996 repealed this combined plan limit for years after 1999, however.[24]

To test compliance with the combined plan limit, for years that it is applicable, the projected annual benefit under the defined benefit plan and the annual additions to the defined contribution plan are converted into fractions, as follows:

- The defined benefit fraction is generally the participant's projected annual benefit (as of the close of the limitation year) divided by 125 percent of that year's applicable defined benefit dollar limit (or 140 percent of final pay if lower—an unlikely situation).

- The defined contribution fraction is determined on a cumulative basis. It is the sum of the annual additions made to the participant's account (as of the close of the limitation year) divided by an accumulated amount. This, in turn, is the sum, for each year of service, of the lesser of: (1) 125 percent of the defined contribution dollar limit for such year, or (2) 140 percent of compensation eligible under the defined contribution plan for such year of service. For this purpose, service is recognized even for years that the plan was not in effect.

These two fractions, when added together, cannot exceed 1.0. If they do, contributions and/or benefits must be reduced until the fractions total 1.0 or less. While reductions can be applied to either

---

22. IRC Section 415(b); IRS Reg. 1.415-3.
23. IRC Section 415(d).
24. IRC Section 415(e); IRS Reg. 1.415-7.

or both plans, most employers have chosen to reduce benefits under the defined benefit plan. For one thing, it is simpler, from a plan design and administration perspective, to make up lost benefits under the defined benefit plan. Another reason was that using the defined contribution plan to the fullest extent possible maximized certain tax benefits, such as taxation of unrealized appreciation on employer stock. The elimination of the combined plan limit for years after 1999 is a further reason for reducing benefits under the defined benefit plan for the few years that remain while the limit applies.

Limit on Compensation

TRA '86 added Section 401(a)(17) to the IRC, limiting the amount of an employee's compensation that can be taken into account in determining contributions and benefits under a qualified plan. This limit was originally set at $200,000 and was indexed to increase with changes in the CPI. By 1993, it had grown to $235,840. The Omnibus Budget Reconciliation Act of 1993 (OBRA '93) reduced the limit to $150,000, beginning in 1994. While this new pay cap is also indexed, it will only increase in $10,000 increments—that is, only when accumulated changes amount to at least $10,000. Because this is an annual limit, a defined contribution plan can provide contributions on pay up to the limit even though the employee does not participate for the entire plan year.

ADDITIONAL REQUIREMENTS

Other requirements that plans must meet to qualify for favorable tax treatment are summarized below.

Nondiversion/Exclusive Benefit Rules

A qualified plan must be established and operated for the exclusive benefit of plan participants and their beneficiaries, and it must be impossible for the employer to divert or recapture contributions before all plan liabilities are satisfied.[25] There are exceptions to this requirement for defined contribution plans. The first is that a plan

---

25. IRC Section 401(a)(2).

or amendment may be established on a conditional basis so that employer contributions are returnable within one year from the denial of initial qualification if the plan is not approved by the IRS. The second is that employer contributions may be made contingent on their tax deductibility and, to the extent a deduction is disallowed, may be returned within one year from the date of disallowance. The third exception permits a return of employer contributions within one year of the time they were made if they were made on the basis of a mistake of fact.[26]

Permanency

Although an employer may reserve the right to amend or terminate a plan at any time, it must establish a plan with the intent that it will be permanent. While employer contributions to a profit-sharing plan need not be made in accordance with a definite predetermined formula, a single or occasional contribution will not be sufficient to meet this requirement. "Permanent" has never been fully defined; as a general rule, however, a plan in existence for at least 10 years is considered to have met the permanency requirement. In any case, the regulations require that substantial and recurring contributions be made if a specific contribution formula is not included in the plan.[27]

Service Counting

Determining an employee's length of service is a critical task in any qualified plan, because many important plan provisions depend on service—including an employee's initial eligibility to participate in the plan, vesting, and, in some situations, the plan's contribution formula.

Basic Principles   For purposes of initial eligibility, vesting, and eligibility for benefit accruals, the law requires that service be determined under specific rules, using one or more alternative

26. Rev. Rul. 91-4.
27. IRS Reg. 1.401-1(b)(2).

methods of compliance.[28] These mandatory rules do not apply in determining service for other purposes, although any method used must be nondiscriminatory in both design and operation. Most employers adopt a single method of determining service for all purposes, since a consistent approach eliminates potential confusion and additional administrative work, and simplifies employee communications.

Under the mandatory rules, an employee must be given credit for a year of service for any computation period during which he or she is credited with at least 1,000 hours of service. Once participation has commenced, the employee must receive a ratable benefit accrual for any computation period during which he or she is credited with at least 1,000 hours.[29] Hours of service and computation periods are defined as follows:

- **Hour of Service:** In general, an hour of service is one for which an employee is paid or entitled to payment for the performance of duties with the employer. It also includes hours for which the employee is paid (or entitled to payment) during which no duties are performed due to vacation, holiday, illness, incapacity, layoff, jury duty, military duty, or leave of absence. Hours for which back pay is awarded or agreed to by the employer are also included. However, a plan need not credit an employee with more than 501 hours of service for any single period during which the employee performs no duties or for which payment is made under workers' compensation, unemployment compensation, or state disability income laws while the employee is not working.

- **Computation Period:** A computation period is a 12-month period and may be a plan year, a calendar year, or the employee's employment year. In the case of service for initial eligibility purposes, however, the initial 12-month

---

28. IRC Section 410(a) and ERISA Section 202(a). Regulations interpreting these service requirements are issued by the Department of Labor (DOL) for both the labor and tax provisions of the law, however. See DOL Reg. 2530.200b-1 through 5.

29. Defined contribution plans can also require that the employee be employed on the last day of the plan year in order to receive a benefit accrual for that year, provided this does not result in prohibited discrimination. See DOL Reg. 2530.200b-1(b) and Rev. Rul. 76-250.

period must begin with the actual date of employment. Subsequent computation periods for eligibility can continue to be employment years or may be changed to plan years, provided the first such plan year includes the first anniversary of the first day on which the employee was credited with an hour of service.

A break in service occurs when an employee is credited with fewer than 501 hours of service in a computation period. If the employee is credited with at least 501 but fewer than 1,000 hours of service in a computation period, the employee will not incur a break in service, but he or she will not be credited with a year of service.

Compliance Methods   The basic method of complying with the service counting rules is the hours counting method, which takes all hours worked plus additional nonworked hours into account. This approach requires employers to keep records of actual hours of service. In lieu of using hours counting, employers may use an equivalency method or the elapsed time method.

There are four alternative equivalency methods. The first uses *hours worked*, determining service on the basis of actual hours worked, including overtime and excluding all other nonworked hours. The second uses only *regular hours worked*, excluding overtime and nonworked hours. The third uses a *time period* selected by the plan—day, shift, week, half-month, or month—and credits the employee with an imputed number of hours for the period involved as long as he or she works at least one hour during the period. The fourth uses *employee earnings*, calculating hours of service on the basis of earnings the employee received during the period involved.

The elapsed time method measures service from the employee's date of employment to date of severance.

An employer that uses an equivalency or the elapsed time method pays a penalty. In the case of a time period equivalency, the penalty is that an employee will be credited with more hours for the period than are usually worked. Hours that must be credited for the various time periods are as follows:

- One day—10 hours.
- One week—45 hours.

- Half-month—95 hours.
- One month—190 hours.
- Shift—actual hours in the shift.

The penalty associated with the other equivalencies is a reduction in the 1,000 and 501 hours standards, as shown in Exhibit 3–5. And service spanning rules under the elapsed time method can require the granting of service for time not worked (but not for benefit accrual purposes) during the year after the employee's severance date.

Other Requirements   For benefit accrual purposes, service need not be counted for periods when the employee was not an active participant or was not making mandatory employee contributions (i.e., contributions required as a condition of participating in the plan). For vesting, service before the year in which the employee turns age 18 may be excluded, along with service when the plan was not in effect or service during years when mandatory employee contributions were not made. Because an employee's elective deferrals to a CODA are considered employer contributions, a plan presumably may not disregard service during years in which an employee did not make such deferrals.

If an employee resumes employment after a break in service, a question arises as to whether prebreak service will have to be aggregated with postbreak service. In general, no aggregation will be required until the employee is credited with one year of postbreak service. When this occurs, pre- and postbreak service must be aggregated if: (1) the employee had any degree of vesting in

E X H I B I T   3–5

Adjustments Required in Hours of Service Under Certain Equivalencies

Equivalency	Year of Service	Break in Service
Hours worked	870	435
Regular hours worked	750	375
Earnings		
Hourly-rated employees	870	435
Other employees	750	375

employer-provided benefits attributable to prebreak service, or (2) the break in service was shorter than five years.

If an employee (male or female) is absent from work due to the employee's pregnancy, the birth of a child, adoption, or child care immediately following birth or adoption, the law requires that the plan—for purposes of determining whether a break in service has occurred—treat as hours of service the lesser of the hours that would have been credited during the absence or 501 hours. If the employee would not have a break in service solely because of this rule, the hours are credited in the year in which the absence began; otherwise, they are credited in the following year.

The law permits what is known as decoupling—the use of different service counting methods within the same plan for eligibility, vesting, and benefit accrual purposes. It also permits the use of different methods for different classes of employees. An employer might use hours counting for part-time employees and use a time period equivalency for all other employees, for example. Decoupling is not permitted if it results in discrimination.

Minimum Participation Rules

As a general rule, a qualified plan cannot require, as a condition of eligibility, that an employee complete more than one year of service.[30] A two-year service requirement is acceptable if a plan provides for full and immediate vesting, except for a CODA.

In addition, a qualified plan cannot require that an employee be older than 21 to participate,[31] and it cannot set a maximum age for participation.

An individual who has reached age 21 and has one year of service must be allowed to commence plan participation by the earlier of: (1) the date that is six months after the date on which the eligibility requirements were met, or (2) the first day of the plan year beginning on or after the date on which the requirements were met.[32]

---

30. IRC Section 410(a)(1).
31. Ibid. The law allows tax-exempt educational organizations to use age 26 as a minimum age requirement in a plan that provides for full and immediate vesting.
32. IRS Reg. 1.410(a)-4(b).

Vesting Requirements

A qualified plan must provide that employees will have a vested right to their benefits under a specific set of rules.[33] The value of aftertax *employee* contributions must be fully vested at all times. The value of elective deferrals must also be fully vested at all times. The value of other *employer* contributions must be vested when an employee reaches the plan's normal retirement age, regardless of the employee's service at that time. Otherwise, the value of these other employer contributions must be vested under either of the following schedules:

- 100 percent vesting after five years of service.
- Graded vesting, with 20 percent after three years of service, increasing by 20 percent per year until 100 percent vesting is achieved after seven years.

Other vesting requirements for defined contribution plans include the following:

- QNECs, QMACs and employer matching contributions made to satisfy the safe harbors for CODA nondiscrimination testing must be fully vested at all times.
- Once vested, no forfeitures are permitted. If a plan has more liberal vesting provisions than the law requires, however, forfeitures are possible up to the time the employee would have to be vested under the law.[34] Thus, for example, a plan with full and immediate vesting could provide for forfeitures during the first five years of service in cases where an employee is terminated for dishonesty.
- Vested amounts of less than $3,500 may be paid in a lump sum at termination without employee consent; otherwise, an employee must consent to a lump sum payment and must have the right to leave his or her account balance in the plan until the later of age 62 or normal retirement age. A plan may not impose a significant detriment on a participant who does not consent to a distribution.[35]

---

33. IRC Section 411.
34. *Noell* v. *American Design, Inc. Profit-Sharing Plan*, 6 EBC 1833 (11th Cir. 1985); *Heppel* v. *Roberts & Dybdahl, Inc. Profit-Sharing Plan*, 2 EBC 2529 (8th Cir. 1980).
35. IRS Reg. 1.411(a)-11(c).

- When a plan is amended to change the vesting schedule, employees with at least three years of service must have the right to elect the former vesting schedule if it is more liberal.[36] As a practical matter, most plans in this situation provide that the participant's benefit will automatically be determined under the more favorable vesting schedule.

- If a participant terminates employment and receives a distribution of a partially vested interest in the value of employer contributions, he or she must be given a buy-back right if reemployed before incurring five consecutive breaks in service. This right allows the employee to repay the amount previously distributed within five years of being reemployed. If this is done, the employer must restore the amount forfeited by the employee on the prior termination, but this amount is not adjusted for any gains or losses that might have resulted had the amount not been forfeited.

Top-Heavy Rules

Special rules apply to any plan that is top-heavy.[37] A defined contribution plan is top-heavy in a plan year if, as of the determination date (generally, the last day of the preceding plan year), the sum of the account balances of all key employees participating in the plan is more than 60 percent of the sum of the account balances of *all* participating employees.

A key employee is defined as: (1) an officer with annual compensation greater than 50 percent of the Section 415 defined benefit dollar limit (or $60,000 for 1996); (2) one of the 10 employees owning the largest interests in the employer and receiving annual compensation greater than the Section 415 dollar limit on annual additions ($30,000 for 1996); (3) an employee who owns more than 5 percent of the employer; and (4) an employee who owns more than 1 percent of the employer and who receives annual compensation in excess of $150,000. Note that the definition of key

---

36. IRS Reg. 1.411(a)(10).
37. IRC Sections 401(a)(10) and 416.

employee is different from the definition of HCE used for other qualification purposes.

For each year that a defined contribution plan is top-heavy, nonkey employees must receive a minimum contribution of at least 3 percent of compensation (but not more than the percentage contributed for key employees). Reallocated forfeitures and elective deferrals under a CODA are considered to be employer contributions for purposes of determining the percentage for key employees. In addition, the plan must meet one of two fast vesting schedules: (1) 100 percent vesting after three years of service, or (2) graded vesting of at least 20 percent after two years of service, increasing in 20 percent increments until 100 percent vesting is achieved after six years.

The combined plan limit under Section 415, for the years applicable, also must be determined using 100 percent (rather than 125 percent) unless the plan meets a concentration test and provides an extra minimum benefit for nonkey employees. The concentration test is satisfied if the value of key employee account balances is not more than 90 percent of the value of all account balances. The extra minimum benefit required for nonkey employees under a defined contribution plan is 1 percent of compensation for each year during which the plan is top-heavy.

Joint and Survivor Requirements

The tax law contains elaborate provisions for the protection of a vested participant's spouse, both before and after retirement. In general, these joint and survivor requirements apply to defined benefit and money purchase pension plans.[38] Profit-sharing, stock bonus, or employee stock ownership plans need not comply with the joint and survivor requirements if: (1) the participant's vested account balance is paid in full upon his or her death to the participant's surviving spouse (unless the spouse consents in writing to

---

38. IRC Sections 401(a)(11) and 417. The rules specify that a married participant's benefit must be paid in the form of a qualified joint and survivor annuity for the benefit of the participant and his or her spouse unless the participant, with spousal consent, elects otherwise. If a vested participant dies before the annuity starting date, benefits must be paid to his or her spouse in the form of a qualified preretirement survivor annuity, unless waived with spousal consent.

the designation of a different beneficiary), (2) the participant has not elected benefits in the form of a life annuity,[39] and, (3) all or any portion of the participant's account balance has not been transferred from a plan subject to the joint and survivor rules. Most CODAs comply with these conditions to avoid the burden of administering and communicating the full joint and survivor rules. Note that spousal consent is not required for plan loans or in-service withdrawals if the participant's account balance is not subject to the joint and survivor rules at the time the loan or withdrawal is made.[40]

Distribution Rules

Unless otherwise requested by the employee, benefit payments must commence within 60 days of the latest of the following three events: (1) the plan year in which the employee terminates employment; (2) the completion of 10 years of participation; or (3) attainment of age 65 or the normal retirement age specified in the plan.[41]

An employee's account balance must be distributed in accordance with the minimum distribution rules. Prior to 1997, these rules required that distributions commence by April 1 following the calendar year in which the employee attains age 70-1/2, even if the employee remained employed. Beginning in 1997, however, qualified plan participants, other than 5 percent owners of the employer, are not required to begin receiving distributions until April 1 of the year following the later of (1) the calendar year in which the employee attains age 70-1/2, or (2) the calendar year in which the employee retires.

Further, the distribution must be completed over the life of the employee (or the joint lives of the employee and his or her beneficiary) or over a period that does not exceed the employee's life expectancy (or the joint life expectancy of the employee and beneficiary). Special rules apply in the case of distributions made on account of death.

---

39. Note, however, that this does not preclude the use of an installment payout that determines payments on the basis of the participant's life expectancy, as recalculated each year.
40. IRS Reg. 1.401(a)-20, Q&A 24.
41. IRC Section 401(a)(14).

Direct Rollovers and Transfers

Plans must provide, as a condition of qualification, that recipients of distributions eligible for rollover treatment may make "direct rollovers" or transfers of these amounts to an IRA or another qualified plan. While plans are required to make such rollovers or transfers for distributees, they are not required to accept them on behalf of new employees.

Assignments/QDROs

In general, a qualified plan must prohibit employees from assigning their benefits to others.[42] Exceptions have been granted for: (1) revocable assignments of up to 10 percent of benefit payments; (2) the use of up to 50 percent of an employee's vested interest as collateral for a loan made from the plan; and (3) assignments made pursuant to qualified domestic relations orders (QDROs).

A QDRO is a domestic relations order that is made in accordance with state domestic relations laws for alimony, child support, or the settlement of marital property rights.[43] Such an order must create or recognize the existence of a right to a benefit for an alternate payee or must assign to the alternate payee the right to receive all or part of the participant's benefit. Only the participant's spouse, former spouse, child, or other dependent may be an alternate payee.

A QDRO must specify the amount or percentage of the participant's benefit that is to be paid to the alternate payee(s) or how it is to be determined, as well as the plan and number of payments or period to which the order applies. The order must also include the name and last known mailing address of the participant and the alternate payee(s).

Although QDROs must be recognized by a plan, they cannot require types or forms of benefits not otherwise provided by the plan, nor can they require the plan to provide increased benefits.

Plans must have written procedures for determining the qualified status of domestic relations orders and for administering these orders. The plan administrator must promptly notify the participant and alternate payee(s) when an order has been received

---

42. IRC Section 401(a)(13); see also IRS Reg. 1.401(a)-(13).
43. IRC Section 414(p).

and must explain the plan's procedures for determining whether the order is a QDRO. The plan administrator must also notify the participant and alternate payee(s) of the determination of whether or not the order is a QDRO. While the determination process is under way, the administrator must account separately for amounts that would be payable to the alternate payee(s) under the order during the determination period. If, within 18 months, it is determined that the order is qualified, these segregated amounts (with interest) are paid to the alternate payee(s); otherwise, they are paid to the person who would have received them absent the order.

A QDRO may require the payment of benefits to an alternate payee while a participant is still employed, provided it does not call for payments to begin before the plan's early retirement age.

Early retirement age is defined as the earlier of (a) the date on which the participant is entitled to a distribution under the plan or (b) the later of the date the participant attains age 50, or the earliest date on which the participant could begin receiving benefits on separation from service. Thus, in certain circumstances, an alternate payee may begin receiving a distribution pursuant to a QDRO when the participant attains age 50, even though the participant may still be employed. This is permissible even in the case of a CODA that prohibits in-service distributions before age 59-1/2 except in case of hardship.

Technical changes made by TRA '86 and three IRS private letter rulings allow a plan to provide for an immediate payout to an alternate payee even before early retirement age.[44] A plan must specifically provide for the earlier payout. Such a provision may be desirable because it helps the administrator avoid maintaining separate accounts for an alternate payee. However, a plan presumably cannot force an immediate payout to an alternate payee; the QDRO, as well as the plan, must provide for immediate payout.

An alternate payee has the option of deferring distribution of the amount awarded in a QDRO. If the alternate payee elects to do so under a plan that offers different investment vehicles, it is unclear whether the plan must permit the alternate payee to choose how to invest this amount. According to the Senate Finance Committee report, alternate payees are considered beneficiaries.

---

44. TRA '86 Conference Committee Report, at II-858. PLR 8744023, 8743102, and 8837013.

Because other beneficiaries are generally not allowed to direct investments, an administrator could argue that an alternate payee should not be entitled to direct investments. In the absence of regulations, some employers are allowing former spouses to select investment vehicles, while other employers are selecting the vehicles themselves. If an employer selects the vehicle, the plan administrator may have fiduciary responsibility for that selection because the former spouse is considered a beneficiary.

It is unclear whether the amount of a loan outstanding at the time a QDRO is entered should be treated as part of the account balance for purposes of determining the award amount, although it seems logical that it should. It is also not clear whether an alternate payee who has an account balance under the plan should be permitted to take out a loan. However, it would seem reasonable for an employer to prohibit an alternate payee from using the plan's loan feature on the grounds that other beneficiaries are not allowed to do so. The plan administrator should make certain that the QDRO makes a clear statement on both issues.

Loans

Many defined contribution plans permit employees to make loans, using their account balances as collateral security. Both the IRC and ERISA except these loans from the prohibited transaction rules if certain requirements are met.[45] If the loan is not considered a prohibited transaction, it will not violate the assignment and alienation prohibition. If a loan is made and these requirements are not met, the plan could be considered to have engaged in a prohibited transaction. Under these circumstances, the loan would not be given an exception to the qualification requirements that benefits cannot be assigned, and the plan could be disqualified.

Plan loans are governed by a number of tax and labor law provisions, and may also be subject to the Federal Truth-in-Lending Act and the Equal Credit Opportunity Act. For ease of reference, all of these requirements are covered in Chapter 9.

---

45. IRC Section 4975(d)(1) and ERISA Section 408(b)(1). DOL Reg. 2550.408b-1 applies for purposes of the Code and ERISA.

Miscellaneous Requirements

Trust   If plan assets are held in trust, the general rule is that the trust must be organized or created in the United States and maintained at all times as a domestic trust.[46]

Leased Employees   Leased employees must be treated as an employee of any employer for whom the leased employee performs services for various qualified plan testing purposes.[47] A leased employee is any person who is not an employee of the recipient and who provides service to the recipient if: (1) such services are provided under an agreement between the leasing organization and the recipient; (2) such person has performed such services for the recipient on a substantially full-time basis for at least one year. For years prior to 1997, the services performed by such person had to be of a type historically performed in the business field of the recipient by employees; for 1997 and subsequent years, the services performed must be under the primary direction or control of the recipient. Leased employees may be ignored for plan qualification requirements if they do not constitute more than 20 percent of the recipient's non-highly compensated work force and they are covered by a plan maintained by the leasing organization that meets the following requirements: (1) the plan is a money purchase pension plan with a nonintegrated employer contribution rate of at least 10 percent of pay; (2) the plan provides for full and immediate vesting; and (3) each employee of the leasing organization immediately participates in the plan.

Anticutback Provisions   The law prohibits a plan amendment from reducing or eliminating an employee's accrued benefit—whether vested or not.[48] In the case of a defined contribution plan, the participant's accrued benefit is generally considered to be his or her account balance. In addition, an optional form of benefit (e.g., a lump sum or installment) may not be eliminated with respect to existing accrued benefits. Future accruals and the application of plan provisions to these future accruals may be changed, provided that existing accrued benefits are protected.

46. IRC Section 401(a); IRS Reg. 1.401-1(a)(3).
47. IRC Section 414(n).
48. IRC Section 411(d)(6).

Generally, these protected benefits may not be eliminated by reason of a transfer between plans.[49] However, *elective* transfers between plans that meet the following requirements are permissible—even if such transfers result in the elimination of a protected benefit:

- The participant makes a voluntary, fully informed election to transfer benefits to another plan of the same employer.
- In the case of a terminating plan, the plan has offered the participant all accrued and protected benefits; in an ongoing plan, the participant has the option of leaving his or her benefit in the plan if such benefit is greater than $3,500.
- In the case of a defined benefit or money purchase pension plan, qualified joint and survivor annuity notice and spousal consent requirements are met with respect to the transfer.
- The participant whose benefits are transferred is entitled to an immediate distribution from the plan.
- The entire nonforfeitable benefit is transferred, equaling at least the greater of the single sum distribution provided under the plan or the present value of the accrued benefit payable at normal retirement age using a rate no greater than the applicable interest rate under Section 417(e) and subject to the Section 415 limits.
- In the case of a transfer from a defined contribution to a defined benefit plan, the defined benefit plan provides a minimum benefit equal to the benefit, expressed as an annuity payable at normal retirement age, based on the transferred amount.[50]

Certain benefits are not protected under this provision. These include: (1) the right to make elective deferrals and aftertax employee contributions; (2) the right to direct investments; (3) the right to make loans; (4) the right to a particular form of investment; (5) allocation dates for contributions, forfeitures, and earnings; (6) the time for making contributions; and (7) valuation dates for account balances. Thus, these features may be eliminated even with respect to existing account balances.

---

49. IRS Reg. Section 1.411(d)-4, Q&A 3(a).
50. IRS Reg. Section 1.411(d)-4, Q&A 3(b).

Under the nondiscrimination rules for benefits, rights, and features discussed earlier, a benefit, right, or feature that is eliminated prospectively will be deemed to be nondiscriminatory in all future plan years if the nondiscrimination requirements are met as of the date the benefit, right, or feature is eliminated and no changes are made to the benefit, right, or feature after that date. For a plan to avail itself of this special rule, the benefit, right, or feature must generally apply with respect to earnings, expenses, gains, and losses on the account balance as of the elimination date. However, in the case of a plan loan provision that is eliminated prospectively, the plan may limit the availability of loans to the participant's account balance on the date the provision is eliminated.

The IRS also takes the position that an optional form of benefit may not be conditioned on employer discretion. In its view, the employer's exercise of discretion to deny a particular form of benefit to a participant would be tantamount to eliminating the optional form with respect to that participant. A plan may condition the availability of an optional form on objective criteria that are specifically set forth in the plan, however. But an employer may not amend a plan to add such objective conditions with respect to account balances existing on the date of the amendment.[51]

Mergers and Consolidations A qualified plan must provide that in the case of any merger or consolidation of plan assets with those of another plan, or in the case of a transfer of plan assets or liabilities, each participant must receive a benefit immediately after the merger, consolidation, or transfer that is equal to or greater than his or her benefit immediately prior to such transaction.[52] Thus, a participant's account balance in a CODA or any other defined contribution plan must be the same after the merger as before the merger. In addition, a plan merger is considered a plan amendment, so optional forms of benefits cannot be eliminated with respect to existing account balances. For example, assume Plan A, which has a lump sum option and a 10-year installment option, is merged with Plan B, which has a lump sum option

---

51. IRS Reg. 1.411(d)-4, Q&A 7.
52. IRC Sections 401(a)(12) and 414(l); IRS Reg. 1.414(l)-1.

and a 15-year installment option, and that the merged plan will offer only a lump sum and a 10-year installment option. Participants from Plan B must still be offered the 15-year installment option with respect to their account balances on the date of the merger. To preserve the special nondiscrimination rule for the 15-year installment option, that option must be available with respect to earnings, expenses, gains, and losses on that account balance as well.

CHAPTER 4

CODAs: Additional Tax Law Requirements

The essence of a CODA is the choice it offers employees as to when they will receive income. Normally, the choice between receiving cash now (as salary or a profit-sharing bonus) or later (by deferring it under the plan) would invoke the doctrine of constructive receipt. This doctrine deems an individual to be in receipt of income in the year it is available without restriction or penalty, even though the individual chooses to defer payment until a subsequent year.

When it enacted Section 401(k), Congress suspended the doctrine of constructive receipt for qualified CODAs, provided certain rules are met.[1] These rules are intended to ensure that HCEs do not derive significantly greater tax advantages from a CODA than NHCEs, and to encourage employees to use these vehicles to save for retirement rather than for the short term.

Thus, a plan that includes a CODA must meet the requirements of Section 401(k) as well as the general qualification requirements discussed in Chapter 3. The Section 401(k) requirements limit the extent to which HCEs can participate relative to NHCEs. They also require that amounts employees electively defer be fully vested at all times and impose restrictions on when these funds

---

1. IRC Sections 401(k) and 402(e)(3); IRS Reg. 1.401(k)-1(a)(3)(v) and 1.402(a)-1(d)(2).

can be distributed to employees. These requirements are the subject of this chapter.

A related IRC provision, Section 401(m), limits aftertax employee and matching employer contributions on behalf of HCEs, whether or not the plan includes a CODA. Because the test used to check compliance with this provision is similar to the test that applies to elective contributions, and because the two tests must be coordinated, it is covered in this chapter rather than in Chapter 3.

TYPES OF CONTRIBUTIONS

A brief summary of the different types of contributions employers and employees can make to a CODA will set the stage for a discussion of the specific requirements of Section 401(k).

Elective (Pretax) Contributions/Deferrals

Elective contributions, also called pretax contributions or elective deferrals, are the amounts an employee authorizes the employer to contribute to a CODA on a pretax basis—either by way of salary reduction in the case of a typical savings plan or through an election to defer in the case of a cash option profit-sharing plan.[2]

It is important to recognize that elective deferrals are treated as though they are *employer* contributions for most federal tax law purposes.[3] Thus, elective deferrals affect the amount of deductible contributions an employer may make to a plan (see Chapter 6, page 124). And, as discussed in Chapter 3, elective deferrals can reduce an employee's annual addition limit under Section 415. Further, elective deferrals are generally not subject to state and local income taxes.[4]

Despite this general tax treatment, elective deferrals are considered wages for social security purposes. Thus, they are subject to social security (FICA) taxes (as well as unemployment insurance

---

2. IRS Reg. 1.401(k)-1(g)(3).
3. IRC Section 401(k)(2)(A); IRS Reg. 1.401(k)-1(a)(4)(ii).
4. Notable exceptions include the Commonwealth of Pennsylvania and the City of Philadelphia.

or FUTA taxes) and are taken into account in determining an employee's social security benefits.[5]

Even though elective deferrals reduce an employee's pay for income tax purposes, an employer may take them into account in determining benefits under other employer-sponsored programs (e.g., defined benefit pension plans or group life insurance plans).

Aftertax Employee Contributions

An aftertax employee contribution consists of money an employee is deemed to have received and taken into income.[6] A CODA does not have to permit aftertax contributions, and many CODAs do not.

Matching Contributions

A matching contribution is a contribution the employer makes when an employee authorizes an elective deferral or makes an aftertax employee contribution.[7] It is common, but not mandatory, for a savings plan CODA to provide for matching contributions.

Nonelective Contributions

A nonelective contribution is an employer contribution made on behalf of eligible employees regardless of whether they have made elective deferrals or aftertax employee contributions.[8] Such contributions, made solely at the employer's election, are sometimes referred to as "profit-sharing contributions" or "401(a) contributions." Both names reflect the fact that they are simply employer contributions to a qualified profit-sharing plan that happens to include a CODA.

Qualified Nonelective Contributions

A qualified nonelective contribution (QNEC) is a nonelective contribution to which two special rules apply: the QNEC must be fully

---

5. IRC Section 3121(v)(1).
6. IRS Reg. 1.401(m)-1(f)(6).
7. IRS Reg. 1.401(m)-1(f)(12).
8. IRS Reg. 1.401(k)-1(g)(10).

vested at all times, and it generally may not be distributed to the employee on an in-service basis for any reason before the employee reaches age 59-1/2.[9] The one exception to this prohibition against in-service distributions would allow QNECs (and earnings thereon) made before the later of December 31, 1988, or the end of the last plan year ending before July 1, 1989, to be withdrawable before age 59-1/2 on account of hardship.[10]

Qualified Matching Contributions

The qualified matching contribution (QMAC) is a matching contribution that meets the same rules a nonelective contribution must meet to become a QNEC (i.e., full vesting and restrictions on in-service withdrawals).[11]

Safe Harbor Employer Contributions

A safe harbor employer contribution is an employer contribution that satisfies one of two safe harbors, eliminating the need to perform ADP testing. A safe harbor employer contribution either (1) provides certain matching contributions to NHCEs, or (2) provides a contribution of 3 percent of compensation for all NHCEs. See SAFE HARBORS—ADP/ACP TESTING, beginning on page 100.

Mandatory/Voluntary Employee Contributions

Employee contributions are often characterized as either mandatory or voluntary. In a sense, these terms are misnomers because employee contributions are voluntary in almost all plans. The distinction usually intended when they are used is between contributions required as a condition for participating in the plan and receiving a matching employer contribution and employee contributions that do not trigger an employer contribution. If a CODA permits an employee to contribute up to 10 percent of pay in 1 percent increments, and the employer makes a 50 percent matching contribution only on the first 6 percent of pay the employee

---

9. IRS Reg. 1.401(k)-1(g)(13)(ii).
10. IRS Reg. 1.401(k)-1(d)(2)(ii).
11. IRS Reg. 1.401(k)-1(g)(13)(i).

contributes, the employee's 6 percent contribution is considered to be mandatory; the remaining employee contributions are viewed as voluntary.

Employees may be permitted to make mandatory and voluntary contributions on an elective or an aftertax basis or both. Some plans give employees a choice; others allow contributions on an elective basis only. Still others require that mandatory contributions be made on an elective basis and allow employees to choose how voluntary contributions will be made. The choice is important because, as discussed later in this chapter, an employee's in-service withdrawal rights will differ depending on whether his or her contributions are elective or aftertax.

ELECTIVE DEFERRAL LIMIT

TRA '86 imposed an annual dollar limit on the elective contributions an employee can make.[12] Initially set at $7,000, the limit is indexed to increase with changes in the CPI. For 1996, the limit is $9,500; for future years, the dollar amount, after adjustment for CPI changes, will be rounded down to the next lowest multiple of $500.

The elective deferral limit:

- Is a plan qualification requirement in the case of plans of related employers (and must be stated in the plan document), as well as a limit that applies to the individual employee.[13]
- Applies only to elective deferrals and not to other employer contributions of any type.
- Applies on the basis of the individual's tax year (almost always a calendar year), not the plan year or the plan's limitation year for Section 415 purposes.
- Is determined without regard to any community property laws and is reduced by other elective deferrals, including those made to a simplified employee pension (SEP), to a tax-sheltered annuity or to another employer's CODA.

---

12. IRC Section 402(g).
13. IRC Section 401(a)(30); IRS Reg. 1.401(a)-30.

Under IRS final regulations, plans must limit an employee's elective deferrals under all plans of the employer (including related employers) for any taxable year to the elective deferral limit.[14] If the limit is exceeded under a plan or plans of the same or *related* employers, the plans will be disqualified unless a corrective distribution of the excess deferrals (including investment income on those deferrals) is made by April 15 of the year following the year in which the excess arose. In this case, the plan may provide either (1) that the employee is deemed to have designated excess deferrals to be refunded, or (2) that the employer may notify the plan of excess deferrals to be refunded.

If an individual defers more than the maximum under plans of two or more *unrelated* employers, neither of the plans will generally be disqualified. In fact, neither of the plans will be aware that an individual made an excess deferral unless and until the individual requests a refund of the excess from the plan. In this situation, the plan may—but need not—provide for a refund of excess deferrals. Assume, for example, that an employee deferred the maximum of $9,500 in 1996 under Company A's plan and also deferred $4,000 in 1996 under unrelated Company B's plan. Company A's plan could, but need not, allow the employee to take a refund of a portion of his $9,500 in elective deferrals in order to reduce his total deferrals to the maximum allowable amount. The administrator of a plan including such a provision would then have to require the employee to certify or provide evidence of the excess deferral in his application for refund.[15]

If the corrective distribution of excess deferrals (including investment income on those deferrals) is not made by April 15 following the year in which the excess arose, the employee will be currently taxed on the excess, even though it was not distributed.[16] Any excess deferral not distributed by April 15 must remain in the plan, subject to all regular withdrawal restrictions, and will be taxed again to the employee when it is later distributed.[17]

---

14. IRS Reg. 1.401(a)-30.
15. IRS Reg. 1.402(g)-1(e)(4).
16. IRS Reg. 1.402(g)-1(e)(8)(iii).
17. The treatment of excess deferrals due to the elective deferral limit should not be confused with the treatment of excess contributions that occurs because of the ADP/ACP tests. See discussion beginning on page 103.

The value of an excess deferral will be taxable to the employee for the year in which the excess deferral was made; the employee will be taxed on the investment income in the year it is distributed.[18] If, for example, an employee made an excess contribution of $1,500 in 1995, and a refund of $1,600 is made to him by April 15, 1996 (including $100 of investment income earned on the excess contribution), the employee will have to report $1,500 as part of his 1995 income; the $100 of investment income will be part of his 1996 income. The corrective distribution is not subject to either the 10 percent penalty tax on early distributions or the 15 percent penalty tax on excess distributions.

The employer will have to take excess deferrals of all HCEs into account in applying the ADP test (see page 91); excess deferrals of NHCEs are not generally considered for this test.[19]

Only excess deferrals that are not distributed within the correction period are counted as annual additions for purposes of Section 415.[20]

PARTICIPATION REQUIREMENTS

As noted in Chapter 3, a qualified plan cannot, as a rule, require that an employee complete more than one year of service as a condition of eligibility; up to two years may be required if the plan provides for full and immediate vesting of employer contributions. The two-year option is not available to CODAs, and the basic one-year rule continues to apply to these plans under all circumstances.[21] Technically, this restriction applies only to the CODA portion of a plan. Thus, a plan could impose a one-year service requirement on participation in the elective deferral portion of the plan, and a two-year service requirement on the right to share in nonelective employer contributions. Dual service requirements could cause administrative difficulties and confusion among employees, however, and are thus uncommon; most plans require one year of service for all eligibility purposes.

---

18. IRS Reg. 1.402(g)-1(e)(8)(i).
19. Reg. 1.402(g)-1(e)(1)(ii).
20. Ibid.
21. IRC Section 401(k)(2)(D); IRS Reg. 1.401(k)-1(e)(5).

Employers cannot use an employee's election to make or not make elective deferrals as a direct or indirect condition for making employee benefits (other than matching contributions) available under any other plan.[22] IRS regulations define employee benefits broadly in this context to include such items as life insurance, health benefits, and stock options. The rule also encompasses aftertax employee contributions; thus, a plan cannot require employees to make elective deferrals before they can make aftertax contributions.

In general, this rule will not apply to nonqualified restoration plans that make up benefits lost because of the elective deferral limit, the ADP test, or Section 415. Such a plan will violate the rule only to the extent that an employee receives additional deferred compensation by deciding to make or not to make elective deferrals under a CODA. Under a special rule in the regulations, employers can prohibit nonqualified deferrals until an employee has made the maximum permitted deferral under the CODA, but they cannot otherwise require or prohibit the nonqualified deferral of amounts that an eligible employee could have contributed to the CODA.

VESTING REQUIREMENTS

The value of elective deferrals must be fully and immediately vested in employees at all times.[23] The value of employer contributions must be vested in accordance with the general vesting rules described in Chapter 3. Any safe harbor employer matching contributions made to satisfy the safe harbors for CODA nondiscrimination testing must also be fully vested and subject to the distribution restrictions that apply to elective deferrals. An employer contribution that is a QNEC or a QMAC is, by definition, fully vested and is also subject to the distribution restrictions described below.

DISTRIBUTION REQUIREMENTS

The IRC permits a qualified profit-sharing plan to make distributions upon retirement, death, disability, and termination of employment and the occurrence of an "event" as described below.

---

22. IRC Section 401(k)(4); IRS Reg. 1.401(k)-1(e)(6).
23. IRC Section 401(k)(2)(C); IRS Reg. 1.401(k)-1(c).

It also permits a profit-sharing plan to make distributions after the expiration of a fixed number of years (interpreted by the IRS to mean two years). Thus, profit-sharing plans can generally provide for in-service withdrawals of employer contributions that have accumulated for at least two years. Events that make in-service withdrawals from profit-sharing plans possible include financial hardship. The term *event* has also been interpreted to include the completion of a five-year period of plan participation.[24]

These general distribution rules apply to nonelective contributions and to most matching employer contributions to a CODA (including the typical savings plan). They generally do *not* apply to elective deferrals, safe harbor employer contributions, or to QNECs or QMACs.[25]

The law permits employees to withdraw aftertax contributions from a profit-sharing plan or a typical savings plan at any time, even if the plan includes a CODA. Nonetheless, many plans impose penalties to discourage employees from making such withdrawals.[26]

An employee can receive a distribution of the value of his or her account, including elective deferrals and QNECs and QMACs, upon separation from service.[27] In-service withdrawals of these items are restricted, however. In general, an employee cannot receive or withdraw amounts from an elective deferral account on an in-service basis unless he or she:

---

24. IRS Reg. 1.401-1(b)(1)(ii); Rev. Rul. 68-24, 71-224 and 71-295.
25. IRC Section 401(k)(2)(B).
26. The IRS has taken the position that a plan that allows an employee to freely withdraw employee contributions that triggered employer matching contributions violated the qualification rules unless penalties were imposed (Rev. Rul. 74-55 and 74-56). The theory was that an employee could manipulate employer contributions, violating the predetermined allocation formula requirement. But in General Counsel Memorandum 35556 (11/8/73), it was noted that prohibited manipulation could not result where employee contributions are made through payroll deduction. Many older plans have retained their penalties, however.
27. IRC Section 401(k)(2)(B)(i)(I); IRS Reg. 1.401(k)-1(d)(1)(i). These distributions might still be subject to the possible imposition of a 10 percent early distribution tax. See Chapter 6. Separation does not include a change from one job to another within a controlled group; an employee's access to his or her elective deferral account will be limited so long as he or she works for the employer that sponsors the CODA or for other members of the controlled group. Thus, if an employee covered under a CODA maintained by Subsidiary A transfers to Subsidiary B, which does not maintain a CODA, the employee cannot receive a distribution solely because of the transfer.

- Has attained age 59-1/2,[28]
- Receives a single lump sum distribution on account of: (1) termination of the plan (without the establishment or maintenance of a successor plan—other than an ESOP or a simplified employee pension (SEP), or (2) certain employer dispositions, or
- Has a hardship.

If the plan provides for safe harbor employer contributions, QNECs or QMACs, it must also provide that—except in situations involving the grandfather provision previously described—these contributions (and investment earnings thereon) are not withdrawable on an in-service basis prior to age 59-1/2.

Restrictions on elective deferrals, QNECs, and QMACs will generally continue to apply to these funds even after they have been transferred to another plan of the same, or a different, employer.[29]

The age requirement referred to above is self-explanatory. The other contingencies mentioned—plan terminations, employer dispositions, and hardships—require additional discussion.

Plan Terminations

Under IRS final regulations, distributions upon termination of a CODA are permitted if a successor defined contribution plan (other than an ESOP or SEP) does not exist during a specified period.[30] For this purpose, a successor plan does not include a plan that does not overlap the CODA (i.e., a plan in which less than 2 percent of employees who were eligible for the CODA at the time of its termination are or were eligible to participate at any time during the 24 months beginning 12 months before the time of termination). Thus, employers that sponsor another defined contribution plan that covers a separate group of employees may distribute CODA account balances upon plan termination.

It should also be noted that the IRS has ruled that a company's disposition of a subsidiary or assets to a *partnership* did not

---

28. IRC Section 401(k)(2)(B)(i)(III); IRS Reg. 1.401(k)-1(d)(1)(ii).
29. IRS Reg. 1.401(k)-1(d)(6)(iv).
30. IRS Section 401(k)(10)(A)(i); IRS Reg. 1.401(k)-1(d)(3).

give rise to a permissible CODA distribution, because the transaction did not meet the literal requirement of the statute: that the disposition be made to—and the participants continue employment with—the acquiring *corporation*.[31]

An impermissible distribution from a terminating plan will not automatically disqualify the successor plan. Elective deferrals under the prior CODA would be currently taxable, however.

Employer Dispositions

CODAs can make distributions upon certain sales of businesses[32] (i.e., the sale of at least 85 percent of the assets used in a trade or business or the sale of the entire interest in a subsidiary to an unrelated employer). In order to make a distribution in such an event, the purchaser must not maintain the seller's plan after the date of sale.[33] The purchaser will be deemed to maintain the seller's plan if:

- It adopts the seller's plan or becomes an employer whose employees accrue benefits under the plan, or
- It merges the seller's plan with, or transfers plan assets to, a plan it maintains.

A purchaser will not be deemed to maintain the seller's plan merely because the purchaser's plan accepts rollover contributions of amounts distributed from the seller's plan.[34]

To be treated as a distribution upon the sale of a business, a distribution must normally be made by the end of the second calendar year after the calendar year in which the sale occurs.[35] In addition, a distribution may only be made to an employee who continues in employment with the purchaser of the assets or subsidiary.[36] The distribution must also be a lump sum distribution.[37]

---

31. PLR 9102044
32. IRC Section 401(k)(10)(A)(ii) and (iii); IRS Reg. 1.401(k)-1(d)(4).
33. IRC Section 401(k)(10)(C); IRS Reg. 1.401(k)-1(d)(4)(i).
34. IRS Reg. 1.401(k)-1(d)(4)(i).
35. IRS Reg. 1.401(k)-1(d)(4)(iii).
36. IRS Reg. 1.401(k)-1(d)(4)(ii).
37. IRC Section 401(k)(10)(B); IRS Reg. 1.401(k)-1(d)(5). In this context, the term *lump sum distribution* is defined somewhat differently from the way it is defined in the context of the taxation of distributions.

When CODA account balances are transferred to the plan of the buyer (other than as an elective transfer under protected benefit regulations discussed in Chapter 3), the buyer's plan will be disqualified if it distributes the transferred CODA account balances without regard to the otherwise applicable distribution restrictions.[38] Exhibit 4–1 shows how these rules apply in various types of transactions.

Hardship Withdrawals

The rules governing hardship withdrawals distinguish between the amounts actually deferred and the investment earnings thereon. All elective deferrals themselves (regardless of when made), plus investment income earned on elective deferrals through a specified date, are withdrawable on account of hardship. This date is specified in the plan and must be no later than the later

EXHIBIT 4–1

Sale of Assets or Subsidiary

	Distribution Permitted	
	Yes	No
Buyer assumes/adopts seller's CODA		X
Seller's plan (or portion thereof) is merged into buyer's existing plan		X
Seller terminates its plan and buyer covers employees under buyer's new or existing plan	X	
Seller terminates its plan and buyer covers employees under buyer's new or existing plan; employees roll over distributions from seller's plan to buyer's plan	X	
Seller terminates its plan and transfers account balances (not under elective transfer rules) to buyer's new or existing plan that covers employees		X
Buyer terminates seller's plan and buyer covers employees under its new or existing plan		X
Seller retains plan and buyer covers employees under its new or existing plan	X	

---

38. IRS Reg. 1-401(k)-1(d)(6)(iv).

of December 31, 1988, or the last day of the plan year ending before July 1, 1989. It appears that safe harbor contributions, like QMACs and QNECs, and related earnings, are not available for hardship withdrawal.

The rules also impose two conditions on hardship withdrawals: (1) there must be an immediate and heavy financial need, and (2) the distribution must be necessary to satisfy the financial need.[39] The regulations allow each of these conditions to be met on a facts and circumstances basis, but also provide the following safe harbors:

Immediate and Heavy Financial Need These four events are deemed to constitute immediate and heavy financial need:[40]

- The incurring of certain medical expenses (as defined in IRC Section 213(d)) by the employee, the employee's spouse, or certain dependents of the employee (as defined in IRC Section 152) or the need for up-front funds to *obtain* certain medical services for these persons.
- Costs related directly to the purchase (excluding mortgage payments) of a principal residence for the employee.
- Payment of room and board, tuition and related educational fees for the next 12 months of postsecondary education for the employee or the employee's spouse or dependents. Related educational fees include such items as lab, library, and music room fees but presumably do not include payments for books.
- The need to prevent the eviction of the employee from his or her principal residence or foreclosure on the mortgage of the employee's principal residence.

Although the regulations do not address the issue, plan administrators should probably verify that one of the safe harbor events has occurred prior to making a distribution. This should not generally be difficult, since each of these events usually lends itself to relatively easy documentation (e.g., foreclosure notices, medical bills, or tuition statements). It is not clear what documentation a

---

39. IRS Reg. 1.401(k)-1(d)(2)(i).
40. IRS Reg. 1.401(k)-1(d)(2)(iv)(A).

plan would need in the case of up-front payments to obtain medical care; a statement from a physician or hospital as to the nature of the treatment and the associated expense would presumably be adequate. If actual expenses exceed estimated costs, the employee might need to request another hardship withdrawal to the extent allowable under the plan.

A plan is not required to limit the hardship events it recognizes to the four identified above. An employer that chooses to move beyond the assurance of the safe harbors may structure its plan to ignore the safe harbor events altogether or add other events to hardship lists. But exclusive use of the safe harbor events is the only way to eliminate the possibility that the IRS will investigate and determine that actual distributions were not due to true hardship.

Necessary to Satisfy Financial Need This condition looks to whether the distribution exceeds the need by focusing on whether the employee can meet the need with any other reasonably available resources. It applies independent of and in addition to the first condition.

There are three ways to approach this second test. The first is to base determinations on facts and circumstances—an approach that could invoke an IRS challenge.

The second approach takes advantage of a regulatory safe harbor that includes four conditions:[41]

- The distribution must not exceed the amount of the employee's immediate and heavy financial need, including amounts necessary to pay any federal, state, or local income taxes or penalties reasonably anticipated to result from the distribution. This would include the 10 percent penalty tax on early distributions and presumably the 15 percent tax applicable to excess distributions.[42]

- The employee must have obtained all distributions (other than hardship distributions) and all nontaxable (at the time of the loan) loans currently available under all plans maintained by the employer.

---

41. IRS Reg. 1.401(k)-1(d)(2)(iv)(B).
42. See Chapter 6.

- The plan, and all other plans maintained by the employer, must provide that the employee's elective deferrals and employee contributions will be suspended for at least 12 months after receipt of the hardship distribution.

- The plan, and all other plans maintained by the employer, must limit the employee's elective deferrals for the calendar year immediately following the calendar year of the hardship distribution to no more than a specified amount—the excess, if any, of that year's elective deferral dollar limit over the amount electively deferred in the year of the distribution.

With respect to the first condition, the final regulations are unclear as to whether the gross-up may only be for taxes and penalties attributable to the distribution of elective contributions or may include taxes on all monies distributed. Based on IRS comments, it appears that the gross-up may be applied to all monies distributed. Thus, for example, a hardship distribution consisting of all of a participant's vested company matching contributions and a portion of his or her elective deferrals can be grossed up to reflect taxes related to *both* the elective contributions and the company matching contributions.

Plan administrators will generally have the responsibility of verifying the amount of the gross-up, though the plan administrator could require the participant to provide an estimate of anticipated taxes. This would make the participant responsible for properly representing his or her personal tax filing status. As an alternative, the plan administrator may want to assume the lowest federal tax bracket applies or simply use the federal withholding rate (10 percent) for nonperiodic plan payments.

The third condition listed above is very broad and applies to all qualified and nonqualified deferred compensation plans maintained by the employer, including stock option and stock purchase plans.[43] Thus, for example, an executive who takes a hardship withdrawal could be prevented from exercising stock options (with the possible exception of a cashless exercise) during the following 12-month period.

---

43. IRS Reg. 1.401(k)-1(d)(2)(iv)(B)(4).

The employer's other plans need not be amended to provide that contributions will be suspended in the event of a hardship withdrawal if the employee is prohibited under a legally enforceable agreement from participating in these plans. To fulfill this requirement, the employer could presumably include a statement on the hardship withdrawal application form. An employee *can* continue to make mandatory contributions to a defined benefit plan and to health and welfare plans (including a cafeteria plan) during the period of suspension, however.[44]

The third approach necessary to satisfy the financial need test is a middle ground between facts and circumstances and the safe harbor. It provides some protection for the plan administrator, but not the absolute protection of the safe harbor. The regulations state that a distribution:

> ... generally may be treated as necessary to satisfy a financial need if the employer relies on the employee's written representation, unless the employer has actual knowledge to the contrary, that the need cannot reasonably be relieved:
>
> 1. through reimbursement or compensation by insurance or otherwise;
> 2. by liquidation of the employee's assets;
> 3. by cessation of elective contributions or employee contributions under the plan; or
> 4. by other distributions or nontaxable (at the time of the loan) loans from plans maintained by the employer or any other employer, or by borrowing from commercial sources on reasonable commercial terms in an amount sufficient to satisfy the need.[45]

If one of the above actions would increase the amount of the need, the need will not be considered relieved by one of the actions.[46] If a participant needs money for a down payment to purchase a principal residence, for example, the participant would not be required to take a plan loan if such a loan would prevent the employee from obtaining the financing to purchase the residence.

Further, if the plan loan would only partially satisfy the financial hardship, the plan may make a hardship distribution to the

---

44. Ibid.
45. IRS Reg. 1.401(k)-1(d)(2)(iii)(B).
46. Ibid.

participant without requiring that he first take a loan. Thus, an employee who needs $10,000 but can only borrow $9,000 from the plan may represent that his need cannot be fulfilled by available borrowing, and a plan loan would not be required. (By contrast, under the safe harbor discussed above, the participant is required to take the maximum plan loan in any event.)

As noted, the employer is entitled to rely on the employee's statement unless the employer has actual knowledge that the employee's representation is untrue. This standard nevertheless requires the employer to check the maximum available plan loan against the amount requested for hardship withdrawal. If the employer knows the employee can take a loan from the plan in excess of the full need, then the employer will not be entitled to rely on the employee's statement.

Changes to Hardship Provisions

Employers may change a plan's hardship withdrawal provisions—adding or revising nondiscriminatory and objective standards for distributions, including eliminating hardship distributions for existing account balances—without causing a prohibited cutback in accrued benefits.[47] This rule is useful where a plan with one set of hardship rules is being merged with a plan that has a different set of hardship rules.

THE ADP AND ACP TESTS

As noted in Chapter 3, the IRS views the actual deferral percentage (ADP) test as the principal means for determining whether contributions to a CODA are nondiscriminatory. The ADP test compares the rates at which highly compensated employees (HCEs) and non-highly compensated employees (NHCEs) authorize elective deferrals. In general, a plan will not pass the ADP test if HCEs make elective deferrals at a rate that is very much higher than the NHCE deferral rate.

The actual contribution percentage (ACP) test, added to the IRC by TRA '86, is identical to the ADP test, but it applies to

---

47. IRS Reg. 1.411(d)-4, Q&A-2(b)(2)(x).

aftertax and matching employer contributions.[48] The following discusses these tests in detail. It should be observed, however, that beginning in 1999, employers will be able to avoid the ADP test by satisfying one of two safe harbors. In addition, the ACP test for employer matching contributions can be avoided by satisfying a safe harbor. These safe harbors are discussed beginning on page 100.

Running the ADP Test

To run the ADP test, the plan sponsor must:

- Divide eligible employees into HCEs and NHCEs, taking all eligible employees into account—even if they have not elected to participate in the plan. (Eligible employees are employees who have met the plan's age and service requirements and are able to make elective deferrals.)[49]
- Construct a fraction for each eligible employee in each group. The numerator is the employee's elective deferral for the plan year; the denominator is his or her compensation for the year up to the $150,000 (indexed) maximum.[50]
- Convert each fraction into a percentage (to four decimal places),[51] counting nonparticipating but eligible employees as zeroes.[52]
- Add the percentages within each group and average them into a single ADP for HCEs and a single ADP for NHCEs.[53]

For years prior to 1997, these steps had to be followed using compensation and deferrals for the current year—both for NHCEs and HCEs. Beginning with the 1997 plan year, employers will be allowed to conduct the ADP test using actual deferral percentages of NHCEs for the prior year. By using prior year results for the NHCEs, the plan sponsor will be able to determine maximum HCE contribution levels at the beginning of the year, rather than

---

48. IRC Section 401(m); IRS Reg. 1.401(m)-1.
49. IRS Reg. 1.401(k)-1(g)(4).
50. IRS Reg. 1.401(k)-1(g)(1)(ii)(A).
51. IRS Reg. 1.401(k)-1(g)(1)(i).
52. IRS Reg. 1.401(k)-1(g)(1)(ii)(A).
53. IRS Reg. 1.401(k)-1(g)(1)(i).

during or after the close of the plan year. Employers are not required to use the prior year percentages; however, if the employer elects to use current plan year percentages, then this election can only be changed in accordance with IRS regulations—to be promulgated at some future time.

If the ADP for HCEs does not exceed the ADP for NHCEs by more than a permitted margin, the plan passes the test. The size of the permitted margin depends on whether the plan sponsor uses the basic ADP test or the *alternative limitation* test.

Under the basic test, the ADP for HCEs cannot be more than 125 percent of the ADP for NHCEs.[54] The alternative limitation can produce a wider margin than the basic test in many situations; it permits the ADP for HCEs to be as much as 2 times the ADP for NHCEs but not more than 2 percentage points higher.[55] Using whichever test produces the best result, the following margins are permitted:

- If the NHCE ADP is 2 percent or less, the HCE ADP can be 2 times the NHCE ADP; for example, if the NHCE ADP is 1.5 percent, the HCE ADP can be any percentage up to 3 percent.

- If the NHCE ADP is more than 2 percent but not more than 8 percent, the HCE ADP can be 2 percentage points higher than the NHCE ADP; for example, if the NHCE ADP is 4 percent, the HCE ADP can be any percentage up to 6 percent.

- If the NHCE ADP is more than 8 percent, the HCE ADP can be 125 percent of the NHCE ADP; for example, if the NHCE ADP is 10 percent, the HCE ADP can be any percentage up to 12.5 percent.

These margins are also shown in Exhibit 4–2.

If there are no HCEs, or no NHCEs, the plan is deemed to pass the ADP test.[56]

In general, the percentages of HCEs eligible to participate in more than one employer-sponsored CODA (on a controlled group basis) are aggregated, and the same percentage is used for the HCE

---

54. IRS Reg. 1.401(k)-1(b)(2)(i)(A).
55. IRS Reg. 1.401(k)-1(b)(2)(i)(B).
56. IRS Reg. 1.401(k)-1(b)(2)(i).

E X H I B I T   4-2

Permissible ADPs for HCEs

If the ADP for NHCEs is:	Then the ADP for HCEs May Not Exceed:
1%	2%
2	4
3	5
4	6
5	7
6	8
7	9
8	10
9	11.25
10	12.50

in all of the plans. This is not the case for plans that cannot be aggregated (e.g., ESOPs and non-ESOPs).[57]

Conditions

Elective deferrals must meet two conditions to be counted in the ADP test for a given plan year.[58] First, they must be allocated to the accounts of participants as of a date within that plan year. (Thus, an allocation cannot be contingent on the participant's performance of service on any date following the date of allocation.) Second, they must be paid to the trust no later than 12 months after the end of the plan year to which the contribution relates.

The elective deferrals for a given plan year must also relate to compensation that either would have been received by the participant in the plan year but for the elective deferral, or is attributable to services performed by the individual in the plan year and, but for the election to defer, would have been received by the individual within two and a half months after the end of the plan year.[59]

---

57. IRS Reg. 1.401(k)-1(g)(1)(ii)(B).
58. IRS Reg. 1.401(k)-1(b)(4)(i)(A).
59. IRS Reg. 1.401(k)-1(b)(4)(i)(B).

Compensation used for purposes of the ADP test must meet one of the definitions deemed acceptable under Section 414(s) of the IRC, regardless of the definition used to determine plan contributions.[60]

For testing purposes, a plan sponsor may determine an employee's compensation for either the plan year or the calendar year ending within the plan year, but it must use the same period to determine compensation for all eligible employees for a particular plan year.[61] If a plan year is December 1 through November 30, for example, the compensation to be used in the denominator of the ADP test for the December 1, 1995, through November 30, 1996, plan year could be based on calendar year 1995 compensation. Thus, the denominators to be used in the ADP test would be known only one month into the plan year. The calendar year alternative may be helpful for an employer with a noncalendar year plan year that has difficulty capturing the required 414(s) test compensation on a noncalendar year basis.

Beginning with the 1999 plan year, the ADP test can be performed excluding any NHCEs who participate before attaining age 21 and completing one year of service (the maximum statutory eligibility requirements permitted), as long as the plan separately passes the Section 410(b) coverage tests for all participants in that age/service group.

Employers can also calculate the ADP based solely on compensation while an employee is eligible to participate, ignoring periods before the employee meets the plan's eligibility requirements.[62] This could improve test results when two conditions exist: (1) the plan does not provide for immediate eligibility upon hire, and (2) the percentage of each year's newly eligible NHCEs exceeds the percentage of HCEs. Even if both conditions are met, the impact on test results may be too small to justify a change in existing payroll procedures.

If the employer makes QNECs and/or QMACs, it can add these contributions to the elective deferrals made by employees when performing the ADP test.[63] In fact, employers may choose to

---

60. See page 37.
61. IRS Reg. 1.401(k)-1(g)(2)(i).
62. Ibid.
63. IRS Reg. 1.401(k)-1(b)(5).

make such contributions for the express purpose of meeting the ADP test when the plan would otherwise fail.[64] It should be noted, however, that:

- Employer contributions of this type are fully vested at all times and are subject to in-service withdrawal restrictions.[65]
- If a QNEC or QMAC is used to help pass the ADP test, it cannot be used for any other nondiscrimination test—for example, the amount test of Section 401(a)(4).[66]
- There could be a financial difference between solving an ADP problem with QNECs and solving it with QMACs. The group of individuals that will share in the QNEC is usually composed of all eligible employees, whether or not they have authorized elective deferrals; the group sharing in a QMAC usually consists only of those employees who have actually made elective deferrals for the year in question—typically a smaller group.

An example will help to clarify this last point. Suppose that Company X maintains a CODA with 1,000 eligible NHCEs and that the ADP for this group is 3.5 percent, derived as follows:

	Number of NHCEs	Total Compensation	Average Deferral Rate	Total Percentage Points
NHCEs participating	700	$21,000,000	5%	3,500
NHCEs not participating	300	6,000,000	0	0
Total	1,000	$27,000,000		3,500

The total percentage points contributed by the participating NHCEs is 3,500 (700 times 5 percent), and these points, divided by the total number of NHCEs (1,000), yields an ADP of 3.5 percent. If the ADP for HCEs is assumed to be 6 percent, the plan fails the

---

64. To be used for the ADP test in a particular plan year, QNECs and QMACs generally must be made by the end of the 12-month period following the plan year to which they relate IRS Reg. 1.401(k)-1(b)(4)(i)(A)(2) and (b)(5)(v).
65. IRS Reg. 1.401(k)-1(g)(13)(iii).
66. IRS Reg. 1.401(k)-1(e)(7).

test. It could pass the test if the ADP for the NHCEs were raised to 4 percent or, to express this in another way, if the total percentage points for NHCE group were increased to 4,000.

There are at least two ways for Company X to increase the ADP for the NHCEs. One is to make a QNEC for all 1,000 NHCEs; another is to make a QMAC for only the 700 NHCEs who are participating. A level percentage of pay QNEC would have to equal one half of 1 percent of the entire payroll of $27,000,000, a cost of $135,000 ($27,000,000 times .005). By contrast, a level percentage QMAC that would achieve the same result would cost $150,000. (This is derived from a QMAC of .007143 of the $21,000,000 payroll of the participating NHCEs. This supplemental QMAC, plus the elective deferrals of .05, total .057143. This percentage, multiplied by the 700 NHCEs, yields 4,000 percentage points or an ADP of 4 percent.)

In this example, the QNEC is less expensive for the employer than the QMAC. This would not be the case if the payroll base of the 700 participating NHCEs was larger than $30,000,000 and if the payroll base of the nonparticipating employees remained at $6,000,000.

Running the ACP Test

As noted earlier, the ACP test is identical to the ADP test, except that it applies to employee aftertax and employer matching contributions. All employees eligible to make an aftertax contribution and receive an allocation of matching contributions must be included in the test. However, where the ACP test includes only matching contributions, an employee who is not entitled to a year-end matching contribution due to failure to fulfill a service requirement presumably would not have to be counted at all.

Just as the ADP test can be run either with elective deferrals, or with elective deferrals plus QNECs and QMACs, in the numerator, the numerator in the ACP test can also be structured in several ways. Normally, the numerator in the ACP test consists of aftertax employee contributions and matching employer contributions. It can also include QNECs or elective deferrals that represent a cushion in the ADP test for the plan (i.e., any portion of these contributions not needed to pass the ADP test).[67] Exhibit 4–3 shows the

---

67. IRS Reg. 1.401(m)-1(f)(1)(ii).

E X H I B I T   4–3

Assignment of Contributions to ADP/ACP Tests

ADP Test	Type of Contribution	ACP Test
X ⬅═══════	Elective Deferral ═══════➤	X
	Aftertax Employee Contribution ═══════➤	X
	Matching Contribution ═══════➤	X
X ⬅───────	QNEC ───────➤	X
X ⬅───────	QMAC ───────➤	X

tests to which different types of contributions can or must be assigned. The double-line arrows indicate that the contribution must be assigned to a test; the single-line arrows indicate that the contribution may be assigned to a test.

How contributions are assigned for testing purposes will not change their basic nature for regular plan purposes and record-keeping.

MULTIPLE USE OF THE ALTERNATIVE LIMITATION

As a general rule, a plan that is subject to both the ADP and ACP tests must pass at least one of them using the basic or 125 percent test. In other words, multiple use of the alternative limitation described above is prohibited.[68]

Employers can apply an aggregate limit test in situations where they can pass each test only by using the alternative limitation, however. The aggregate limit test works as follows:[69]

- Step 1: add the ADPs and ACPs for HCEs to arrive at the aggregate HCE percentage.

- Step 2: multiply the *larger* of the ADP or ACP for NHCEs by 1.25.

- Step 3: multiply the *smaller* of the ADP or ACP for NHCEs by 2.

---

68. IRC Section 401(m)(9)(A); IRS Reg. 1.401(m)-2(b)(1).
69. IRS Reg. 1.401(m)-2(b)(3)(i).

- Step 4: compare the product in Step 3 with the sum of 2 plus the *smaller* of the NHCE ADP or ACP. Add the lesser of the two results to the result in Step 2.

If the resulting sum in Step 4 equals or exceeds the aggregate HCE percentage in Step 1, then the plan passes the aggregate limit test.

The aggregate limit test can also be run by reversing the items described above, using the same basic mathematics. The smaller of the NHCE ADP or ACP would be multiplied by 1.25, and the larger of the NHCE ADP or ACP would be multiplied by or added to 2.

An employer can run the aggregate limit test either way and use whichever approach produces the best result. In general, if the NHCE ADP and ACP are both lower than 2 percent, the second approach will be more beneficial. If the plan fails the test and the employer does not return excess contributions as described below, however, then it must correct the ADPs or ACPs for either HCEs or NHCEs—or both—to pass the aggregate limit test.

ADP/ACP TESTING UNIT

In general, employers must test each single plan, as defined in IRC Section 414(l), to determine whether it meets the ADP/ACP test. To be a single plan under Section 414(l), all of the assets of the plan must be available to pay all the benefits under the plan. A defined contribution plan will not fail to meet this test merely because it has separate written documents and separate trusts or provides separate accounts and permits employees to direct the investment of their accounts. Thus, for example, if a single plan has two CODAs covering different groups of employees (e.g., hourly and salaried) both CODAs would have to be tested together even though one allowed deferrals up to 6 percent of pay and the other allowed deferrals of up to 10 percent of pay.

Disaggregated Plans

The mandatory disaggregation rules for coverage discussed in Chapter 3 also apply for ADP/ACP test purposes. If a plan containing a CODA passes the coverage requirements on a qualified separate line of business (QSLOB) basis, for example, the plan sponsor would have to perform a separate ADP test with respect to each QSLOB. Separate ADP/ACP testing is also required of the ESOP and non-ESOP portions of a plan.[70]

Separate ADP/ACP tests also apply if a CODA covers both union and nonunion employees. The ADP/ACP tests would be performed separately on the nonunion portion of the plan. The rules described below apply to the union portion of the plan.

Collectively bargained plans did not have to satisfy the ACP test and were exempt from ADP testing until the 1993 plan year.[71] For plan years beginning in 1993, a collectively bargained CODA must satisfy the ADP test in order for the CODA to be qualified, that is in order for employees to exclude their elective deferrals from income. For plan years beginning before 1993, such a plan was treated as satisfying the ADP test even if the CODA did not meet the ADP test.

Employees' elective deferrals for pre-1993 years, as well as post-1992 years, are nevertheless limited by the $7,000 (indexed) dollar limit on elective deferrals in effect for the applicable year.[72]

Permissive Aggregation

If an employer aggregates two single plans containing CODAs and arrangements subject to Section 401(m) testing for coverage purposes (e.g., a salaried and an hourly plan), it will have to perform the ADP/ACP tests on an aggregated plan basis.

SAFE HARBORS–ADP/ACP TESTING

A CODA plan sponsor will no longer have to worry about nondiscrimination tests for elective contributions starting in 1999 if the employer satisfies one of two safe harbors by either: (1) providing certain matching contributions to NHCEs, or (2) making a contribution of 3 percent of compensation for all NHCEs, regardless of whether these employees contribute to the plan. The safe harbor

---

70. See Chapter 5.
71. IRS Reg. 1.401(k)-1(a)(7); 402(a)-1(d)(3)(iv); 1.401(k)-1(f)(7), Ex. 4; 1.401(m)-1(a)(3).
72. IRS Reg. 1.402(g)-1(g)(2).

matching contribution must be at least 100 percent of the first 3 percent of pay contributed and 50 percent of the next 2 percent of pay contributed. Other formulas for matching contributions will qualify for this safe harbor treatment if the formula provides an amount of matching contribution at least as large as the safe harbor formula and the percent matched does not increase as the employee's contribution increases. In addition, the rate of match for HCEs cannot be greater than the rate of match for NHCEs.

Also, ACP testing will not be required for matching contributions starting in 1999 if:

1. The plan makes safe harbor employer contributions that meet either of the ADP safe harbors.
2. The plan does not match pretax or aftertax employee contributions above 6 percent.
3. The rate of match does not increase with increasing rates of pretax or aftertax employee contributions.
4. The match rate for HCEs is no greater than that for NHCEs at each rate of contribution.

The ACP test will still be required, however, for aftertax employee contributions.

To meet the safe harbor, eligible employees must be informed of their opportunity to participate in the CODA prior to the beginning of the year and the safe harbor employer contributions must be fully vested and subject to the same restrictions on distributions as elective contributions—i.e., they can be distributed only on account of separation from service, death, disability or attainment of age 59-1/2.

While these safe harbors eliminate the need and expense of annual testing as well as the necessity of recharacterizing or refunding excess contributions, they can result in additional plan costs due to the required employer contribution, full vesting, and annual notice requirements.

CURING EXCESSES THROUGH RESTRUCTURING

For plan years beginning before 1992, an employer was permitted to restructure a CODA or the 401(m) portion of a plan on an employee group basis. This enabled the employer to perform the

ADP/ACP tests on an employee group basis rather than testing the plan as a whole, provided each component plan satisfied the coverage requirements.

Unlike the employee group restructuring process that applies for coverage testing purposes, as described in Chapter 3, the employees in a group for ADP or ACP testing purposes must share some common attribute *other than* similar allocation or accrual rates. Thus, a CODA or the 401(m) portion of a plan could have been restructured by employee groups based on the following common attributes: work site, job classification, same division or subsidiary, same unit acquired in a merger or acquisition, hire date during a specified period, or coverage under the same benefit or contribution formula. A plan could not be restructured based on employees whose only attribute is the same or similar deferral ratios, or another attribute having substantially the same effect.

The IRS will not allow the employer to restructure on an employee group basis for plan years beginning in 1992 and later.[73] But employers interested in retaining the advantages of restructuring (i.e., separate ADP/ACP testing) on a permanent basis should consider splitting their plans into two or more single plans covering different groups of employees. As discussed above, the single plans could still be covered by one plan document, and the plans' assets could be held in one master trust. Separate Forms 5500 would be required, however.

CURING EXCESSES WITH QNECs and QMACs

As discussed earlier with regard to the ADP or ACP test, the employer can attempt to cure the failure of the multiple use test by making extra contributions (typically for NHCEs only) in the form of QNECs or QMACs to offset HCE excesses. (Chapter 13 includes a detailed discussion of approaches and options in this regard.) However, the plan sponsor may also choose to refund excesses as described in the next section.

RECHARACTERIZATION

Plan sponsors can recharacterize contributions that exceed the ADP limit as aftertax employee contributions.[74] These recharacter-

---

73. IRS Reg. 1.401(k)-1(b)(3)(ii).
74. IRS Reg. 1.401(k)-1(f)(3).

ized contributions must be then tested under the ACP test for the year the contributions were originally made.

Recharacterization is permitted only to the extent that the recharacterized amounts plus the aftertax employee contributions actually made under the plan do not exceed the plan's cap on aftertax contributions.[75] If a plan permits 6 percent of compensation to be contributed on an aftertax basis and 5.50 percent has actually been contributed, for example, only 0.50 percent of excess contributions can be recharacterized.

Excess contributions must be recharacterized within two and a half months after the end of the plan year. Whether this requirement is met is determined according to the date on which the last affected employee is notified of the recharacterization.[76]

Recharacterized contributions are treated as aftertax contributions for tax purposes.[77] Thus, such contributions will be includable in the employee's gross income on the earliest date that amounts deferred for the plan year being tested would otherwise have been received in cash. Under a plan with a plan year ending June 30, 1996, for example, an employee who has made deferrals since July 1, 1995, will have any recharacterized contributions taxed as of July 1, 1995, even if total elective contributions did not exceed the ADP limit for the 1995 plan year until March 15, 1996, and were not recharacterized until August 15, 1996.

Although the recharacterized contributions are treated as aftertax contributions for purposes of ACP testing and individual income taxation, they are treated as elective employer contributions for other qualified plan purposes, most notably under Sections 404 and 415.[78] However, final regulations clarified that recharacterized excess contributions are not subject to the restrictions on in-service distributions applicable to elective deferrals discussed above.[79]

REFUNDING EXCESS CONTRIBUTIONS

If a plan fails the ADP, ACP, or multiple use test and the employer does not cure excesses with QNECs or QMACs, the plan must

---

75. IRS Reg. 1.401(k)-1(f)(3)(iii)(B).
76. IRS Reg. 1.401(k)-1(f)(3)(iii)(A).
77. IRS Reg. 1.401(k)-1(f)(3)(ii)(A).
78. IRS Reg. 1.401(k)-1(f)(3)(ii)(B).
79. IRS Reg. 1.401(k)-1(f)(3)(ii)(A).

return any excess contributions made by HCEs, together with any investment earnings on such contributions. Any matching employer contributions generated by excess deferrals or excess contributions generally must be forfeited even though the employee is otherwise vested;[80] vested matching contributions may be distributed to correct an ACP problem, whereas nonvested matching contributions presumably must be forfeited.[81]

The excess attributable to a failure of the ADP test is called an excess contribution;[82] the excess attributable to a failure of the ACP test is called an excess aggregate contribution.[83] The term *excess contribution* will be used hereafter to include both types unless it is necessary to make a distinction.

Refund Deadlines

There are two critical dates in returning excess contributions. The first of these dates is two and a half months after the end of the plan year in which the excess occurred. If excess contributions and investment earnings on such contributions are returned to HCEs by that time, the amount will be taken into income on the earliest date that amounts deferred for the plan year being tested would have otherwise been received in cash.[84] Distributions are *not* subject to FICA and FUTA taxes; they will be subject to withholding if distributed more than two and a half months after the end of the plan year.[85] A return of aftertax contributions will not be taxable; other returned amounts, including investment income on both aftertax and elective contributions, will be taxable as income but will not be subject to any penalty taxes that might normally apply to early distributions from a qualified plan.[86]

---

80. IRC Sections 401(k)(8)(E) and 411(a)(3)(G); IRS Reg. 1.401(k)-1(f)(5) and 1.401(a)(4)-4(e)(3)(G).

81. IRS Reg. 1.401(m)-1(e)(1), (3) and (4).

82. IRC Section 401(k)(8); IRS Reg. 1.401(k)-1(g)(7)(i).

83. IRC Section 401(m)(6); IRS Reg. 1.401(m)-1(f)(8).

84. IRS Reg. 1.401(k)-1(f)(4)(v); 1.401(m)-1(e)(3)(v); a *de minimis* rule provides that if the total principal amount of the excess contributions is less than $100 and is distributed within two and a half months after the close of the plan year, excess amounts (plus earnings) will be included in income in the year of distribution. IRS Reg. 1.401(k)-1(f)(4)(v)(B); 1.401(m)-1(e)(3)(v)(B).

85. IRS Notice 87-77

86. IRS Reg. 1.401(k)-1(f)(4)(v)(A); 1.401(m)-1(e)(3)(v)(A).

The second critical date is the last day of the plan year following the plan year in which the excess occurred. If the required amounts are distributed after the first critical date (two and a half months after the close of the plan year) and before this second critical date, the amount returned is taken into income by the HCEs in the year of distribution. (Again, a return of aftertax employee contributions is not taxable.)[87] In addition, the employer is subject to a 10 percent penalty tax on the amount of principal involved (but not investment earnings).[88]

Missing the Deadlines

Serious consequences ensue when excesses are not returned by this second critical date. If the excess is an excess contribution, the CODA portion of the plan loses its qualified status for the plan year for which the excess contributions were made and for all subsequent plan years in which the excess aggregate contributions remain in the plan.[89] Disqualification of the CODA portion of the plan means that all employees are taxed on amounts they could have elected to receive in cash but chose to defer to the plan during the year.

The situation is much more serious if the excess is an excess aggregate contribution. In this case, the *plan* will be treated as failing to satisfy Section 401(a)(4) for the plan year in which the excess aggregate contributions were made, and for all subsequent plan years in which the excess aggregate contributions remain in the plan.[90] The consequences are severe: the employer could lose its deductions, plan investment income could be taxable and employees could be taxed on their vested account balances.

Coordinating Refunds

The regulations make an effort to coordinate the return of multiple types of excesses. It is clear that returns of excess contributions and excess deferrals are coordinated; the return of elective deferrals to

---

87. Ibid.
88. IRC Section 4979(b); IRS Reg. 1.401(k)-1(f)(6)(i); 1.401(m)-1(e)(5)(i).
89. IRS Reg. 1.401(k)-1(f)(6)(ii).
90. IRS Reg. 1.401(m)-1(e)(5)(ii).

cure either type of excess is counted toward curing the other excess.[91] Thus, for example, if an excess deferral has already been cured by the return of elective deferrals (and earnings thereon) to a particular HCE, and it is subsequently determined that there is an excess contribution problem requiring the return of elective deferrals to the same individual, the amount to be returned to cure the excess contribution problem is reduced by the amount that was already returned to cure the excess deferral problem.

The Refund Process

Refunds must be made according to the method specified in the law. Beginning in 1997, excess contributions must be refunded starting with those HCEs who have made the highest dollar amount of contribution, rather than those whose contribution rate is the highest as was the case under prior law.

The actual amount deferred by the HCE with the highest dollar amount of contribution is reduced until one of the following occurs: (1) the ADP or ACP problem is cured; or (2) the reduced contribution equals the amount contributed by the next highest HCE(s). If the latter result occurs first, then the amount contributed by all HCEs at this level will be reduced until the problem is cured or until the next level is reached, and so forth.

If refunds are required on the ADP side, the plan should return unmatched elective deferrals before it returns elective deferrals that have attracted a matching employer contribution if at all possible. The same is true of the ACP test; unmatched after tax contributions should be refunded first.

Assume, for example, that a plan provides a 50 percent matching contribution on the first six percent of employee contributions, whether elective or aftertax. An HCE earning $100,000 a year contributes 12 percent on an elective basis for half the year; this means he has contributed a total of $6,000, and $3,000 of this amount has attracted a matching contribution of $1,500. If this HCE's ADP for the year is six percent but must be lowered to four percent to comply with the ADP test, the plan could refund $2,000 of unmatched elective deferrals, leaving $3,000 in matched elective

---

91. IRS Reg. 1.401(k)-1(f)(5)(i); 1.402(g)-1(e)(6).

deferrals, $1,000 in unmatched elective deferrals, and $1,500 in matching employer contributions in the account.

Refunding Investment Earnings

The investment earnings to be returned along with excess contributions must be determined for the plan year of excess and, if the plan so provides, for the gap period—the time between the end of the year and the date of distribution.[92] For purposes of determining the earnings that should be returned along with the excess contributions, a plan may use the same method it uses to allocate income to participants' accounts, provided the method is used consistently to determine all corrective distributions during the plan year and is nondiscriminatory.[93]

As an alternative, investment earnings may be determined by multiplying a dollar amount by a fraction. The dollar amount equals earnings allocable to the type of contribution being distributed. The numerator of the fraction is the participant's excess for the plan year. The denominator is the participant's account balance as of the beginning of the plan year plus contributions made during the plan year and the gap period if gap period income is allocated.[94]

A simpler method may be used to determine earnings for the gap period.[95] Under this method, earnings that were calculated for the year are multiplied by the product of 10 percent times the number of calendar months that have elapsed since the end of the year.

Aggregate Limit Test

If an excess results from failure to meet the aggregate limit test, refunds must be made until the test is met. The regulations do not specify an order for cutting back; the plan can make adjustments on either the ADP or ACP side. It is not clear whether adjustments may be made on both the ADP and ACP sides.[96]

---

92. IRS Reg. 1.401(k)-1(f)(4)(ii)(A); 1.401(m)-1(e)(3)(ii)(A).
93. IRS Reg. 1.401(k)-1(f)(4)(ii)(B); 1.401(m)-1(e)(3)(ii)(B).
94. IRS Reg. 1.401(k)-1(f)(4)(ii)(C); 1.401(m)-1(e)(3)(ii)(C).
95. IRS Reg. 1.401(k)-1(f)(4)(ii)(D); 1.401(m)-1(e)(3)(ii)(D).
96. IRS Reg. 1.401(m)-2(c)(1).

It generally makes sense to meet the aggregate limit test by first refunding aftertax employee and associated matching contributions that are vested. Assume, for example, that a CODA provides for a 50 percent match on the first 6 percent of employee contributions. The plan allows elective contributions of up to 5 percent of compensation, and aftertax contributions of up to 11 percent of compensation. In the current plan year, there is only one HCE; she receives $130,000 in compensation. This HCE made elective contributions of 5 percent of pay ($6,500) during the year and received a matching employer contribution of 2.5 percent or $3,250. She also made aftertax contributions of 1 percent of pay ($1,300), attracting a match of $650 (0.5 percent).

The ADP/ACP test results for the year are as follows:

	ADP	ACP
HCE	5.00%	4.00%
NHCEs	3.28	2.65

Because the plan will pass both the ADP and ACP tests only by applying the alternative limitation, it must comply with the aggregate limit calculated as follows:

$$3.28 \text{ times } 1.25 = 4.10$$
$$2.65 \text{ plus } 2.00 = \underline{4.65}$$
$$\text{Aggregate limit} = 8.75$$

Because the percentage for the HCE is 9.00 percent (5.00 plus 4.00), the plan fails the aggregate limit test.

If the plan sponsor decides to correct the excess by making an ACP refund, the refund is calculated as follows. The excess rate (9.00 percent minus 8.75 percent) is multiplied by compensation ($130,000). The result of this step (.25 percent times $130,000) yields a refund of $325. This total refund is apportioned between aftertax employee contributions and employer matching contributions— $216.67 and $108.33, respectively. Assuming the HCE is fully vested, the employer refunds the entire amount. (The refund could be made entirely from matching contributions, but the allocation described minimizes taxes because aftertax employee contributions do not constitute a taxable distribution.) After the refund, the HCE's ACP will be 3.75 percent [($5,200 minus $325) divided by

$130,000]. Added to the HCE's ADP of 4.00 percent, this yields a total of 8.75 percent, which is the percentage permitted by the aggregate limit test.

By contrast, a correction made through an ADP refund would reduce the HCE's account by $487.50. The refunded amount would still be $325 (.25 times $130,000), but the HCE would also have to forfeit the employer matching contribution of $162.50.

It should be noted that excesses can be corrected by reducing the ADP or ACP of the HCEs, or a combination of both.

Nonqualified "Wrap-Around" Plans

Wrap-around plans are arrangements that allow executives to make up on a nonqualified basis exactly the amounts that cannot be deferred to a CODA because of the ADP test. These plans, if they are to be exempt from most of the labor law requirements of Title I of ERISA, must be unfunded and maintained primarily for the purpose of providing deferred compensation for a select group of management or highly compensated employees. Even though the group involved is, by definition, highly compensated under the tax law, it does not automatically follow that they will all be considered as highly compensated under the labor law. Thus, it may not be possible to extend the plan to all individuals whose contributions are restricted by the ADP test.

In a private letter ruling,[97] the IRS approved a type of wrap-around arrangement that works as follows: Executives elect in year one to defer a fixed percentage of their compensation in year two into a nonqualified plan. After the employer performs the ADP test for year two early in year three, the employer actually contributes money on behalf of the executives to the CODA to the extent allowable under the ADP test. Then, the deferral amounts in excess of the amount allowable under the ADP test are left in the nonqualified wrap-around plan. Matching contributions would operate in a similar manner.

The wrap-around arrangement is relatively easy to administer. In many cases, it eliminates refunds to executives of amounts contributed to the CODA in excess of the ADP test, and it may eliminate the need to monitor the ADP test on a frequent basis.

---

97. PLR 9530038.

AVERTING PROBLEMS

There are a number of steps an employer can take to avert problems with he ADP and ACP tests. Using the contribution percentages of the NHCEs for the prior plan year allows maximum HCE contribution levels to be determined at the beginning of the current year, for example. An employer who utilizes the safe harbors for nondiscrimination testing will also avoid ADP/ACP problems. Other steps that might be taken include setting limits on contribution rates at the beginning of the year and conducting prospective testing in advance of year end so as to anticipate problems.

CHAPTER 5

ESOPs and KSOPs

This chapter provides an overview of the special tax law and ERISA provisions that apply to employee stock ownership plans (ESOPs). The discussion also covers leveraged ESOPs and KSOPs; a KSOP is a plan created by the marriage of a CODA and an ESOP.

ESOPs

An ESOP is a qualified plan that is designed to invest primarily in qualifying employer securities, something that must be explicitly stated in the plan document.[1] While the government has not expressly defined what the quoted phrase means, most practitioners believe this requirement will be met if more than 50 percent of plan assets are so invested, when examined over the life of the plan. Common stock and preferred stock convertible into common stock are the employer securities typically used in these plans.[2]

Only a stock bonus plan or a combination stock bonus plan and money purchase pension plan can be designed to be an ESOP;[3] a profit-sharing plan or a stand-alone money purchase plan cannot. Stock bonus plans are generally subject to the same

---

1. IRC Section 4975(e)(7); IRS Reg. 54.4975-11(b).
2. IRC Sections 4975(e)(8) and 409(1).
3. IRC Section 4975(e)(7)(A).

qualification rules as profit-sharing plans; the primary difference is that distributions under a stock bonus plan must be available in the form of employer securities.

LEVERAGED ESOPs

In a leveraged ESOP, the plan borrows money—either directly from a lending institution, or via a back-to-back arrangement in which the employer borrows the money and lends it to the plan. The plan uses this money to purchase employer stock—in most cases directly from the company.

Employer stock is held in a plan suspense account and is typically pledged as collateral for the loan. Because the plan cannot generate income (other than investment income), and because of certain restrictions on the lender's ability to realize on the collateral in the event of a default, the employer must usually guarantee any loan between the plan and the lending institution.

The employer then makes contributions to the plan for the benefit of employees. The plan uses those contributions to repay the loan (including interest). Under certain circumstances loan repayments are made with cash dividends on the stock acquired with the loan proceeds. As the loan is repaid, shares of stock are released from the suspense account and are allocated to the accounts of eligible participants.

The plan sponsor can determine how many shares to release as the loan is repaid using either of two methods. The fractional method is most common; the number of shares released reflects the ratio of the amount of the current principal and interest payment to the total current and future principal and interest payments on the loan. Under the second or principal-only method, the number of shares released reflects the ratio of the current amount of principal being repaid to the total current and future principal repayments. This method cannot be used when the term of the loan is more than 10 years; certain other conditions also apply. Under either method, the value of the stock at the time the release takes place is not taken into account when determining the number of shares being released.

Many employers find leveraged ESOPs attractive because they can put relatively large blocks of company stock into presumably friendly hands. While this could be an advantage in the event of a takeover attempt, a leveraged ESOP must exist primarily for employee benefit purposes, and takeover protection can only be incidental.[4]

Employers who are considering a leveraged ESOP should analyze the accounting implications very carefully. In general, however, a leveraged ESOP can be structured without significant dilution in earnings per share.

KSOPs

A KSOP is a CODA in which employer matching contributions are made to an ESOP; a loan transaction may also be structured to prefund future employer matching contributions. The ESOP can be a stand-alone plan with a CODA, or it can be part of a program consisting of two plans, one of which is a profit-sharing or stock bonus plan that is not an ESOP. As a rule, elective deferrals and aftertax employee contributions are made to the non-ESOP portion of the program, and the employer match is made to the ESOP portion.[5]

Many employers with conventional CODAs that provide for investing the company matching contributions in company stock are interested in establishing an ESOP for the employer stock portion of the plan (whether or not leveraged) in order to obtain a tax deduction for the payment of dividends that are either passed through to employees or, in the case of a leveraged arrangement, used to repay the loan.[6] Further, prior employer contributions that have been invested in employer stock can be converted under the plan and defined as part of the ESOP, thus generating a tax deduction for dividends passed through to employees. The ability to deduct dividends can create significant tax savings for an employer. If, for example, the employer is in a 34 percent tax bracket and the dividends passed through on the KSOP stock

---

4. *NCR Corp.* v. *American Telephone & Telegraph Co.*, Case No. C-3-91-78, slip op. (S.D. Ohio, March 19, 1991); *Shamrock Holdings, Inc.* v. *Polaroid Corp.*, 559 A.2d 257 (Del. Ch. 1989).
5. In TAM 9503002, the IRS took the position that a CODA with an ESOP feature could allow a participant to direct that his or her pre-tax contributions be used to repay an exempt loan. The IRS stated that this provision would not violate the exclusive benefit rule. On January 16, 1996, however, the DOL asked the IRS to reconsider its position since the DOL believes that the use of participant pre-tax contributions to repay the exempt loan would raise fiduciary issues and possibly be a prohibited transaction.
6. See page 119 for a discussion of the treatment of dividends used in this fashion.

amount to $1,000,000, the employer will save $340,000 as a result of being allowed this deduction.

When establishing the fund/account structure of a KSOP, it is important to determine whether leveraged KSOP shares need to be separated from nonleveraged shares. This would be necessary if the employer wants to take advantage of special tax rules that apply only to leveraged shares: dividends on allocated shares that are used to repay the loan are deductible, and forfeitures of leveraged shares, when allocated among remaining participants, are not considered to be part of the annual addition for Section 415 purposes.[7]

OVERVIEW OF TAX AND ERISA CONSIDERATIONS

ESOPs must generally satisfy all of the plan qualification requirements described in Chapter 3. Unique tax law requirements and special ERISA provisions that apply to these arrangements are summarized below.

Diversification Exemption

There is a special exception to the general fiduciary requirement that assets of a plan be invested in a diversified portfolio of investments for eligible individual account plans, including ESOPs.[8] Under this exception, ESOPs can be invested primarily in employer securities. The prudence requirement of ERISA continues to apply, except to the extent this rule might require diversification; the exclusive benefit fiduciary rule also applies to these plans.

Joint and Survivor Requirements

Money purchase plans are generally subject to the qualified joint and survivor rules. However, a money purchase plan that is part of an ESOP is exempt from these rules to the same extent as any other defined contribution plan, that is, in general, if: (1) the participant's vested account balance is paid in full to his or her surviving spouse (unless the spouse consents in writing to another beneficiary), and

---

7. See page 120.
8. ERISA Section 404(a)(2).

(2) the participant does not, or is not allowed to, elect benefits in the form of a life annuity.[9]

Integration With Social Security; Permitted Disparity

An ESOP cannot be integrated with social security benefits and thus cannot take advantage of the disparity in contributions otherwise permitted under Section 401(l).[10]

Coverage and Nondiscrimination Tests

Employers cannot combine ESOPs with other plans in applying the nondiscrimination and coverage rules,[11] except for purposes of the average benefit percentage test.[12] Similarly, for plan years beginning on or after 1990, the portion of a plan that is an ESOP and the portion that is not must be treated as separate plans.[13]

Voting Rights

If the employer's stock is publicly traded, employees must be given pass-through voting rights for the shares allocated to their accounts.[14] If the employer's stock is privately held, voting rights

---

9. IRC Section 401(a)(11)(C). Note also that the plan cannot be a transferee plan with respect to the participant. IRC Section 401(a)(11)(B)(iii)(III) and IRS Reg. 1.401(a)-20, Q&A 3.
10. IRS Reg. 54.4975-11(a)(7)(ii) and IRS Reg. 1. 401(l)-1(a)(4). See Chapter 3.
11. IRS Reg. 1.401(a)(4)-1(c)(8); IRS Reg. 54.4975-11(e); IRS Reg. 1.410(b)-7(c)(2) and IRS Reg. 1.410(b)-7(d)(2).
12. IRS Reg. 1.410(b)-7(e)(1).
13. The fact that ESOPs are tested separately from other plans may make advance testing for nondiscrimination difficult if the plan permits employee contributions to be made to both the ESOP and nonESOP portions of the plan. An example will illustrate this. If a participant makes a pretax contribution of 6 percent and directs that 50 percent of that contribution be invested in the ESOP, the two ADP tests (one for the ESOP and one for the nonESOP portion) will each reflect a 3 percent deferral rate for the participant. However, if the participant decides to change his or her investment direction election, the deferral percentages for the ESOP and nonESOP portions of the plan will change even though the overall deferral by the participant remains the same. This adds further complexity to advance testing for discrimination because the test results will vary not only on the amount that the participant contributes but by the participant's investment direction.
14. IRC Section 409(e).

must be passed through only for such matters as the approval or disapproval of any corporate merger or consolidation, recapitalization, reclassification, liquidation, dissolution, or sale of substantially all of the firm's assets.[15] If the shares of the closely held company were acquired with the proceeds of a loan (generally made after July 10, 1989, and before August 21, 1996) where the lender was able to exclude 50 percent of the interest from income, however, all voting on allocated shares must be given to participants.

Employee Diversification Rights

Employees nearing retirement (those age 55 or over with at least 10 years of participation) must be given the opportunity to diversify their investments by transferring from the employer stock fund to one or more of three other investment funds.[16] The right to diversify need be granted only for a 90-day window period following the close of the plan year in which the employee first becomes eligible for the right and following the close of each of the next five plan years. This right is limited to shares acquired after 1986, and is further limited to 25 percent of such shares until the last window period, when up to 50 percent of such shares may be eligible for diversification.

Distribution Requirements

In general, an ESOP is required to make distributions to participants in the form of employer securities.[17] As an alternative, cash may be the normal form of distribution, but the participant must have the right to elect to receive stock. This requirement does not apply to the extent the participant has elected to diversify his or her account balance.

---

15. This voting requirement can be satisfied by providing each participant with one vote, regardless of the number of shares actually allocated, and voting all shares held by the plan (whether or not allocated) in proportion to the vote.
16. IRC Section 401(a)(28). Alternatively, amounts subject to the right of diversification may be distributed from the plan.
17. IRC Sections 409(h) and 4975(e)(7). If the employer is a privately held company whose charter or bylaws restrict ownership of substantially all of its securities to employees and qualified plans, participants need not be given the right to receive stock. The employer can distribute either cash or stock subject to a right of first refusal in its favor.

ESOPs are subject to the rules that prohibit the forced distribution of an employee's account (if more than $3,500) until normal retirement age or age 62, if later. Unlike other qualified plans, however, ESOPs are required to permit accelerated distributions for stock acquired after 1986 when participants terminate employment. Specifically, and unless otherwise requested by the participant, ESOPs must distribute such stock by the end of the year following: (1) the year in which the participant dies, retires, or becomes disabled, or (2) the fifth plan year following the year of termination for any other reason.[18] However, the employer may delay distribution of securities acquired under a loan until the plan year following the plan year in which the loan has been repaid *in full*. If the general qualified plan distribution rules would require distributions earlier than these special ESOP rules, the general rules apply.

Rights of First Refusal

Stock acquired with an ESOP loan may be made subject to a right of first refusal in favor of the employer, the plan, or both.[19] The stock must not be publicly traded at the time the right is exercisable. Further, the selling price and other terms under the right must not be less favorable to the seller than the greater of: (1) the value of the stock, or (2) the purchase price and other terms offered by a buyer other than the employer or the plan who makes a good faith offer to purchase the stock. The right of first refusal must lapse no later than 14 days after the security holder gives written notice that an offer to purchase the stock has been made by a third party.

Put Options

If employer securities are not publicly traded when they are distributed, they must be subject to a put option—that is, the employee must have the right to require the employer to repurchase the

---

18. IRC Section 409(o). Longer periods are allowed if the employee's account balance
    exceeds $500,000 (adjusted for increases in the cost of living).
19. IRS Reg. 54.4975-7(b)(9). See also Footnote 16, above, re: stock of privately held
    companies.

stock.[20] This put option must be exercisable only by the employee (or his or her donee, the employee's estate, or a distributee from the employee's estate). The put option may not bind the plan, but it may grant the plan the option to assume the rights and obligations of the employer at the time it is exercised.

The put option must be exercisable for at least 60 days following the distribution of the stock and, if not exercised, for a second period of at least 60 days in the plan year following the distribution. The price must be determined under a fair valuation formula.

If an employer is required to repurchase employer securities that are distributed to the employee as part of a total distribution (of the entire amount in the employee's account within one taxable year), the payment may be made in substantially equal periodic payments over a period not exceeding five years. The payments may not be made less frequently than annually and must begin no later than 30 days after the exercise of the put option. In addition, the employer must provide adequate security and pay reasonable interest on the unpaid amounts. If the employer is required to repurchase employer securities as part of an installment distribution, it must pay for the securities in full within 30 days after the employee exercises the put option. A separate put option exists for each installment.

Deductibility of Contributions

The annual deduction limit for a nonleveraged ESOP is 15 percent of payroll. In a leveraged ESOP, the employer may deduct all contributions used to repay interest on the loan and up to 25 percent of payroll for contributions used to repay principal.[21]

Deductibility of Dividends

Corporate employers are generally not allowed a tax deduction for dividends and must pay those dividends to shareholders out of aftertax income. If cash dividends are passed through or paid out

20. IRC Section 409(h).
21. IRC Section 404(a)(9).

to participants under an ESOP, however, the employer can deduct them on its income tax return.[22]

Employers must consider a number of issues in administering a dividend pass-through feature. Is the pass-through elective on the part of employees, for example? If it is, the employer will not receive a deduction for dividends that employees elect to have reinvested under the plan. A recent private letter ruling shows employers a way to obtain a tax deduction for dividends without forcing employees to receive these dividends.[23] Under this arrangement, dividends are passed through at the election of employees, but they are granted an automatic increase in their salary reduction to exactly offset the extra cash received. This approach, of course, will not work for any employee whose elective deferral is at the maximum allowed. It also could create ADP testing problems since it would tend to raise the ADP for highly compensated employees. A further problem is that the net effect of doing this is to collect social security (FICA) taxes on dividend payments that are not otherwise subject to this tax.

There are other administrative issues involved with a dividend pass-through feature. Will minimums be imposed on the pass-through? Are the appropriate plan accounts clearly designated as ESOP accounts and eligible for the dividend pass through? Will it be necessary to coordinate the pass-through with concurrent in-service withdrawals? Are dividends to be passed through for terminated participants? These questions illustrate the administrative considerations involved when including a pass-through provision in an ESOP.

Cash dividends are also generally deductible if they are used to repay an ESOP loan. Where such dividends relate to *allocated* shares, however, participants must receive an allocation of employer securities with a fair market value of at least the amount of such dividends. For stock acquired after August 4, 1989, however, only dividends on stock acquired with the ESOP loan that are used to repay *that* loan are deductible.

---

22. IRC Section 404(k). The dividends must be paid out no later than 90 days after the end of the plan year in which they were paid. In addition, any dividends passed through are taxable income to the employees; they are not subject to the 10 percent early distribution tax, however. See IRC Section 72(t)(2)(vi).
23. PLR 9523034.

The use of dividends to repay an ESOP loan can further enhance the already favorable treatment accorded ESOPs under Section 415, as discussed below.

Interest Exclusion

When a leveraged ESOP owns at least 50 percent of each class of the employer's stock (or the total value of all outstanding stock), a partial interest exclusion was available to a qualified lender (bank, insurance company, investment company),[24] permitting the lender to exclude 50 percent of the interest received on the ESOP loan from its taxable income. This provision of the law was repealed for loans made after August 20, 1996. The repeal does not apply to the refinancing of loans made on or before August 20, 1996, or pursuant to a binding contract in effect on June 10, 1996, nor does it apply to loans made pursuant to a binding contract that was in effect on June 10, 1996.

Section 415 Limits

Calculation of the Section 415 limit is based on employer contributions to the leveraged ESOP—not on the market value of shares at the time they are allocated to participant accounts.[25] Further, repayments of interest on the loan and reallocated forfeitures derived from leveraged shares are not part of the annual addition if no more than one third of the deductible employer contribution for the year is allocated to HCEs.[26] Dividends, as a form of plan earnings, are not annual additions under Section 415. This is presumably true even where dividends are used to repay principal on the loan.

This favorable treatment can result in additions to participants' accounts that are significantly greater than would be the case in a non-ESOP.

Consider the following example, which focuses on the sixth year an ESOP loan is outstanding, uses the fractional method of

---

24. IRC Section 133.
25. IRS Reg. 54.4975-7(b)(8)(iii).
26. IRC Section 415(c)(6).

releasing shares, and assumes that no more than one third of the employer contribution is allocated to HCEs:

Amount of loan	$100,000
Term	10 years
Total shares initially purchased	10,000
Shares remaining in suspense account	5,000
Cost basis per share	$10
Current share value	$17
Total current and future year payments	$81,500
Employer loan repayment (year 6)	
Principal	$10,100
Interest	6,200
Total	$16,300

The number of shares to be released under the fractional method depends on the amount of the loan repayment. The first step in this process is to develop a fraction. The numerator of this fraction is the amount of the current year's repayment ($16,300); the denominator is total current and future payments under the loan ($81,500). This fraction (1/5) is then multiplied by the total number of shares in the ESOP suspense account at the beginning of the year (5,000). Thus, 1,000 shares (1/5 times 5,000) would be released in this situation.

In this example, the employer's contribution that represents an interest payment will not be part of the annual additions for participants. Their aggregate annual additions will be only $10,100, the amount of the principal repayment, even though the employer's total contribution was $16,300. Further, since the share value had increased to $17 at the time of release and allocation to participant accounts, the total value added to the accounts would be $17,000 (1,000 times $17), but the annual additions to their accounts would still be only $10,100.[27]

Any forfeitures attributable to leveraged shares could increase the actual value of the amounts being allocated to participant accounts without increasing their annual additions or, alternatively, could further *decrease* annual additions if used to reduce

---

27. The employer's deduction would be limited to the $16,300 payment. The additional $700 attributable to growth in the value of the stock would not be deductible.

employer contributions to repay loan principal. If forfeitures in this example were $1,000, employees would either have this value added to their accounts (with their annual additions staying at $10,100) or have the same account values but with annual additions reduced to $9,100.

As noted, dividends are viewed as a form of plan earnings, and are thus not part of an employee's annual addition. If dividends were $8,500 and were applied to repayment of principal, for example, only $1,600 of the $16,300 total payment (i.e., the $10,100 principal repayment less $8,500 of dividends and none of the $6,200 interest payment) would be considered to be annual additions. Again, participants would receive the full value of the released shares ($17,000), but only the lesser amount of $1,600 would be charged to their annual additions limits.

ADP/ACP Testing

Assuming that matching contributions can be used to repay an ESOP loan,[28] it is not clear how the ADP/ACP tests described in Chapter 4 are to be applied. A strong argument can be made that testing should be based on the amount of employer contributions rather than the value of the shares released from the suspense account. (This would be consistent with the treatment under Section 415.) Whether dividends used to repay an ESOP loan should be taken into account is also not clear. What is clear is that the ADP, ACP, and multiple use tests are applied *separately* to the ESOP and non-ESOP portions of a plan.[29]

---

28. See Footnote 5, above.
29. IRS Reg. 1.401(k)-1(g)(11)(iii)(B); 1.401(m)-1(f)(14); 1.401(m)-2(b).

CHAPTER 6

Other Tax Law Provisions

In addition to imposing the qualification requirements discussed in Chapters 3 and 4, the tax code includes a number of other provisions that apply to defined contribution plans and CODAs. This chapter begins with a discussion of provisions governing the deductibility of employer contributions. After a brief review of the prohibited transaction rules and the taxation of unrelated business income, it concludes with a discussion of how employees are taxed when they receive benefit distributions.

DEDUCTIBILITY OF EMPLOYER CONTRIBUTIONS

The maximum tax-deductible amount an employer may contribute to a profit-sharing plan or stock bonus plan each year is 15 percent of the compensation of employees covered under the plan.[1] For this purpose, compensation is defined as the amount actually paid or accrued to the participants for the employer's taxable year in question; it is not limited to compensation used to determine plan contributions, nor is it the compensation used in testing the plan for qualification purposes.[2]

---

1. IRC Section 404(a)(3)(A).
2. Rev. Rul. 80-145.

The compensation used to determine deductible contributions does not include elective deferrals made by employees. Because the deduction limit is expressed as a percentage of participant compensation, a lower level of compensation will reduce the maximum available deduction. Further, employees' elective contributions are considered employer contributions, so they also reduce the amount the employer can otherwise contribute.

Assume, for example, that the participants in a CODA have gross company compensation (before elective contributions) of $1,000,000 and have elected to defer $100,000 in the aggregate. The deductible limit (15 percent of covered compensation for a profit-sharing plan) is applied to the net compensation—$900,000. Thus, the maximum deductible contribution the employer can make to the plan is $135,000 (15 percent times $900,000). Had the plan been a traditional profit-sharing plan with no elective deferrals, the limit would have been $150,000. The elective deferrals also use up $100,000 of the $135,000 the employer can contribute, reducing the additional employer contribution to $35,000.

An employer contribution in one taxable year that is greater than the deduction limit for that year creates a contribution carryover. An employer may deduct any such carryover in a succeeding taxable year if it does not bring the total deduction to more than 15 percent of covered payroll for that succeeding year. A 10 percent penalty tax will be levied on the amount of any excess or nondeductible contribution for the year in which it was made and for each succeeding year until it is either returned to the employer or becomes deductible under the carryover rules.[3]

The law also permitted credit carryforwards for profit-sharing plans until 1987. When the amount contributed and deducted for a year was less than 15 percent of covered payroll, the employer could accumulate unused deductions and use them in a later year when contributions exceeded the 15 percent limit. The overall deduction limit for the later year, including the credit carryforward, could be as high as 25 percent of compensation for that later year. TRA '86 eliminated credit carryforwards on a prospective basis; carryforwards accumulated before 1987 can still be used as permitted by prior law.

---

3. IRC Section 4972.

While there is no percentage-of-pay deduction limit, as such, for money purchase pension plans, the Section 415 annual addition limit of 25 percent of pay effectively establishes the maximum amount that can be contributed to such a plan.

If an employer maintains both a defined benefit pension plan and a defined contribution plan covering at least one employee in common, the total amount deductible in any taxable year under both plans cannot exceed the greater of 25 percent of the compensation paid or accrued to employees who are in either plan for such year or the amount of contributions to the defined benefit plan required to meet the minimum funding standards.[4] This additional 25 percent limit does not eliminate the requirement that a currently deductible profit-sharing or stock bonus plan contribution must not exceed 15 percent of participating payroll, nor does it operate to increase the amount that would otherwise be an allowable deduction for contributions to the defined benefit plan.

To be deductible for a given year, contributions must be made no later than the due date for filing the corporate tax return for that year, including any extensions.[5]

PROHIBITED TRANSACTIONS

Both labor law (Title I of ERISA) and the IRC prohibit certain transactions between the plan and disqualified persons.[6] A disqualified person is broadly defined to include any plan fiduciary, a person providing services to the plan, any employer or employee organization whose employees or members are covered by the plan, a direct or indirect owner of 50 percent or more of the business interest of the employer, a relative of any of the above, an officer, director, and

---

4. IRC Section 404(a)(7). The limit can exceed 25 percent if the pension plan is a defined benefit plan and the required contribution to meet minimum funding standards exceeds 25 percent of compensation. In that case, however, no deductible contribution could be made to the profit-sharing or stock bonus plan.
5. IRC Section 404(a)(6).
6. IRC Section 4975, ERISA Section 406. The IRC refers to transactions between the plan and disqualified persons. ERISA refers to transactions between the plan and "parties in interest." For the most part, IRC and ERISA provisions are similar, although the penalties for engaging in a prohibited transaction differ. This portion of the text discusses the IRC provisions only; the fiduciary provisions of ERISA are discussed in Chapter 7.

certain highly compensated employees, or a person having 10 percent or more of the ownership interest in any of the above.[7]

The following transactions between the plan and a disqualified person are prohibited:

- The sale, exchange, or leasing of property.
- Lending money or extending credit (including funding the plan by contributing debt securities).
- Furnishing goods, services, or facilities.
- A transfer to or the use of plan assets.
- In the case of a fiduciary, dealing with plan assets/income or receiving compensation for his own account.

These prohibitions apply even to arm's length transactions and even though the plan is fully protected.

An initial excise tax of a percentage of the amount involved in a prohibited transaction may be levied on the disqualified person who engages in the transaction. For prohibited transactions that occurred before August 21, 1996, the initial excise tax was 5 percent of the amount involved; for prohibited transactions occurring after August 20, 1996, this initial excise tax is 10 percent of the amount involved. If the situation is not corrected within the time allowed (90 days after notification by the IRS unless extended by the IRS), a further excise tax of 100 percent of the amount involved may be imposed. Engaging in a prohibited transaction, however, will generally not cause the plan to be disqualified.

UNRELATED BUSINESS INCOME

While the investment income of a qualified trust established in conjunction with a qualified plan is generally exempt from tax,[8] all or part of this income could be subject to tax if it is considered to be unrelated business income.[9]

Unrelated business income is the gross income derived from any unrelated trade or business regularly carried on by the trust, less allowable deductions directly connected with the carrying on

---

7. Under the fiduciary provisions of ERISA, an employee is also considered to be a party in interest for purposes of the prohibited transaction rules.
8. IRC Section 501(a).
9. IRC Section 501(b).

of such trade or business, with certain exclusions.[10] An unrelated trade or business is any trade or business carried on by the trust.[11]

Only income resulting from the direct operation of the unrelated trade or business is subject to tax. Thus, for example, if the trust owns all the stock of a corporation but the corporation directly operates the business, the stock dividends received by the trust will not be subject to tax.

The following income is not considered to be unrelated business income: dividends, interest, annuities, royalties, most rents from real property, and gains from the sale or exchange of noninventory property, except if such income is attributable to debt-financed property. Thus, care should be taken to avoid the trust borrowing to purchase property. (For example, a piece of rental real estate subject to a mortgage would be debt-financed, making the rents subject to unrelated business income tax.)

Unrelated business income must be reported by the trustee on Form 990-T. Generally speaking, most qualified trusts will be taxed on unrelated business income at the rates imposed on trusts and estates.

TAXATION OF DISTRIBUTIONS

The general tax principles that apply to distributions from qualified plans can be summarized as follows:

- Amounts distributed will generally be taxed as ordinary income under Sections 72 and 402 of the IRC.
- Portions of distributions that are considered attributable to amounts previously taxed (e.g., aftertax employee contributions) will be considered the employee's cost basis and generally will be recovered tax free.
- Lump sum distributions before the year 2000 and lump sum distributions made to individuals born before January 1, 1936 may qualify for special income-averaging treatment.
- The doctrine of constructive receipt is not applicable; for example, the fact that an employee has the right to receive a

10. IRC Section 512.
11. IRC Section 513(b).

distribution in a lump sum will not give rise to constructive receipt of the entire amount if the employee elects some other form of payment.

- Death benefits (unless they consist of pure term insurance) will generally be taxable to the beneficiary. They will also be includable in the employee's gross estate for federal estate tax purposes.

Special tax treatment applies to the distribution of annuity contracts and to the unrealized appreciation on any employer securities that are part of a distribution.

Determination of Cost Basis

In most situations, an employee's cost basis—or "investment in the contract" in IRC terminology—will consist simply of his or her own aftertax contributions to the plan.

Other items may be included in an employee's cost basis, however.[12] In plans that permit employees to use their account balances to purchase life insurance, for example, part of the amount paid as a life insurance premium is considered to have been distributed to the employee in the year in which the premium is paid. This is the portion of the premium used to purchase current term insurance protection (i.e., the difference between the face amount of the insurance and its cash value). Even though the employee does not receive cash, he or she will have received the value of the insurance protection, and it is this value that is considered to have been distributed and thus taxable. The law permits previously taxed insurance costs to be added to the employee's cost basis for any subsequent distributions made under the insurance policy, but these cannot be considered part of the employee's cost basis if the contract is surrendered and the proceeds are distributed.[13]

An employee's cost basis could also include other employer contributions that had been previously taxed to the employee— for example, benefits under a nonqualified plan that was later

---

12. IRC Section 72(c); IRS Reg. 1.72-6.
13. Compare Regs 1.72-16(b) with Rev. Rul. 67-336, 1967-2 C.B.66. These costs are often called PS 58 costs after the number of the original IRS ruling that published rates for determining the taxable amounts involved.

qualified. It could also include amounts taxable to HCEs for years in which a plan failed to meet the coverage tests.

In-Service Distributions

When an employee receives an in-service cash distribution of the entire value of his or her account, the amount of the distribution that exceeds the employer's cost basis will be taxable in the year of distribution as ordinary income. In addition, it may be subject to the early and excess distribution taxes discussed later in this chapter. A distribution that occurs after age 59-1/2 may be eligible for special averaging treatment if it meets the requirements for a qualifying lump sum distribution, as discussed on page 132.

If the in-service distribution represents only a part of the employee's account, it will still be taxed as ordinary income, with a pro rata tax-free recovery of the employee's cost basis.[14] The amount of the distribution that is considered a recovery of cost basis is determined by multiplying the distribution amount by a fraction. The numerator is the employee's total cost basis; the denominator is the value of the employee's vested account balance. If the value of the employee's total vested account balance is $10,000 and he has a cost basis of $1,000, the fraction is 1/10. If the employee's partial distribution is $2,000, 1/10 of this amount, or $200, would be considered a tax-free recovery of cost basis; $800 would be taxed as ordinary income. It should be noted that this result occurs no matter how the plan describes the withdrawal. Thus, even though the plan permits only a withdrawal of aftertax employee contributions, and an employee perceives that only his own money is being returned, the distribution will be taxed as described above.

TRA '86 mandated the pro rata recovery of an employee's cost basis. The basis recovery rules of prior law treated all distributions as a return of cost basis until that basis was fully recovered; all distributions thereafter were taxable. In plans that permitted in-service withdrawals on May 5, 1986, and had separate accounting for employee contributions, pre-1987 employee contributions can be withdrawn under the old rules until exhausted; thereafter, the new rules apply.

---

14. IRC Section 72(c)(8).

TRA '86 also provided some relief for defined contribution plans by permitting them to categorize the portion of the employee's account balance attributable to aftertax contributions as a separate contract for purposes of the basis recovery rules.[15] In effect, this permits employers to make distributions only from the account or separate contract that consists solely of aftertax employee contributions plus earnings. Thus, while the pro rata distribution rule still applies, calculations are based on the ratio of aftertax employee contributions to the value of the separate contract that consists of these contributions and earnings thereon. To use this approach, the plan must maintain adequate separate accounts by keeping separate records of aftertax contributions and earnings and by allocating earnings, gains, losses, and other credits between the separate account and other portions of the plan on a reasonable and consistent basis.

Employer options for establishing contracts under a plan are discussed in more detail in Chapter 9.

Annuity Distributions

If a plan distributes an annuity contract to an employee, the employee will recognize taxable income only when he or she receives actual payments under the contract.

If the employee has no cost basis, all annuity payments will be taxable as ordinary income when received.

If the employee has a cost basis, part of each distribution will be considered a tax-free recovery of that cost basis. If annuity payments are being made on a nonlifetime basis, each payment will be multiplied by an exclusion ratio or fraction to determine the amount that is tax free and the amount that is taxable. The numerator of the fraction is the total cost basis; the denominator is the employee's expected return under the annuity agreement. Thus, for example, if the employee is to receive annuity payments of $12,000 for 10 years, his expected return is $120,000 (10 times $12,000). If the employee's cost basis is $10,000, his tax-free recovery each year will be $1,000 or 1/12th ($10,000/$120,000) of $12,000.

---

15. IRC Section 72(d)(2).

This concept of determining an exclusion ratio was also applicable to life annuities with an annuity starting date before November 19, 1996. It remains applicable for annuities that commence on or after age 75 and have a guaranteed period of five or more years. For other life annuities with an annuity starting date of November 19, 1996 or later, a simplified method is used to determine the portion of each payment that is a tax-free return of cost basis. The nontaxable portion received each month will be the employee's cost basis, divided by the following number of anticipated payments:

Age of Primary Annuitant on Annuity Starting Date	Number of Payments
Up to 55	360
Over 55, up to 60	310
Over 60, up to 65	260
Over 65, up to 70	210
Over 70	160

Installment Distributions

If an employee's account balance is payable in installments and there is no cost basis, all payments will be taxable as ordinary income when the employee receives them. If the employee has a cost basis, the tax treatment of installment payments is less than clear. In order for the payments to be taxed as an annuity, as described above, either the total amount payable or the period for which the payments are made must be determinable when payments begin.[16] Installment payments under a defined contribution plan will generally not be able to meet these criteria, however, because fluctuations in the value of a participant's account will vary both the term and the total amount of the payments. In addition, plans typically allow an employee to direct that the remaining balance be paid as a lump sum, thus changing the period over which payments are made. As a result, employers should probably treat installment payments as in-service withdrawals, as discussed above, grandfathering pre-1987 aftertax contributions as necessary.

---

16. IRS Reg. 1.72-4(b)(1).

Lump Sum Distributions

Lump sum distributions, whether in-service or at retirement or other termination of employment, will be taxed as ordinary income in the year of distribution to the extent they exceed the employee's cost basis.[17]

Under certain circumstances, however, lump sum distributions may qualify for favorable tax treatment. This favorable tax treatment is only available for lump sum distributions made before the year 2000 or to employees who were born before January 1, 1936. In addition, the distribution must:

- Be made after the employee reaches age 59-1/2.
- Be payable on account of the employee's death, after the employee reaches age 59-1/2 or on account of separation from service.
- Represent the full amount then credited to the employee's account under the plan and all plans of the employer of a like kind (i.e., all pension plans or all profit-sharing plans).
- Be received by the employee within one taxable year.

If the employee has participated in the plan in at least five tax years before the year of distribution and if the distribution occurs before 2000 and meets the above requirements, the employee may elect to have the distribution taxed under a five-year averaging rule. The tax is calculated as follows:

- Step 1: determine the initial taxable amount—the gross distribution less the employee's cost basis.
- Step 2: if the initial taxable amount is less than $70,000, calculate a minimum distribution allowance. If the taxable amount is less than $20,000, the allowance is 50 percent of the distribution; if the taxable amount is $20,000 or more, the allowance is $10,000 reduced by 20 percent of the amount by which the distribution exceeds $20,000. Subtract this minimum distribution allowance from the initial taxable amount to determine the net taxable amount.
- Step 3: divide the net taxable by 5.

---

17. IRC Section 401(e).

- Step 4: calculate the tax on the amount arrived at in Step 3 for a single taxpayer with no exemptions or deductions and with no other income.
- Step 5: multiply the amount arrived at in Step 4 by 5 to determine the total tax due.

Exhibit 6–1 calculates the tax payable on a qualifying lump sum distribution of $50,000 to an employee with a cost basis of $10,000.

An employee can elect five-year averaging only once and only after age 59-1/2. To determine whether there has been a qualifying lump sum distribution, all plans within a given category (pension, profit sharing, and stock bonus) must be aggregated and treated as a single plan. Thus, for example, if an employer maintains two profit-sharing plans—a conventional CODA and a tax credit employee stock ownership plan qualified as a profit-sharing plan—the employee must receive a full distribution of his or her entire account balance under *both* plans and in the *same* taxable year. Otherwise, five-year averaging would be available only to the distribution made from the second plan in a subsequent year.

If a distribution includes an annuity contract and/or employer securities, some part of the distribution may not be currently taxable. As noted earlier, the value of the annuity will not be taxed when distributed, and the employee will be taxed only on annuity payments when actually received. Similarly, any unrealized appreciation on employer securities will not be taxable in the year of distribution unless the employee so elects. The fact that some part of the distribution is not currently taxable in either of

E X H I B I T   6–1

Lump Sum Distribution: Five-Year Averaging

Gross distribution:		$50,000
Cost basis:	minus	10,000
Initial distribution allowance:		$40,000
Minimum distribution allowance:	minus	6,000
Net taxable amount:		$34,000
One fifth of net taxable amount:		6,800
Tax on $6,800 (15 percent):		1,020
Total tax due ($1,020 x 5):		5,100

these situations will not preclude five-year averaging. This treatment will still be available for the balance of the distribution if it otherwise qualifies; however, the values not currently taxable will be taken into account in determining the marginal tax rate on the amount that is being taxed.

Grandfathering provisions of TRA '86 apply to individuals who were born on or before January 1, 1936. These individuals have several choices as to distributions made before 2000:

- They can treat the entire distribution under the five-year averaging rules.
- They can treat the entire distribution under the former 10-year averaging rules using 1986 tax rates in effect prior to TRA '86.
- If they participated in the plan prior to 1974, they can treat the portion of the distribution attributable to this participation as a long-term capital gain, with either 10-year or 5-year averaging on the balance. (For this purpose, the old long-term capital gain maximum tax rate of 20 percent applies.)

For distributions made in 2000 or later, these individuals may elect 10-year averaging (with or without the capital gains option, if available); the option to use five-year averaging will no longer be available.

Long-term capital gains treatment can produce very favorable results where it is available. In general, 10-year averaging will produce lower taxes for smaller distributions; it is apt to produce higher taxes for larger distributions, because the marginal tax rate in the calculation can reach 50 percent. This pattern is illustrated in Exhibit 6–2, which compares 5- and 10-year averaging for net taxable distributions ranging from $25,000 to $1,000,000.

Distributions of Employer Securities

Employer securities distributed from a qualified plan are likely to have appreciated in value since they were acquired by the plan, that is, the market value of the stock at the time of distribution will probably exceed the cost of the stock when it was purchased by the plan. For lump sum distributions, the employee has the option of

EXHIBIT 6–2

Comparison of 5- and 10-Year Averaging

	Aftertax Proceeds*	
Taxable Distribution	**5-Year Averaging**	**10-Year Averaging**
$ 25,000	$ 22,600	$ 23,199
50,000	43,100	44,126
75,000	63,750	64,695
100,000	85,000	85,529
150,000	123,178	125,430
200,000	159,178	163,078
300,000	230,660	233,670
400,000	299,660	297,398
500,000	368,660	356,318
750,000	533,148	490,632
1,000,000	693,148	617,790

*Based on 1996 tax rates

treating the portion of the distribution that represents net unrealized appreciation (NUA) as taxable income at the time of the distribution or when the stock is subsequently sold.[18] Assume, for example, that an employee receives a qualifying lump sum distribution and chooses to defer taxation on the employer securities included in the distribution. In the year of distribution, the employee will be taxed only on the cost basis of the stock (plus any other assets distributed). Upon a subsequent sale of the stock, the employee will be taxed on the NUA at the time of distribution plus any gains between the date of distribution and the subsequent sale.[19]

---

18. IRC Section 402(e)(4)(B).
19. The NUA at the time of distribution is treated as long-term capital gain, and any gain between the date of distribution and subsequent sale will be treated as long-term or short-term capital gain depending upon the time the stock is held after distribution. Although TRA '86 reduced favorable tax treatment for long-term capital gains, a long-term capital gain is taxed at a maximum rate of 28 percent. In addition, a long-term capital gain can be offset by capital losses and any resulting capital loss can be used to offset up to $3,000 of ordinary income.

The amount of NUA that receives this special tax treatment depends on whether the securities are part of a qualifying lump sum distribution or a distribution that would otherwise have qualified as such a distribution if five-year averaging tax treatment had not been repealed for distributions in the year 2000 or later. If the distribution so qualifies, but without regard to the requirement that there be five years of participation, all NUA on employer securities distributed may be excluded from current year taxation; otherwise, only the NUA attributable to employee aftertax contributions is excluded from current year taxation and that exclusion is automatic (i.e., the taxpayer cannot elect to pay tax currently).

If the stock is held until the employee's death, the employee's heirs will have a cost basis in the stock equal to its market value at the time of death (i.e., the appreciation in value unrealized at the time of death will not be taxed as income). The full value will be included in the employee's gross estate for estate tax purposes, subject to marital deduction credits and the like.

Early Distribution Tax

If an employee receives a distribution from any qualified plan before age 59-1/2, the distribution may be subject to a penalty tax of 10 percent.[20] This tax, if applicable, is levied in addition to any tax otherwise due on the distribution.

The following are *not* subject to the early distribution tax:

- Distributions that are part of a scheduled series of substantially equal periodic payments for the life (or life expectancy) of an employee (or the joint lives of the employee and his or her beneficiary).
- Distributions on account of death.
- Distributions on account of disability (if the employee is unable to engage in any substantial gainful activity by reason of a physical or mental impairment that is expected to result in death or be of long-continued and indefinite duration).

---

20. IRC Section 72(t).

- Distributions to an employee who separated from service after reaching age 55.[21]
- Hardship distributions for deductible medical expenses that exceed 7-1/2 percent of adjusted gross income.
- Distributions to an alternate payee under a qualified domestic relations order (see Chapter 3).
- Dividends on ESOP stock that are paid in cash.

An early distribution tax will not be imposed on any amounts rolled over into an IRA; however, subsequent distributions from the IRA could be subject to this tax unless they are made at a time or for a reason that qualifies for an exemption that applies to IRA distributions.

Minimum Distribution Excise Tax

The minimum distribution rules covered in Chapter 3 require that payments be made by certain dates and over prescribed time periods. If actual distributions fail to meet these rules, the employee may be subject to an excise tax of 50 percent of the shortfall.[22] The tax may be waived if the shortfall was due to reasonable error and reasonable steps were taken to remedy the situation. In this situation, the employee must file Form 5329 (Return of Additional Taxes), pay the tax, and attach a letter requesting a refund, including an explanation of the reasonable error and the steps that have been (or will be) taken to remedy the shortfall. If the IRS grants the waiver, it will refund the excise tax to the employee.

Excess Distribution Tax

TRA '86 imposed an excess distribution tax of 15 percent on distributions that exceed certain stipulated dollar amounts.[23] Distributions from all tax-sheltered arrangements are aggregated for purpose of this tax. Thus, for example, taxable distributions from

---

21. Although the statutory language suggests that the separation must actually occur after age 55, the IRS has taken the position that a distribution will be exempt from the tax if it is made after separation and the separation occurred during or after the calendar year in which the employee attained age 55. See IRS Notice 87-13.
22. IRC Section 4974; IRS Prop. Reg. 54.4974-2.
23. IRC Section 4980A; IRS Temp. Reg. 54.4981A-1T.

tax-sheltered annuities, IRAs, and all qualified plans—of all employers—are taken into account. An individual will not be subject to the tax with respect to distributions to an alternate payee under a qualified domestic relations order, if included in the alternate payee's income, or, in the year of distribution, to any amounts that are rolled over into an IRA on a timely basis. Other items not subject to this tax include distributions of annuity contracts that are not currently taxable, distributions of excess contributions (whether due to limits on elective deferrals or application of the ADP and ACP tests), and distributions of health coverage or medical benefits under Section 401(h) of the IRC.

In general, the excess distribution tax is imposed on distributions (not including qualified lump sum distributions) received during the employee's calendar year to the extent they exceed the then current threshold amount. For 1996, this amount is $155,000. The threshold amount is indexed to increase with changes in the CPI. As with the Section 415 dollar limitations, this dollar amount is rounded to the next lower multiple of $5,000.

A separate 15 percent tax applies to a lump sum distribution that qualifies for income-averaging treatment (or would otherwise have qualified for this treatment had it not been repealed) to the extent the lump sum distribution exceeds a threshold amount. For 1996, this amount is $775,000 and it, too, will increase for changes in the CPI in the same manner as the annual threshold amount.

This excess distribution tax has been suspended for distributions made during the years 1997, 1998, and 1999.

It appears that unrealized appreciation on employer securities, though not necessarily taxable in the year of distribution, will be subject to this excise distribution tax.

When an employee is subject to the 10 percent early distribution tax on the same distribution, the 10 percent tax may be offset against the 15 percent excess distribution tax.

It should be noted that the 15 percent excise tax does not apply to amounts payable upon the death of an employee; an equivalent 15 percent tax is imposed as an additional form of estate tax. Items such as the unified credit, the marital deduction, and charitable contributions will not operate to reduce this tax. Thus, it is possible that the 15 percent tax could be levied in situations where no other estate tax is payable.

It should also be noted that although the excess distribution tax was suspended for distributions made during the years 1997,

1998, and 1999, this suspension does not apply to distributions made on account of the death of the employee; in this situation, the 15 percent additional estate tax will be levied.

Death Benefits

Any death benefits payable from a qualified plan are included in the employee's gross estate for federal estate tax purposes.[24] The marital deduction applies to any amount payable to the employee's spouse, however

In general, distributions to a beneficiary will be taxable to the beneficiary to the same extent and in the same manner as if they has been distributed to the employee. The beneficiary will have a cost basis equal to that of the employee, plus for deaths occurring before August 21, 1996 (and unless otherwise used) the beneficiary may have the employee death benefit exclusion provided by Section 101(b) of the IRC up to a maximum of an additional $5,000. This death benefit exclusion has been repealed for deaths occurring after August 20, 1996.[25]

If any portion of the distribution consists of life insurance proceeds and the employee either paid the insurance cost or reported this cost as taxable income, the pure term insurance elements (the difference between face amount and cash value) will be paid to the beneficiary free of income tax. The cash value portion of the insurance policy, along with any other cash benefits, will be considered to be taxable income to the beneficiary.[26]

Rollovers

Lump sum distributions from a qualified plan (excluding any after tax employee contributions) can be rolled over to an IRA or to another employer's qualified plan (as long as that plan accepts rollover contributions). For this purpose, it does not matter whether the distribution qualifies for income-averaging tax

---

24. IRC Section 2039(a).
25. The Section 101(b) exclusion was available in the case of qualifying lump sum distributions regardless of whether the employee's rights to the amounts were forfeitable or nonforfeitable immediately prior to death. For other distributions, this exclusion was available only to the extent the employee's rights were forfeitable.
26. IRC Section 72(m)(3)(c); IRS Reg. 1.72-16(c).

treatment. Partial distributions and installments made over a period of less than ten years may also be rolled over or transferred to another employer's qualified plan.[27]

Any amounts rolled over will not be taxed in the year of distribution, and early or excess distribution taxes are not applied to these amounts. Distributions from the IRA or other plan will of course be taxable and will also be subject to early and excess distribution taxes where applicable. Note, however, that distributions from the IRA will be taxable as ordinary income, while distributions from another qualified plan could be eligible for income averaging if the employee has five years of participation in that plan at the time of distribution and the other conditions are met.

The rollover to the IRA or another qualified plan must take place within 60 days after receipt of the distribution. Further:

- If the amount is distributed to the employee who then makes the rollover, the distribution will be subject to automatic withholding of 20 percent even though the total amount of the distribution may not be subject to taxation because of the rollover; any excess taxes withheld could then be claimed as a tax refund when the employee's tax return for the year is filed.
- If the amount is transferred directly by the plan to an IRA or another employer's qualified plan, no withholding will take place.
- If the distribution is noncash property, all of the property must be transferred, but the property may be sold and all or any part of the sales proceeds may then be transferred to the IRA.
- Amounts transferred to the IRA can be subsequently transferred to another qualified plan.
- The transfer may be made to an existing or a new IRA, but if an existing IRA is used, and if it contains contributions that are not qualified plan distributions—that is, conventional IRA contributions—the amount transferred may not be later transferred to another qualified plan.

---

27. IRC Section 402(c)(4).

- A spouse can make a rollover to an IRA in the case of a death benefit distribution.

- If a partial distribution is taken and rolled over, the balance remaining in the employee's account in the qualified plan, as well as similar plans, will no longer qualify for income-averaging tax treatment.

- If part of a distribution is rolled over and the balance taken in cash, this balance will not qualify for income-averaging tax treatment.

When a distribution from a qualified plan is eligible for rollover or direct transfer to another employer's qualified plan, the plan administrator, within a reasonable period of time before making the distribution, must send a notice to the participant or beneficiary explaining the rollover and direct transfer rules, the tax withholding requirements of distributions that are not directly transferred, and how taxes can be reduced or deferred (i.e, through rollover or income averaging).[28] In general, the timing of the notice must meet the same requirements that apply to notifying participants of their rights as to the qualified joint and survivor annuity under a defined benefit pension plan.

---

28. IRC Section 402(f); IRS Reg. 1.402(f)-2T.

CHAPTER 7

Non-Tax Legal Requirements

While most of the legal issues involving defined contribution plans arise under tax law, employers must also be concerned about the effect of other laws. This chapter covers prohibitions against age and sex discrimination; ERISA's reporting, disclosure, and fiduciary responsibility requirements, and its overall application to nonqualified plans; Securities and Exchange Commission (SEC) requirements that apply to plans that permit employees to invest in employer stock; and matters relating to collective bargaining.

AGE/SEX DISCRIMINATION

The Age Discrimination in Employment Act (ADEA), as amended, prohibits discrimination on the basis of age against employees age 40 and older. As a result of ADEA, employees cannot be forced to retire at any specified age, including the plan's normal retirement age.[1] Further:

- An employee cannot be excluded from participating in a defined contribution plan because of age. Use of a

---

1. There is a limited exception for bona fide executives whose annual employer-provided retirement benefit from all sources is $44,000 or more. An employer can force these individuals to retire at age 65.

minimum age of up to 21, as permitted under the tax law, is acceptable; use of any maximum age is prohibited.

- A protected employee cannot be required to contribute more or at higher levels than other employees, nor can employer contributions be decreased because of age. Changes attributable solely to length of service are acceptable, however.

- As long as a participating employee remains employed, he or she must be eligible to continue full participation in the plan.

Title VII of the Civil Rights Act of 1964, as amended, prohibits discrimination on the basis of sex (or sex-related conditions such as pregnancy). In a defined contribution plan, this means that:

- Different employee and/or employer contributions cannot be required or made on account of the employee's sex.

- There can be no distinction in any plan eligibility requirements—for initial participation, rights to certain options or benefits, treatment of leaves of absence, and the like—on account of sex.

- A plan that offers annuity or lifetime installment benefits can make no distinction in annuity or installment costs and/or benefits on account of sex; these costs and benefits must be based on unisex mortality tables.

TITLE I OF ERISA

Many of the labor law provisions in Title I of ERISA are virtually identical to the tax law provisions that were enacted at the same time. Thus, for example, Title I also includes minimum participation, funding, and vesting requirements, as well as joint and survivor protection for the spouses of employees. For the most part, jurisdiction and administration of these provisions has been assigned to the IRS under the tax provisions, although the DOL has jurisdiction over the determination of service for eligibility, vesting, and benefit accrual purposes.

Title I also contains provisions on reporting and disclosure and on fiduciary requirements. Except for some restrictions on prohibited transactions, these provisions have no counterpart in the tax law.

Reporting and Disclosure

Title I specifies information that plan sponsors must disclose to participants and their beneficiaries and report to the government. These requirements generally apply to most defined contribution plans, regardless of the number of participants involved. There are a limited number of exemptions. For example, the rules do not apply to unfunded excess benefit plans—plans maintained to provide employees with benefits that would have been available under a qualified plan but for the Section 415 limits. In addition, the sponsor of an unfunded plan maintained for the exclusive benefit of a select group of management or highly compensated employees need only notify the DOL of the existence of the plan and the number of employees that it covers.[2]

Title I's reporting and disclosure provisions require that certain items be filed with the government, that others be given to employees, and that still others be made reasonably available to employees on request. Items that must be filed with the *government* include:

- The summary plan description (SPD)—the booklet, folder, or binder given to employees describing the plan.
- Any summary of material modifications (SMM)—a summary of any plan amendment or change in information that must be included in the SPD after the initial SPD has been issued.
- The plan's annual financial report, filed on Form 5500 or one of its variations.

Items that must be distributed to *employees* include:

- The plan's SPD.
- Any SMMs.
- A summary annual report (SAR)—a summary of the plan's annual financial report.

---

2. DOL Reg. 2520.104-23.

- A statement of benefits for all employees who terminate employment.
- A written explanation to any employee or beneficiary whose claim for benefits is denied.[3]

Certain other items must be given to employees on request and/or made available for their examination at the principal office of the plan administrator and at other locations convenient for participants. These items include supporting plan documents and a complete copy of the plan's annual financial report.

Employers must make these documents available at all times in their principal offices. The documents must also be available at any distinct physical location where business is performed and at least 50 participants work. Plan materials need not be kept at each location as long as they can be provided there within 10 working days after a request for disclosure.[4] The employer may charge for reproduction of all materials requested unless the materials fall in a category that must be furnished automatically.[5] Any item that must be furnished to participants and beneficiaries must be sent by a method that reasonably assures actual receipt, for example, personal delivery at the work site or first class mail.[6]

In addition, the plan sponsor must furnish a personal benefits statement (on written request but no more than once every 12 months). If the sponsor furnishes such statements on its own initiative within this timeframe, then it need not respond to requests from individual participants.

Key disclosure items are described in more detail below.

Summary Plan Description   Employers must give the SPD to new employees within 90 days after they become participants and to beneficiaries within 90 days after they start receiving benefits.[7] If a plan is new, the employer must give the initial SPD to

---

3. Other provisions of the law also require that other items be given to employees—for example, notice of the right to elect or reject survivor benefits (if applicable), notice of tax treatment for distributions eligible for IRA rollover treatment, and notice that a plan or amendment has been filed with the IRS for qualification purposes. Such notices are not required under the disclosure provisions of ERISA.
4. DOL Reg. 2520.104b-1(b)(3).
5. DOL Reg. 2520.104(b)-1(b)(3).
6. DOL Reg. 2520.104b-1(b)(1).
7. DOL Reg. 2520.104b-2(a).

participants within 120 days after the plan becomes subject to Title I, filing it with the DOL at the same time. A new, complete SPD must be filed and distributed at least every 10 years. If there have been material changes since the last SPD was issued, however, the employer must file and distribute a new SPD every five years.[8]

The SPD must be in permanent form and must be current regarding all aspects of the plan and the information required by DOL regulations.[9] The SPD must include the following:

- The plan name and the type of plan (e.g., profit sharing).
- The type of plan administration (e.g., trustee).
- The name (or title) and address of the person designated as agent for the service of legal process, as well as a statement that legal process may also be served on a plan trustee or the plan administrator.
- The name, address, and telephone number of the plan administrator.
- The name and address of the employer (or employee organization) that maintains the plan.
- The name, title, and business address of each trustee.
- The employer identification number (EIN) assigned by the IRS and the plan number assigned by the plan sponsor.
- In the case of a collectively bargained plan maintained by at least one employer and one employee organization, or in the case of a plan maintained by two or more employers, the name and address of the most significant employer or organization plus either of the following: (1) a statement that a complete list of sponsors may be obtained on written request to the plan administrator and is available for review, or (2) a statement that, on written request, participants may receive information about whether a particular employer or organization is a sponsor and, if so, the sponsor's address.
- If a collective bargaining agreement controls any duties, rights, or benefits under a plan, a statement that the plan is maintained in accordance with the agreement and that a

---

8. DOL Reg. 2520.104b-2(b).
9. DOL Reg. 2520.102-3.

copy of the agreement may be obtained on written request to the plan administrator and is available for examination.

- Plan requirements as to eligibility for participation and benefits (e.g., age or service requirements, retirement age).
- A description of the provisions for nonforfeitable benefits.
- Information about years of service for eligibility, credited service, breaks in service, and vesting.
- A description of any joint and survivor benefits and any action necessary to elect or reject them.
- A description of the circumstances that may result in disqualification, ineligibility, denial, loss, forfeiture, or suspension of benefits.
- A statement that, as a defined contribution plan, the plan is not insured by the Pension Benefit Guaranty Corporation (PBGC).
- The source of contributions to the plan, the method by which contributions are determined, and the identity of any organization through which the plan is funded or benefits are provided.
- A description and explanation of plan benefits.
- The date of the end of the plan year for purposes of maintaining the plan's fiscal records.
- The procedures to be followed in presenting claims for benefits under the plan and the remedies available under the plan for the redress of claims that are denied in whole or in part.
- A statement of participants' rights under Title I that must appear as a consolidated statement with no information omitted; the regulations contain suggested language that, if used, will assure compliance.

The SPD must be "written in a manner calculated to be understood by the average plan participant" and be "sufficiently accurate and comprehensive" to inform employees and beneficiaries of their rights and obligations under the plan.[10] The explanations provided by legal plan texts and insurance contracts will probably not meet these standards. DOL regulations recommend the use of

---

10. DOL Reg. 2520.102-2.

simple sentences, clarifying examples, clear and liberal cross-references, and a table of contents in the SPD. Further, varying sizes and styles of type may not be used when they may mislead employees.

If a plan covers 500 or more people who are literate only in a language other than English, or if 10 percent or more of the participants are literate only in a non-English language (25 percent or more where the plan covers fewer than 100 participants), the SPD must include a prominent notice in the familiar language offering employees assistance—which may be oral—in understanding the plan.

When different classes of participants are covered with different benefits under the same plan, the employer may elect to prepare a different SPD for each class of participants. In such cases, prominent notice must appear on the first page of the text listing the various classes for whom different SPDs have been prepared.[11]

Retired and terminated vested participants, as well as beneficiaries receiving benefits, come under Title I's definition of participants. Nonetheless, plan sponsors need not furnish these participants with updated SPDs, provided certain notice requirements are met. In addition, these participants need not receive information on plan changes unless the changes affect their rights under the plan.[12]

Annual Report   A plan sponsor must file the plan's annual financial report with the IRS on Form 5500 (or one of its variations) within seven months after the close of each plan year. Employers who have received extensions from the IRS for income tax filings will automatically be granted identical extensions for the plan's annual financial report, provided the plan year and the employer's tax year coincide. Employers may also request an extension of up to two and a half months by filing Form 5558 before the normal due date of the annual report.

The annual report is designed to elicit a complete disclosure of all financial information relevant to the operation of the plan. It requires such items as a statement of assets and liabilities presented by category and valued at current value, changes in assets

---

11. DOL Reg. 2520.102-4.
12. DOL Reg. 2520.104b-4.

and liabilities during the year, and a statement of receipts and disbursements. The reporting form requests details, where applicable, on transactions with parties in interest, loans and leases in default or uncollectible, and on certain reportable transactions (e.g., transactions involving more than 5 percent of the current value of plan assets). The report also requires information on plan changes made during the reporting period and on employees included or excluded from participation.

Certain financial statements in the report must be certified by an independent qualified public accountant. Insurance companies and banks are required, within 120 days after the end of the plan year, to furnish any information necessary for the plan administrator to complete the annual report.[13]

Plans that are fully insured are granted limited exemptions from certain requirements.[14] These plans do not have to complete the financial information sections of the form, nor need they engage an accountant for audit or include an accountant's opinion. Plans with fewer than 100 participants can file simplified versions of Form 5500.

Summary Annual Report An SAR—a simplified summary of the full annual report—must be distributed to plan participants within two months after the due date for Form 5500 when an extension has been granted or nine months after the end of the plan year.[15] The plan administrator may use language prescribed in current DOL regulations and incorporate information from the current Form 5500 in the sample language in accordance with instructions in the regulations.

Summary of Material Modification When a plan sponsor makes material modification to a plan, it must distribute a summary description of that change, written in clear language, to all affected participants and beneficiaries and file the SMM with the DOL.[16] Neither the statute nor the regulations define what constitutes a material modification; the SMM requirement is triggered by any change affecting any information that must be disclosed in the

---

13. DOL Reg. 2520.103-5.
14. DOL Reg. 2520.104-44.
15. DOL Reg. 2520.104b-10.
16. DOL Reg. 2520.104b-3 and 2520.104a-4.

SPD. The SMM must be furnished within 210 days after the end of the plan year in which the change is adopted.

Plan Documents   Plan documents include the text of the plan itself and any collective bargaining agreement, trust agreement, contract, or other document under which the plan is established or operated.[17] Plan participants and beneficiaries are entitled to receive copies of these documents within 30 days of making a written request. The DOL may request copies of these documents at any time.

Benefit Statements for Terminating Employees   Each participant who terminates service with a vested right in his or plan benefits must be provided with a clear statement of these benefits and the percentage that is vested.[18] (All terminating CODA participants will fall into this category because they have a vested right to their elective deferrals.) The statement should include the amount of the participant's account balance, the vested percentage, and the amount of the vested account balance, as well as certain other information. Any participant who has had a break in service of one year is automatically entitled to receive a similar benefit statement. Employers must give statements to vested terminated employees within 180 days after the end of the plan year in which they terminate service or incur a break in service.

The law also requires that a statement be given to an employee who terminates or incurs a one-year break in service without a vested interest, clearly communicating that the individual is not entitled to receive benefits under the plan.[19] For example, an employee who never chose to participate in a savings plan CODA would receive such a statement.

Personal Benefits Statement   Plan participants and beneficiaries may request a written statement of their own benefits, but not more often than once in any 12-month period.[20] The statement should include the total benefits accrued and the portion, if any, that is vested, or if benefits are not vested, the earliest date on

---

17. ERISA Section 104(b)(2) and 502(c)(1).
18. ERISA Section 209(a); DOL Prop. Reg. 2520.105-2.
19. Ibid.
20. ERISA Sections 105(a) and 209(a).

which they will become vested. Under DOL proposed regulations, employers can meet this requirement by providing participants with an annual benefits statement automatically.

Claim Denials   Anyone denied a claim under any plan is entitled to a written statement of the reasons for the denial, usually within 90 days.[21] This explanation should be a clear, comprehensible statement of the specific reasons for the denial, including pertinent plan provisions on which the denial was based. It must also include a description of any material or information necessary for the claimant to pursue the claim, the reasons this additional material is needed, and a full description of the plan's appeal procedure. The claimant must be given at least 60 days thereafter to appeal the claim and is entitled to a final decision in writing within 60 days of the appeal (120 days in special circumstances).

Fiduciary Requirements

Fiduciary provisions are set forth in Part Four of Title I of ERISA, although the definition of fiduciary is found in Part One of ERISA in Section 3(21). A brief overview of these provisions appears below; further discussion of fiduciary responsibilities with respect to plan investments appears in Chapter 12.

Definition of Fiduciary   A person (or corporation) will be considered a fiduciary under ERISA if that person exercises any discretionary authority or control over the management of the plan, any authority or control over assets held in the plan or over disposition of plan assets, renders investment advice for direct or indirect compensation (or has any authority or responsibility to do so), or has any discretionary authority or responsibility for the administration of the plan.

The trustee of a plan is clearly a fiduciary. So are officers and directors of a corporation who have responsibility for certain fiduciary functions, for example, the appointment and retention of trustees or investment managers. Individuals whose duties are purely ministerial (e.g., applying rules of eligibility and vesting) are clearly not fiduciaries.

---

21. ERISA Section 503; DOL Reg. 2560.503-1(e)-(g).

Fiduciary Responsibilities   A fiduciary must discharge all duties solely in the interest of participants and beneficiaries and for the exclusive purpose of providing plan benefits and defraying reasonable administrative expenses. In addition, a fiduciary is charged with using the care, skill, prudence, and diligence that a prudent person in a like capacity who is familiar with such matters would use under the circumstances then prevailing—a standard that has come to be called the *prudent expert* rule. A fiduciary is also responsible for diversifying investments so as to minimize the risk of large losses unless it is clearly prudent not to diversify.[22] Finally, a fiduciary must act in accordance with the documents governing the plan and must invest only in assets subject to the jurisdiction of U.S. courts.

Prohibited Transactions   As noted in Chapter 6, certain transactions are prohibited both by the tax law and by Title I of ERISA. The labor provisions prevent the plan from dealing with a party in interest; the tax law uses the term *disqualified person* to prohibit the same transactions. The labor provisions include employees as parties in interest; they are not considered disqualified persons under the tax law.

The labor law's prohibited transaction rules limit the investment of plan assets in qualifying employer securities and real property. Qualifying employer securities include stock; marketable obligations (e.g., bonds and notes) are also considered to be qualifying employer securities if certain requirements are met. Qualifying employer real property is real property that is dispersed geographically, is suitable for more than one use, and has been leased to the employer.

In general, defined benefit and money purchase plans cannot invest more than 10 percent of the fair market value of plan assets in qualifying employer securities. Deferred profit-sharing plans (including CODAs) that specifically so provide may invest without limit in qualifying employer securities or real property; if the plan does not so specify, however, a 10 percent limit will apply. Stock

---

22. Investments in employer securities in accordance with the prohibited transaction rules are also permitted under the diversity requirement; they must comply with the prudence and exclusive benefit of employee standards.

bonus plans are primarily invested in employer securities, of course.

Even though investment in qualifying employer securities and real property is permitted under the prohibited transaction rules (and under the fiduciary requirements for diversity), investments of this type must still satisfy the overriding requirement that they be for the exclusive benefit of employees. Moreover, they must also satisfy the fiduciary requirement of prudence.

Fiduciary Liabilities Apart from being liable for payment of any excise taxes that might be imposed because of a prohibited transaction under the tax law, a fiduciary will be personally liable for any losses to the plan resulting from any breach or violation of responsibilities and will be liable for the restoration of any profits made through the use of plan assets.[23]

In addition, the DOL may impose a 20 percent penalty on any fiduciary who is found liable for a breach of the fiduciary rules.[24] The penalty is applied to the recovery amount, that is, the amount recovered from the fiduciary on behalf of the plan or its participants pursuant to either an out-of-court settlement with the DOL or court order under a judicial proceeding instituted by the DOL. The DOL may waive or reduce the penalty in cases where the fiduciary acted reasonably and in good faith or where the fiduciary will not be able to restore all losses to the plan absent the waiver or reduction. The penalty is automatically reduced for prohibited transactions by the initial excise tax imposed in those cases.

A fiduciary may also be liable for the violations of a cofiduciary if the fiduciary knowingly participates in or conceals a violation, has knowledge of a violation and does not make reasonable efforts to remedy the breach, or by the fiduciary's own violation enables the cofiduciary to commit a violation.[25] If a plan uses separate trusts, however, a trustee of one trust is not responsible for the actions of the other trusts' trustees. Further, a fiduciary will not be

---

23. ERISA Section 409. Note that the excise tax is paid by the borrower if the prohibited transaction is a loan.
24. ERISA Section 502(1). The penalty may also be imposed on other persons, such as actuaries or consultants, who are found liable for the breach and knowingly participate in the breach.
25. ERISA Section 405.

responsible for the acts of a duly appointed investment manager (except to the extent that the fiduciary did not act prudently in selecting or continuing the use of the investment manager). A trustee will not be liable for following the direction of named fiduciaries in making investment decisions if the plan so provides.

Delegation of Authority   A fiduciary can delegate noninvestment activities if the plan permits delegation and clearly spells out a procedure for doing so. Under the prudent expert rule, however, fiduciaries remain responsible for persons to whom they have delegated those responsibilities. Similarly, they remain responsible for the acts of their agents in performing ministerial duties.

Participant-Directed Accounts   Section 404(c) of ERISA exempts plan sponsors and other plan fiduciaries from liability for investment returns in profit-sharing, CODA and savings plans that permit employees to direct the investment of their own accounts, provided certain requirements are met. These requirements are spelled out in regulations issued by the DOL.[26] Failure to comply with these requirements does not necessarily mean the fiduciaries will be liable for investment performance in plans with participant-directed accounts; it simply means that regulatory protection under 404(c) will not be available to them.

The regulations are designed to ensure that participants have control over their assets and have the opportunity to diversify their holdings. Key provisions are summarized below:

- **Investment Instructions**. The regulations require the plan to provide participants with reasonable opportunities to give investment instructions to the plan fiduciary, who is obligated to comply with these instructions.
- **Descriptive Material.** Each participant must be provided with or have the opportunity to obtain sufficient information to make informed decisions as to investment alternatives under the plan, as well as financial information concerning these alternatives. This includes, among other things:

---

26. DOL Reg. 2550.404c-1.

1. A general description of the investment objectives and risk and return characteristics of each investment alternative.
2. An explanation of how to give investment instructions and of any limitations on such instructions.
3. An identification of investment managers.
4. An explanation of voting, tender, and similar rights.
5. A description of transaction fees and expenses that could affect the participant's account balance.
6. The name, address, and phone number of the plan fiduciary.
7. Where appropriate for the investment alternative, any applicable prospectus.
8. A notice that the plan is intended to comply with ERISA Section 404(c) and that fiduciaries' liability is thereby limited.

- **Investment Options**. Plans must offer at least three diversified categories of investment—with materially different risk and return characteristics—that collectively allow participants to construct a portfolio with risk and return characteristics within the full range normally appropriate for a plan participant and which allow for diversification. This rule implies that all plans must offer an investment alternative that reasonably assures the preservation of capital.

  Look-through investment vehicles, such as mutual funds or bank commingled funds and guaranteed investment contracts, qualify as diversified categories of investment because the underlying assets are diversified. Thus, a plan sponsor may meet the requirements by offering three appropriately diverse pooled investment funds, for example, a bond fund, an equity fund, and a money market fund. The plan fiduciary has an ongoing duty to consider the suitability of the look-through investment choices (or investment managers) offered by the plan.

  An investment option consisting of a single equity—employer stock, for example—does not qualify as a diversified category of investment, and an employer stock fund would have to be offered in addition to the three required investment options. The regulations provide some liability protection if employer stock is publicly traded and if certain other conditions are met.

- **Transfers.** Plans must establish specific rules governing participant transfer elections, allowing at least quarterly elections for transfers in or out of the three diversified investment options discussed above. More frequent transfers may be required if appropriate in light of the volatility of a particular investment.

  Investment offerings in addition to the three required options are not subject to the quarterly transfer requirement, but the permitted frequency of transfers in and out of these options is subject to the volatility standard. Sponsors must permit transfers for the least volatile of the three investment options at least as frequently as for the most volatile option, even if the most volatile option is not one of the three required by the rules.

  Because employer stock is a potentially volatile investment vehicle, a plan may have to give participants the ability to transfer in and out more frequently than once a quarter. If so, the plan would have to permit transfers in and out of the least volatile diversified investment category offered under the plan, such as a short-term fixed income fund, with the same frequency.

Employee Investment Education Almost all defined contribution plans let participants direct how their account balances will be invested. While employers recognize the need to encourage employees to save, they have been reluctant to provide extensive education about investing these savings. This reluctance has been due to the fiduciary provisions of ERISA which impose both responsibility and liability on those who provide investment advice for a fee or other compensation, and to the potential application of the Investment Advisors Act of 1940. The concern for these employers has been to distinguish between investment education and investment advice, recognizing that some efforts to provide only education may end up being interpreted as investment advice.

In June of 1996, the DOL issued an interpretive bulletin to enable employers and providers to distinguish between education and advice. This bulletin specifies four types of investment-related information that employers can provide without fear of exposing themselves to fiduciary liability in the view of the DOL.[27] These safe harbors are:

- **General Plan Information.** This includes information about plan features and operations, the benefits of participating in the plan and descriptions of the plan's investment alternatives, including investment objectives, risk and return characteristics, and historical information—as long as such information does not address the appropriateness of particular investment options for a given participant or beneficiary.

- **General Financial and Investment Information.** Information about general investment concepts may be provided— for example, risk and return, diversification, dollar-cost averaging, and the advantages of tax-favored saving. It is also acceptable to provide information as to historical differences in rates of return between different asset classifications, investment time horizons, and estimates of future retirement income needs.

- **Asset Allocation Models.** Participants and beneficiaries can be provided with asset allocation models illustrating the projected performance of hypothetical asset allocations using varying time horizons and risk profiles.

- **Interactive Investment Material.** Acceptable material here includes such items as questionnaires, worksheets, computer software, and other materials that employees can use to estimate their retirement income needs and the potential impact of various investment strategies on their ability to meet those needs.

---

27. The Securities and Exchange Commission (SEC) has indicated that employers whose educational efforts conform to these four "safe harbors" will not be subject to registration or regulation under the Investment Advisors Act of 1940 (unless, of course, they hold themselves out as investment advisors or otherwise meet the definition of advisors in the 1940 law).

To qualify for safe harbor treatment, asset allocation models and interactive materials must be based on generally accepted investment theories and their underlying assumptions must be disclosed (or, in the case of interactive materials, selected by the participant). And if an allocation model or interactive materials identify a specific asset classification such as long-term growth and identify an investment alternative under the plan that matches that classification—and there are other investment alternatives available under the plan that match that same classification—a statement must be made that other investment alternatives are available under the plan, identifying where information regarding these other alternatives may be obtained. Further, models and interactive materials must be accompanied by a statement explaining that participants should consider all of their other income, assets, and investments in applying the model or using the interactive tool (although interactive materials are excused if they take these additional assets into account).

The bulletin also points out that employers may be able to provide investment education that falls outside these safe harbors without automatically being viewed as providing investment advice.

Remittance of Employee Contributions   The DOL has taken the position that participant contributions become plan assets as of the earlier of the date they can be segregated from the employer's general assets. For many years, the outside deadline for depositing such contributions was 90 days. However, the DOL issued final regulations in August 1996 that shorten this outside limit to the 15th business day following the month in which the employee contribution is received or withheld. A procedure is set forth under which an employer can obtain an additional 10 business days if certain conditions are met. This new rule is generally effective February 3, 1997, although for collectively bargained plans this is extended to the first day of the plan year after the latest bargaining agreement in effect on August 7, 1996, has expired.[28]

---

28. DOL Reg. 2510.3-102.

Miscellaneous Requirements

Plan provisions that purport to relieve a fiduciary of responsibilities are void and have no effect.[29] However, a plan, employer, union, or fiduciary may purchase insurance to cover the fiduciary's liability. If the plan purchases this insurance, the insurer must have subrogation rights against the fiduciary. An employer or union may also agree to indemnify a fiduciary against personal liability.

If convicted of certain specified crimes (e.g., embezzlement, arson, robbery) a person cannot serve as a plan administrator, fiduciary, officer, trustee, custodian, counsel, agent, employee, or consultant for 13 years after conviction (or the end of imprisonment, if later). This prohibition will not apply if citizenship rights have been restored or if approved by the United States Board of Parole.

All fiduciaries and persons who handle plan funds or other plan assets are to be bonded for 10 percent of the aggregate amount handled, subject to specified minimum and maximum dollar amounts.[30]

Employers must establish and maintain a plan pursuant to a written instrument that specifically provides for one or more named fiduciaries.[31] Each plan must specify a procedure for establishing and carrying out a funding policy and a method to achieve plan objectives and must describe any procedure for allocating operational and administrative responsibilities. Plans must also include a provision that sets forth the amendment procedure and identifies the persons who have authority to amend the plan and a provision specifying the basis on which payments are made to and from the plan.

Nonqualified Plans

ERISA's broad definition of "pension plan" encompasses any plan, fund, or program maintained by an employer that, by its express terms or as a result of surrounding circumstances, provides

---

29. ERISA Section 410.
30. ERISA Section 412.
31. ERISA Section 402.

retirement income to employees or results in a deferral of income for periods extending to termination of employment or beyond.[32]

Thus, any plan of deferred compensation that does not meet the tax law requirements for a qualified plan will still come under the purview of Title I and, unless exempted, must comply with minimum participation, funding, and vesting requirements, joint and survivor provisions, and the like. If a non-tax-qualified plan becomes subject to the funding and vesting requirements, employees will be taxed on the value of vested benefits that are funded. Thus, most employers prefer to design programs that qualify for one of the available exemptions.

One specific exemption from Title I applies to unfunded excess benefit plans.[33] (Defined contribution excess plans generally include the value of contributions that exceed the Section 415 annual additions limit.) These plans may be funded or unfunded. If unfunded, they are completely exempt from Title I requirements. If funded, they are partially exempt and need comply only with Title I's reporting, disclosure, and fiduciary rules. If the plan is funded, participants will, of course, be currently taxable on the value of any vested benefits.

Another exemption applies to plans that are "unfunded and maintained by an employer primarily for the purpose of providing deferred compensation for a select group of management or highly compensated employees." (These plans are still subject to the reporting and disclosure requirements of Title I, although they need comply only with the minimum disclosure requirements.)[34] The DOL has never clarified the quoted phrase, so there is some uncertainty as to who is in the "select group" and can thus be covered under a top-hat plan. The concern, of course, is that the entire plan could become subject to all Title I provisions if the group was deemed not to come within this exemption.

Despite this uncertainty, many employers have established supplemental executive benefit programs that rely on this exemption. Many of them are restoration plans that restore qualified plan

---

32. ERISA Section 3(2)(A).
33. ERISA Section 4(b)(5).
34. A partial exemption from reporting and disclosure has been provided by the DOL for these plans. In essence, all that is required is that the DOL be notified of the existence of any such plan and the number of individuals it covers.
    DOL Reg. Section 2520.104-23.

benefits lost due to restrictions other than Section 415 (e.g., the limit on pay that can be used to determine contributions and benefits or the annual limit on elective deferrals).[35]

Other plans are much broader in scope, encompassing all forms of deferred compensation and providing benefits for executives that are clearly in addition to those contemplated by broad-based plans.

Veterans' Rights Provisions

Although prior law required employers to give vesting and eligibility credits for periods of military service under all types of retirement plans, benefit accruals were clearly required only under defined benefit (DB) pension plans. The Uniformed Services Employment and Re-employment Rights Act of 1994 (USERRA) broadens veterans' pension rights by requiring employers to also make retroactive contributions for periods of military service to defined contribution (DC) plans upon the employee's return to work. This will likely create added administrative complexity with respect to DC plans.

For a 401(k) plan or a plan permitting aftertax employee contributions, the returning employee must be allowed to make up missed deferrals or contributions over a period equal to three times the period of military service—up to a maximum of five years. And if the employee makes up any missed contributions or deferrals, the employer must make up any missed matching contributions. The measure also requires employers to contribute any missed profit-sharing plan allocations for employees returning from military service. However, employers are not required to make up earnings and forfeitures with respect to any missed contributions.

The amounts credited to employees under salary-based plans must be based on the compensation rate the employee would have received "but for" the absence, thus including any wage increases the employee would have received had he or she not taken military leave. If the compensation that would have been paid is "not

---

35. Because the elective deferral limit may affect employees who are not in the "select group," employers should exercise caution in implementing such an arrangement, making sure it complies with the terms of the top-hat exemption.

reasonably certain," the credit could be based on the employee's pay for the 12-month period preceding the military service.

The Small Business Job Protection Act of 1996 (SBA) included technical corrections to the Internal Revenue Code that allow employers to comply with the requirements of USERRA. Among these, makeup contributions are limited by relevant sections of the IRC, as determined for the year to which the contributions relate, not the year in which they are contributed. The relevant IRC sections are 402(g), 415 and 404(a). In applying these limits, the returning employee is deemed to have received compensation in accordance with the rules governing the determination of compensation for purposes of calculating the maximum amount of makeup contributions, described above. In addition, a plan will not fail any of the nondiscrimination tests (e.g., ADP, ACP, etc.) by reason of makeup contributions.[36] For this purpose, these contributions are simply ignored. The SBA also clarifies that a plan is permitted to suspend loan repayments by an individual who is performing military service, although it is not required to allow such suspensions. There will be no deemed taxable distribution on account of any such suspension, nor will it trigger a prohibited transaction.

While the law's provisions regarding retirement plans generally take effect for all reemployments initiated 60 days after enactment, employers have up to two years to amend their plans to comply with the new rules.

SECURITIES LAWS

The Securities and Exchange Commission (SEC) administers and enforces several laws that affect employee benefit and executive compensation plans, including the Securities Act of 1933 and the Securities Exchange Act of 1934.

Offering Securities

In general, any offer to sell securities must be registered with the SEC unless it qualifies for an exemption. The registration requirements are designed to ensure that purchasers receive material information about the stock being offered.

---

36. IRC Section 414(u).

For purposes of determining whether the registration requirements apply, employee benefit plans can be divided into two groups: those in which *employee* contributions are invested in employer stock and all other plans. Aftertax contributions are always considered employee contributions for this purpose. The treatment of elective contributions depends on how they are made. An elective contribution via salary reduction is considered to be an employee contribution (notwithstanding the fact that it is considered an employer contribution for tax law purposes). Deferral of a year-end profit-sharing contribution into the plan is treated as an employer contribution for both securities and tax law purposes.[37]

A plan that does not involve the investment of employee contributions in employer stock need not be registered with the SEC, such as an ESOP funded entirely with employer contributions. But any employee benefit plan in which employee contributions may be invested in employer stock is considered an offer to sell securities. Thus, the employer must register the plan with the SEC (and distribute certain information about the plan) unless the plan fits within an exemption. While an exemption is rarely available for plans of publicly traded companies,[38] most plans can make use of a simplified registration process using the SEC's Form S-8.[39]

Form S-8 is not really a form; it is a description of information employers must file with the SEC and/or communicate to participants in connection with the registration of the plan. In lieu of using a prospectus, an employer can meet its disclosure requirements through a variety of documents (including SPDs) that, together, provide the information described below.[40] An SPD alone will not provide sufficient disclosure for SEC purposes.

Employers must provide the following information to employees to meet S-8 disclosure requirements:

---

37. SEC Release No. 33-6281.
38. Plans of private companies may be exempt from registration under Rule 701, which permits an employer to grant up to $5 million worth of stock to employees annually without registration. This rule also requires that employees be given a copy of the plan document and that they receive adequate disclosure of material information. Further, the SEC must be notified within 30 days after sales total $100,000 and annually thereafter.
39. Form S-8 is available to employers subject to periodic reporting requirements under Sections 13 or 15(d) of the 1934 Act who have filed all required reports during the preceding 12 months.
40. SEC Release No. 33-6867.

- General information on the plan, including its nature and purpose, its duration and provisions for amendment and termination, whether it is subject to ERISA, and information about the plan administrators.
- The type and amount of securities to be offered under the plan.
- Eligibility criteria for participation in the plan.
- The method of purchasing stock under the plan, including the maximum amount of contributions and the nature and frequency of reports to participants about the status of their accounts.
- Any resale restrictions.
- The tax implications of participating in the plan, for example, the tax treatment of qualifying lump sum distributions.
- Information about the investment funds available to participants under the plan if funds other than employer stock are offered. This must include financial data on investment performance for the prior three years.
- The rights of employees to withdraw from the plan.
- Provisions that relate to vesting or otherwise relate to potential forfeitures or other penalties under the plan; charges and deductions and liens therefor.
- Any unusual risks not otherwise disclosed.
- A statement that certain other documents are available upon request—including the employer's latest annual report on Form 10-K.

If an SPD or other document is used, it must be dated, contain a legend noting that Securities Act registration is included, and be delivered in a timely manner for securities law purposes. Thus, if the SPD is used for purposes of securities law disclosure, it would have to either precede or accompany the offer or sale of employer securities. In the case of a CODA that provides for elective deferrals to an employer stock fund, for example, the SPD would have to precede or accompany any sign-up materials. This would require much earlier distribution of the SPD than is required under ERISA.

Similarly, information about material changes to the plan should be furnished to participants before the changes become effective. As with the original information, there is no prescribed format, provided the materials are dated and contain the required legend. An SMM may suffice, but it would have to be delivered in a timely manner; the ERISA deadline would not qualify as timely.

Plans that are registered with the SEC must file an annual report with the Commission on Form 11-K, which requires disclosure of the plan's financial condition. Plans with fewer than 300 participants need not file after the initial filing.

Insider Trading Restrictions

Section 16(b) of the Securities Exchange Act prohibits an insider from buying and selling, or selling and buying, company stock with a six month period. Insiders who violate this six month trading restriction are required to return all short-swing profits made on such a transaction to the company.

These insider trading rules are not relevant to a variety of broad-based retirement and allied makeup plans covering insiders—for example, defined benefit plans. However, they must be considered for any such plans that are individual account plans and provide for investments in actual or phantom employer stock by insiders. In this case, transactions that increase the amount of stock allocated to an insider are "purchases" and transactions that decrease the amount of stock allocated to an insider are "sales."

The SEC completely revised the insider trading rules with respect to broad-based plans in 1996. The revised rules, and their application to defined contribution and other plans, are discussed in the following paragraphs.

Blanket Exemption

Nearly all transactions under broad-based plans are now exempt without any conditions—other than that the plan involved satisfy one of the definitions so as to be a "qualified plan," an "excess benefit plan," or a "stock purchase plan"—or unless they constitute a discretionary transaction, as described in the next section.

1. **Qualified Plan:** To be a qualified plan, the plan must satisfy the coverage and participation requirements of Section 410 of the IRC.[41]

---

41. See the discussion of these requirements in Chapter 3. Note that a plan does not have to meet all of the tax-qualification requirements—just those relating to coverage and participation.

2. **Excess Benefit Plan:** This type of plan is defined as one that is operated in conjunction with a qualified plan and that provides *only* the benefits or contributions that cannot be provided under the qualified plan because of the limitations of Sections 401(a)(17), 415 and any other applicable contribution or benefit limit set forth in the IRC.[42]

3. **Stock Purchase Plan:** A stock purchase plan is defined as a plan that meets the coverage and participation requirements of Sections 423(b)(3) or 423(b)(5), or, in the alternative, Section 410 of the IRC. The purpose of including this alternative is to make the exemption available to plans that do not satisfy Section 423 but nonetheless cover a broad base of employees—for example, a plan that is limited to nonunion employees and that does not qualify under Section 423 could still qualify for the exemption if the minimum coverage requirements of Section 410 are satisfied.

Consistent with the broad exemptive relief provided to tax-conditioned plans, all purchases under a stock purchase plan are exempt and will not be matched with any other sale during the preceding or succeeding six-month period for purposes of determining any short-swing profit. However, an open market sale of stock acquired in an exempt purchase under a stock purchase plan is matchable with any nonexempt purchase—e.g., an open market purchase during the relevant six-month periods.

Because of this blanket exemption, a variety of purchases and sales of stock that may occur under a qualified plan are now unconditionally exempt.[43] For example, insiders can enroll, receive stock distributions, change the level of their contributions, cease contributions, or change the amount of future contributions invested in employer stock without any special restrictions. Only transactions that are defined as "discretionary transactions" must

---

42. Excess benefit plans would appear to include nonqualified plans that permit 401(k) deferrals in excess of the $7,000 limit (as adjusted) or allow contributions to make up for limitations resulting from ADP or ACP nondiscrimination tests. However, many types of deferred compensation plans (e.g., a plan permitting an executive to defer a percentage of base pay or bonus) would not be included. Also, deferred compensation plans for outside directors could never qualify as excess plans under this definition because a company cannot sponsor a qualified plan for its outside directors.
43. Rule 16(b)-3(c).

satisfy added conditions to be exempt—even under a tax-conditioned plan.

The regulations also provide a separate, unconditional exemption for purchases and sales of employer stock made pursuant to domestic relations orders (DROs), as defined under ERISA and the IRC.[44] This exemption applies both for purposes of the short-swing profit restriction and for reporting purposes.[45] It should be noted that DROs do not have to meet the more stringent requirements of QDROs imposed under the tax law. This means that potentially more transactions could be exempted—for example, those under nonqualified plans.

Exhibit 7–1 lists typical transactions in a CODA that contains an employer stock fund and summarizes the treatment that is provided under the current regulations.

Discretionary Transactions.

For qualified, excess benefit and stock purchase plans, the only types of transactions that must satisfy an extra condition in order to be exempt are so-called discretionary transactions. These are defined as involving either:

- an intra-plan transfer (i.e., a transfer of an existing account balance from one plan fund to another where one of the funds involves actual or phantom employer stock); or
- a cash distribution funded by a sale of such employer stock.

These transactions are only subject to this extra condition if made at the election of an insider. Hence, an involuntary distribution from an employer stock fund triggered by an ADP, ACP or Section 415 limit failure is not subject to this special rule. Also, transactions are exempt from the extra condition if made "in connection with" the insider's death, disability, retirement, or termination of employment or if they are required to be made available to the insider pursuant to the IRC.[46]

---

44. Rule 16a-12.
45. This exemption is not just limited to transactions under tax-conditioned plans. For example, it would also cover shares of stock that an insider acquired under a long-term incentive program that are disposed of in connection with a divorce.
46. Examples of this last category of transactions include an ESOP diversification election or an age 70-1/2 minimum required distribution.

E X H I B I T   7-1

Insider Trading Rules

Transaction	Rule 16(b) Treatment
(1) Election to make contributions used to purchase stock	Exempt purchase
(2) Election to change level of contribution	Exempt purchase
(3) Change investment of existing account into employer stock fund (is a discretionary transaction—"purchase")	Exempt purchase if no opposite-way discretionary transaction ("sale") under any plan in the preceding six months
(4) Change investment of existing account out of employer stock fund (is a discretionary transaction—"sale")	Exempt distribution if no opposite-way discretionary transaction ("purchase") under any plan in the preceding six months
(5) Liquidation of investment in employer stock fund to make plan loan to participant (is a discretionary transaction—"sale")	Exempt distribution if no opposite-way discretionary transaction ("purchase") under any plan in the preceding six months
(6) In-service withdrawal of stock	Exempt distribution
(7) Liquidation of investment in employer stock fund to make in-service withdrawal or hardship distribution (is a discretionary transaction—"sale")	Exempt distribution if no opposite-way discretionary transaction ("purchase") under any plan in the preceding six months
(8) Distribution of stock after employment terminates	Exempt distribution
(9) Sale of stock to make distribution in cash after employment terminates	Exempt distribution
(10) Employer matching contribution used to purchase stock	Exempt purchase
(11) Employer nonelective contribution used to purchase stock	Exempt purchase
(12) Rollover contribution used to purchase stock	Exempt purchase
(13) Plan loan repayments used to purchase stock	Exempt purchase
(14) Sale of stock to make corrective distributions (e.g, due to ADP or ACP test failures)	Exempt distribution
(15) Sale of stock to make minimum required distributions after 70-1/2	Exempt distribution
(16) Sale of stock to effect diversification or distribution under ESOP for participant aged 55 with 10 or more years of service	Exempt distribution
(17) Sale of stock to comply with QDRO	Exempt distribution

Even for discretionary transactions, the condition for exemption is relatively easy to satisfy and administer. All that is required is for every election of a discretionary transaction to occur at least six months after the most recent preceding election of a discretionary transaction that is the "opposite way." As long as six months have elapsed between the elections by the insider to make such transactions, they will be exempt. It should be noted that the focus is on the date of the elections, not the transactions themselves.[47]

Unlike the prior rules, the new rule does not require an irrevocable election six months in advance of the discretionary transaction being elected (i.e., the dates of the election and the transaction itself can occur within a six-month period or even simultaneously). Rather, the focus is on the timing of elections for "opposite way" transactions—i.e., they must occur more than six months apart. A purchase and a sale are opposite-way transactions. In order for a purchase-type discretionary transaction to be exempt, any previous sale-type discretionary transaction must have occurred at least six months earlier. If this rule is violated, the second transaction is not exempt, but the first transaction would still be exempt (assuming it was not elected within less than six months after another opposite-way discretionary transaction).

An example of a purchase-type discretionary transaction is a transfer of an existing account balance in a plan from a fixed income fund to the employer stock fund. An example of a sale-type discretionary transaction is the transfer of an existing account balance out of an employer stock fund into any other investment vehicle offered under the plan. Another example of a sale-type discretionary transaction is an in-service distribution of cash to a plan participant resulting from the liquidation of some or all of the participant's account balance invested in the employer stock fund under the plan. However, if the distribution is made in connection with termination of employment, it will not be considered discretionary. Also, a withdrawal in kind of employer stock is not, in itself, a discretionary transaction since there is no sale.[48]

It is important to note that discretionary transactions can occur under any kind of plan, not just under a tax-conditioned

---

47. Rule 16b-3(f).
48. The preamble to the SEC regulations specifically notes that a plan loan "funded" by a reduction in an employer stock fund of a participant generally will be characterized as a cash distribution—and thus a discretionary sale—for purposes of these rules.

plan, and that such a transaction in one plan can be matched, for the six-month requirement, with an opposite-way transaction occurring under another plan. Therefore, the search for opposite-way transactions must encompass all discretionary transactions under all plans of the employer.

Reporting Requirements.

Insiders are generally required to file periodic reports and annual reports (on Forms 4 and 5 respectively) with the SEC concerning their transactions in employer stock

The new regulations liberalize the scheme for reporting transactions in tax-conditioned plans. Most transactions under qualified, excess benefit and stock purchase plans—those covered by the blanket exemption—will be completely exempt from reporting. Only intraplan transactions and cash distributions would be subject to annual reporting on Form 5. An executive can choose, however, to voluntarily report discretionary transactions on an earlier Form 4—within ten days after the close of the calendar month in which the transaction occurs—rather than at year-end on Form 5. Discretionary transactions must be reported even though they qualify for the conditional exemption.

COLLECTIVE BARGAINING

Employee benefits are a mandatory subject of collective bargaining under the National Labor Relations Act (NLRA). Thus, employers may not refuse to discuss benefits for employees represented by a collective bargaining unit and must negotiate in good faith.

In union plans covering only employees of one employer, the negotiations typically cover such design issues as eligibility, contribution levels, and vesting provisions; funding issues usually remain under the employer's control. On occasion, a union's proposal may be for coverage under a joint labor-management trust fund—typically referred to as a multiemployer or Taft-Hartley plan. The law requires that such plans have equal labor and management representation on the board of trustees. For the most part, however, multiemployer plans have been limited to defined benefit plans and health and welfare programs.

Plan Design and Operational Issues

CHAPTER 8

Plan Design—Employer and Employee Contributions

Although tax and other legal considerations drive much of the design of CODAs, employers have considerable latitude in determining how to structure many plan features. This chapter focuses on the factors plan sponsors should take into account in deciding how—and how much—employees and the company should contribute to savings and profit-sharing plans. Plan provisions that govern employees' rights to their benefits, including vesting, distribution, in-service withdrawal, and loan provisions, are the subject of Chapter 9. Chapter 10 summarizes provisions on service determinations, plan amendments, responsibilities of the plan committee, and the like. Investment and administrative considerations are treated in Chapters 11 through 13. Chapter 14 covers employee communication.

SAVINGS PLAN CODAs

The conventional savings plan CODA requires employees to contribute as a condition of participating in the program. These mandatory contributions are usually matched, to some extent, by employer contributions. A plan may also permit employees to make voluntary or additional contributions that do not attract employer matching contributions.

Mandatory Employee Contributions

In designing a plan that requires employee contributions, employers need to address these basic questions:

- Should employees contribute on a pretax basis, or should they be allowed to choose between pretax and aftertax contributions?
- How much should employees be allowed to contribute?
- Should they be permitted to change their contribution rates, and if so, how frequently?
- How should the plan define the compensation on which contributions are based?

Elective Versus Aftertax   Some plans require that mandatory contributions be made on a pretax basis (elective deferrals); others permit employees to choose whether they are made pretax or aftertax. Still others use a mixture (e.g., elective deferrals up to some level and a choice between elective deferrals and aftertax contributions thereafter).[1]

Elective deferrals obviously create tax advantages for employees, reducing current income tax and enabling them to earn investment income on amounts that would otherwise have been paid as taxes. But elective deferrals are also subject to withdrawal and distribution restrictions, something that some employees—particularly younger ones—may see as a disadvantage. If employees can only contribute by making elective deferrals, they may be discouraged from participating, and the plan may have difficulties passing the ADP test. (Loan and hardship provisions may help mitigate this result, however.)

Employers also have to consider the fact that elective deferrals reduce the compensation base used to determine the company's maximum deductible contribution and can reduce the amount the company can actually contribute within that maximum, as noted in Chapter 6. And special communication efforts may be necessary in plans that require or permit elective deferrals, since some employees will be suspicious of any program that appears to require a "cut" in pay.

---

1. A savings plan could also be structured to permit aftertax contributions only, but it would not be a CODA.

Offering employees the opportunity to make aftertax contributions has several potential advantages. In-service withdrawals of aftertax contributions need not be restricted, although these contributions are subject to an ACP test. Aftertax contributions will not reduce the amount of the employer's allowable deductible contributions. Further, NHCEs may be more inclined to participate if they can choose which type of contribution to make, and their participation could help the plan pass the nondiscrimination tests. On the other hand, restrictions on the multiple use of the alternative limitation in nondiscrimination testing (see Chapter 4) may come into play when employees are permitted to choose which type of contributions to make. Choice will also create additional administrative effort because the administrator will have to keep separate records for each type of contribution, including records for payroll and tax reporting and for such plan purposes as in-service withdrawals. By definition, contributions in excess of the maximum permitted dollar amount of elective deferrals ($9,500 in 1996) must

E X H I B I T   8–1

Factors in Determining Basis of Mandatory Contributions

Elective Contributions Only	
Advantages	**Disadvantages**
Tax benefits for employees	Withdrawal restrictions apply
	ADP test applies
	Communication difficulties
	Reduction in deductible employer contributions

Elective and Aftertax Contributions	
Advantages	**Disadvantages**
Likelihood of higher NHCE participation	Loss of tax benefits for some employees
No withdrawal restrictions on aftertax contributions	ACP test applies to aftertax contributions; multiple use test may also apply
Employer deductible contributions may be reduced to lesser extent	Additional administrative requirements

be made on an aftertax basis and can be made only in plans that allow employees to make both types of contributions. Exhibit 8–1 (page 177) summarizes these issues.

Contribution Levels While some plans specify that all employees must contribute at a single flat rate, most plan sponsors offer employees a choice among several different levels of participation; a plan might allow employees to contribute from 1 percent to 6 percent of pay in 1 percent increments, for example. (Employee contributions can also be set as dollar amounts, rather than as percentages of compensation, though this is relatively uncommon.)

ADP/ACP test considerations will often dictate whether the plan sponsor should permit a choice of contribution levels—and if so, how much choice. The more flexibility, the more likely it is that NHCEs will participate.

To achieve reasonable average contribution or deferral percentages for NHCEs, plans often set some minimum participation rate such as 2 percent of pay. Most plans also specify a maximum level of mandatory contributions as well: 6 percent of pay is common. Such a provision helps control costs because it establishes a maximum employer contribution level. It may also help a plan satisfy the ADP/ACP tests, because HCE participation tends to increase as permitted contribution levels increase, while the reverse is often true for NHCEs.[2]

Contributions can also vary with service. Employees with fewer than 10 years of service might be permitted to contribute at a base rate (or rates), for example, while employees with 10 to 20 years of service can contribute at 150 percent of the base rate(s), and employees with more than 20 years can contribute at 200 percent. However, plans like this could have problems meeting the ADP/ACP tests and the nondiscrimination test on benefits, rights, and features. Employer matching contributions set at a fixed percentage of an employee's contribution will automatically produce

2. There is also some historical basis for use of a maximum. The IRS once took the position that mandatory contributions in excess of 6 percent could be burdensome and could cause discrimination in favor of the highly paid. TRA '86 supplanted this position with the ADP/ACP tests, but many plans established before 1987 retain some type of maximum.

higher dollar amounts for employees with longer periods of service,[3] and longer service tends to correlate with higher pay.

Changing Contribution Rates   Permitting employees to choose how much to contribute gives them flexibility in meeting their individual needs. Permitting them to increase or reduce their contribution rates from time to time, or to suspend contributions, gives them additional flexibility.

Some plans permit employees to exercise their right to change rates or suspend contributions only at the beginning of each quarter; others permit changes at the beginning of each pay period, provided reasonable notice is given. Employers interested in reducing administrative burdens can limit the number of times such changes can be made—to one or two times in any 12-month period, for example. Sponsors may also want to include a provision requiring an employee who suspends contributions to do so for some minimum period of time such as 6 months or one year.

Compensation   As noted earlier, contributions can be based on any definition of compensation that does not result in discrimination in favor of HCEs.[4] Most plan sponsors use either:

- W-2 pay less certain noncompensation items such as moving expenses but including overtime, bonuses, shift differential, or
- Base salary or wages.

A broader definition could produce higher dollar amounts of employee contributions and thus higher employer contributions. But a total pay definition could also aggravate ADP/ACP problems because HCEs might tend to contribute on the basis of total pay, while NHCEs are apt to contribute on the basis of base pay only.

---

3. Some plans achieve this same result by holding employee contributions constant, regardless of service, and by increasing the level of the employer match as service increases.
4. Specific definitions of compensation are required for nondiscrimination testing, deduction and annual addition limits, and the like. These may or may not be the same as the definition used for determining employee and employer contributions. See the discussion of these requirements in Chapter 3.

The way a plan defines pay may also have administrative implications. A definition that does not track the pay bases used for other purposes (taxes, other employee benefits) could require special records and handling, for example.

Prevalence Data Exhibit 8–2 provides information on various plan contribution provisions in 596 savings plan CODAs in Towers Perrin's EBIC database.

Voluntary Employee Contributions

Before TRA '86, an employee could voluntarily contribute up to 10 percent of current pay to a savings plan in addition to any mandatory contributions, so long as the opportunity to make voluntary contributions was available to plan participants on a nondiscriminatory and uniform basis.[5] The limit was cumulative, permitting a contribution of 10 percent of current pay times years of prior service, less any previous voluntary contributions. As a result of TRA '86, the ADP and ACP tests determine whether employee contributions are being made on a nondiscriminatory basis, and the old 10 percent rule no longer applies.[6]

Plans that permit voluntary aftertax contributions may have difficulty in meeting the ACP test; NHCEs are less likely than HCEs to make voluntary contributions—because they cannot afford to, or because they have no incentive in the form of employer matching contributions. These same factors could create problems in meeting the ADP test for plans that permit voluntary pretax contributions.

Nonetheless, many plans permit voluntary contributions, relying on testing and administrative procedures to make sure contribution amounts stay within acceptable parameters. Some allow voluntary contributions on an elective deferral basis only; others permit the employee to choose between elective deferrals and aftertax contributions. Still others permit employees to make voluntary contributions only on an aftertax basis. Limits on voluntary contributions—10 percent of pay, for example—are common (see

---

5. IRS Rev. Ruls. 80-307 and 80-350.
6. Preamble to IRS Prop. Reg. 1.401(k)-1, August 8, 1988.

E X H I B I T   8–2

Prevalence of Various Contribution Provisions in 596 Savings Plan CODAs

Provision	Number of Plans Reporting
Definition of Compensation	
▪ Total W-2 pay	215
▪ Base pay only	189
▪ Base pay, overtime and commissions	45
▪ Base pay and commissions	52
▪ Base pay and overtime	40
▪ Base pay, overtime and bonus	23
▪ Base pay, commissions and bonus	14
▪ Other	18
Employee Contributions	
▪ Mandatory (matched) on elective basis only*	288
▪ Mandatory (matched) on elective or after-tax basis, at employee choice	238
▪ Mandatory (matched) permitted at:	
▪ One level only	1
▪ Two to four levels	106
▪ Five or more levels	400
▪ Level varies by service	16
▪ Fixed dollar amount	3
▪ Voluntary (unmatched) contributions permitted: 3	
▪ Elective basis only*	221
▪ After-tax basis only	19
▪ Elective or after-tax basis, at employee choice	333
▪ Maximum mandatory employee contributions**	
▪ Under 7% of pay	466
▪ From 7% to 10% of pay	47
▪ 11% of pay or higher	10
▪ Fixed dollar amount	3

*Up to maximum elective deferral limit under law
**Most common maximum is 6%

E X H I B I T   8–2 *(Continued)*

Provision	Number of Plans Reporting
■ Maximum voluntary employee conributions***	
■ Under 7% of pay	94
■ From 7% to 10% of pay	289
■ 11% of pay or higher	290
Employer Contributions	
■ No matching contribution	32
■ Match is less than 25%	1
■ Match is 25% to 49%	29
■ Match is 50% to 99%	172
■ Match is 100% or more	97
■ Employer match varies****	221
■ No company contribution	44

***Most common maximum is 10%
****E.g., varies based on profits or service or uses different base and supplemental percentages

Exhibit 8–2). In some cases, total contributions of up to some limit such as 10 percent of pay are permitted, with the first 6 percent mandatory and matched and the balance voluntary.

Matching Employer Contributions

Employers are not required to make matching contributions to a savings plan CODA, but, as Exhibit 8–2 indicates, most of them do.

Tax law once required that employer contributions to profit-sharing plans be made from current or accumulated profits. Most savings plans were qualified as profit-sharing plans and thus included a plan provision to this effect. TRA '86 eliminated this requirement, and the matching contribution formula in a savings plan need not refer to profits.[7]

---

7. IRC Section 401(a)(27).

Structuring the Match   Matching employer contributions to a savings plan CODA are typically expressed as a percentage of what employees have contributed on either an elective or an after-tax basis. As Exhibit 8–2 indicates, contributions may vary from as little as a 10 percent match to as much as 100 percent or 200 percent of what the employee contributes; the most common match level is 50 percent to 99 percent. The *level* of an employer's contribution will reflect its compensation philosophy and any specific objectives the employer has for the plan, as discussed in more detail in the following pages.

In some plans, the employer's overall contribution for the year may be discretionary or it may be based on a profit-sharing formula; once determined, it is usually allocated to employees in proportion to their compensation and/or contributions. Other plans include a basic employer match and an additional profit-sharing match, for example, a base match of 25 percent, increasing to 50 percent, 75 percent, or 100 percent as net profits reach stipulated levels. Still other plans authorize the board of directors to declare an additional discretionary contribution or higher matching rate as warranted by profits. Additional contributions based on profits are usually declared at year end and are allocated on a retroactive basis. Some plans tie the allocation to employees' mandatory contributions; in others, the allocation goes to all eligible employees regardless of whether they have contributed.

In addition to making basic matching and/or profit-sharing contributions, employers may choose to make QNECs, QMACs, or additional matching contributions, or safe harbor contributions, to forestall ADP and/or ACP problems, as discussed in Chapter 4.

Meeting Specific Objectives   An employer's decision to make fixed or variable contributions will reflect its objectives on cost control, funding flexibility, and employee incentives. The level at which it chooses to contribute may also reflect specific objectives.

One such objective for many employers is actively encouraging employees to participate in the plan, for example, to ensure that they accumulate additional funds for retirement, to avoid ADP/ACP problems by increasing NHCE participation, or both. A generous contribution formula is one means to this end.

Others include:

- Use of a weighted formula—one that provides a higher level of employer matching contributions at lower levels of employee contributions.
- Providing some level of employer contribution for all employees on an ongoing basis, regardless of whether they contribute, plus an additional matching contribution for those who elect to make contributions.
- Front-loading the employer contribution by making it higher during early years of participation.

For a discussion of contribution levels in the context of other specific objectives—using CODA assets to pay for postretirement medical coverage, for example—see Chapter 2.

Additional Considerations   Because most employees will become eligible to participate during the course of a plan year, plan sponsors must decide whether to recognize a participant's pay for the entire year for plan purposes or only for that portion of the year after participation commences. The question resolves itself if employer contributions are made on a matching basis; the employee does not contribute until he or she becomes a participant, and employer contributions are a function of how much the employee contributes. When the employer contribution is not a match, it is typically based on pay earned after participation begins.

What about employer contributions for the year in which a participant terminates employment? The employer can require that the employee be employed on the last day of the plan year in order to be eligible to share in the employer's contribution. Some plans—particularly those with profit-sharing contribution formulas—apply such a condition to year-end contributions but generally not to terminations due to retirement, death, or disability. Employer contributions are generally tied to the actual amount contributed by the employee even in a year of termination, however.

Forfeitures

An employee who terminates employment without full vesting forfeits the nonvested portion of his or her account balance attributable to employer contributions. The IRC permits employers to use these forfeited amounts to reduce employer contributions or to reallocate them among remaining participants as if they were additional employer contributions. Most savings plan CODAs use the former approach.

PROFIT-SHARING CODAs

In a cash option deferred profit-sharing plan, the employer determines how much it will contribute for eligible employees each year and makes this contribution available to them either in cash or as a contribution to the plan. Employees are generally not *required* to contribute to receive a profit-sharing allocation.

Profit-sharing CODAs differ from conventional savings plan CODAs in several ways. First, employer contributions are likely to be higher in a profit-sharing plan; contributions of from 8 percent to 10 percent of pay are not uncommon, compared with typical savings plan contributions of 1-1/2 percent to 3 percent of pay. In addition, employers' profit-sharing contributions are typically made only once a year. As a result, employees are apt to view a profit-sharing contribution as a cash bonus, and many of them will elect cash rather than defer the money into the plan. Thus, NHCE participation levels sufficient to satisfy the ADP test may be more difficult to achieve in profit-sharing plans than in conventional savings plans.

Employer Contributions

As with savings plans, employers should consider such factors as annual costs, contribution flexibility, and the ultimate purpose of the plan in determining company contributions to a profit-sharing CODA. Employer objectives may be quite different for profit-sharing CODAs than for savings plans, however. For example, higher contribution levels may reflect the role the employer expects the plan to play in tying employees' interests to those of the company and/or in providing for retirement security.

As noted, the IRC does not require use of a predetermined contribution formula in a profit-sharing plan. When employer contributions are made on a discretionary basis, however, they must be "substantial and recurring."[8]

---

8.   IRS Reg. 1.401-1(b)(2).

Use of a discretionary formula gives employers the flexibility to adjust contributions each year in light of current financial circumstances and capital needs, and to make sure contributions will not exceed the maximum deductible amount. Such a formula may be particularly attractive to private companies that do not want to divulge financial information to employees.

A plan can impose minimums and/or maximums on discretionary contributions, for example, by specifying that annual contributions cannot be higher or lower than stipulated percentages of profits.

The major advantage of a *fixed* formula is that it promotes increased morale and a sense of security among employees, since contributions cannot be manipulated by management. The contribution commitment under a fixed formula is generally expressed as a specific percentage of profits or as a sliding scale of percentages that typically increase as profits increase. These percentages are usually applied to net profits before taxes.

Profit-sharing plans usually include a provision stating that the contribution will in no event exceed 15 percent of the payroll of covered employees to stay within deductible limits and avoid a penalty tax. The 15 percent limit applies only to the portion of the contribution that employees defer; for deduction purposes, amounts that employees elect to take in cash are treated as cash compensation. Thus, an employer might contribute more than 15 percent of pay to the overall plan if it expects that amounts actually deferred will be less than the 15 percent limit.

Whether it uses a discretionary or fixed formula, a plan will typically impose some limit on the annual contribution to protect shareholder return on investments. The plan may provide that no contribution will be made in a year in which dividends on stock are less than a certain amount, for example, or provide that no contributions will be made until profits in a year exceed a certain percentage of the employer's capital funds.

Many profit-sharing CODAs make the entire contribution subject to employee election. But a plan may specify that part of the employer's contribution will be deferred automatically, with the balance available to the employee either as cash or a deferral. This approach is attractive to employers who want the plan to meet retirement income needs. Further, the part that is automatically deferred may be integrated with social security benefits. This approach may also produce lower costs because the portion that is automatically deferred need not be fully vested.

Here, too, employers must decide whether to require that employees be on the active payroll at year end in order to receive contributions, and how much of an individual's pay will be taken into account during the first year of participation.

Employee Contributions

It is customary for a profit-sharing CODA to permit voluntary contributions up to the maximum permitted under the ADP and ACP tests. As is the case with savings plan CODAs, the voluntary contribution provision often follows the old 10 percent rule (i.e., employees can contribute up to 10 percent of pay) even though these contributions must now satisfy the ADP/ACP tests.

Allocation Formulas

Although a profit-sharing plan need not follow a specific contribution formula, it must follow a specific formula in allocating employer contributions among employees. The typical plan simply allocates the employer contribution in a way that reflects the relationship of each employee's plan compensation to the total plan compensation of all participants. If an employee's plan compensation is $50,000 and the total plan compensation of all participants is $500,000, for example, the employee will receive 10 percent of the employer's contribution.

It is also possible, though uncommon, to weight the allocation formula to reflect service. This is acceptable to the IRS provided that all applicable nondiscrimination tests are met. For example, such a formula might grant two units for each year of service and one unit for each $100 of compensation; an employee earning $50,000 with 20 years of service would have 540 units (500 for pay and 40 for service). All units of all employees would then be totaled and divided into the employer's contribution to arrive at a unit value. Each employee's units would then be multiplied by this value to arrive at the amount of the employer contribution the employee would receive.

Forfeitures

As noted, savings plans generally use forfeitures of terminating employees to reduce employer contributions; in profit-sharing plans, such forfeitures are usually reallocated among remaining participants. If the plan consists solely of CODA contributions (amounts available as cash but electively deferred), the plan is always fully and immediately vested, and there are no forfeitures.

CHAPTER 9

Plan Design–Benefit Entitlement Provisions

Vesting provisions establish employees' rights to their benefits; distribution, withdrawal, and loan provisions govern how and when they have access to those benefits. The issues employers should consider in designing these benefit entitlement features are the subject of this chapter.

VESTING

Tax law requirements on vesting were described in Chapter 3. In brief: (1) the value of elective deferrals and aftertax contributions must be fully vested at all times; (2) the value of employer contributions must be fully vested at normal retirement age, regardless of length of service; (3) the value of employer contributions must otherwise be vested under either of two vesting schedules (5-year cliff vesting or graded vesting of 20 percent per year starting after 3 years); and (4) top-heavy plans must use an accelerated vesting schedule.

Exhibit 9–1 summarizes vesting provisions in the savings plan CODAs in the Towers Perrin Employee Benefit Information Center database that include company contributions.

Most employers opt for cliff vesting of employer contributions because it is easier to explain to employees and to administer. But, depending on turnover patterns, graded vesting could help

E X H I B I T   9—1

Vesting Provisions

Number of plans	596
Plans with no employer contributions	44
Plans with graded vesting	192
Plans with cliff vesting that is:	
▪ Immediate	198
▪ After one year of service/participation	3
▪ After two years of service/participation	4
▪ After three years of service/participation	23
▪ After four years of service/participation	7
▪ After five years of service/participation	64
Plans with other vesting provisions (e.g., after three and one half years of service)	61

lower employer costs through forfeitures by employees terminating with more than five but less than seven years of service. Turnover during this period is apt to be low for most employers, however, so this potential cost savings may not be significant. In any event, it should be weighed against the additional costs associated with the partial vesting of employees who terminate with less than five years of service.

Employers can adopt vesting schedules that are more liberal than the law requires; examples include full vesting from the first day of plan participation or full vesting after only two or three years of service.

More liberal vesting has cost implications, of course. If a vested employee terminates employment before vesting would have been legally required, the value of his or her vested benefit represents an additional plan cost; absent vesting, the money would have been forfeited and could have been used to reduce employer contributions. Actual turnover patterns during the first five years of employment will determine the magnitude of this cost.

Further, in plans that reallocate forfeitures among remaining employees, a more liberal schedule will mean the loss of some benefits for longer-service employees who would otherwise have had these amounts added to their accounts. Some observers believe it is more equitable to reallocate forfeitures to longer-service employees than to pay out these values to those who terminate with short service.

Cost is not the only issue employers need to consider, however. Liberal vesting provisions might encourage employees to participate in the plan earlier and contribute at higher levels, for example, making it easier for the plan to meet the ADP/ACP tests. Full and immediate vesting eliminates a certain amount of record-keeping and administration and simplifies employee communications—particularly for annual employee statements and at termination of employment.

Plans may base vesting on years of service or a combination of years of service and years of participation. The tax law permits a plan to exclude, for vesting service, years during which an employee does not make mandatory employee contributions. (Because elective deferrals are treated as employer contributions, however, a plan may not disregard years during which an employee does not make elective deferrals.) Even so, some service must be taken into account (e.g., service after age 18 and before eligibility to participate in the plan). Because vesting cannot be based solely on participation, most employers choose to use only years of service for their vesting provisions.

Most CODAs provide for full and immediate vesting in the event of death and usually in the event of disability, regardless of service. Plans that permit accelerated vesting in cases of disability must define what constitutes disability. For administrative convenience, this definition will usually track the definition the employer uses for its long-term disability income plan, though more liberal or conservative definitions may be used.[1]

RETIREMENT AGES

For the most part, the concepts of normal, early, and deferred retirement age are not relevant in defined contribution plans. An employee's benefit at any given time is equal to the value of his or

---

1. Disability benefits could be subject to the 10 percent early distribution tax unless the disability that gives rise to the distribution meets a specific definition set forth in the Code, namely, a disability that renders the employee unable to engage in any substantial gainful activity and can be expected to result in death or to be of long-continued and indefinite duration.

her account balance. Retirement, in effect, is just another form of termination of employment.

Nonetheless, defined contribution plans include a provision specifying normal retirement age which establishes a full vesting point under tax law. It is also desirable to define normal retirement age in a manner consistent with the employer's defined benefit plan.

Plans often specify an early retirement eligibility age as well, even though there is no difference in the value of the employee's account if early retirement requirements are not satisfied at the time of termination. A common provision requires the employee to have completed at least 10 years of service and reached age 55.

An early retirement definition will enable the plan sponsor to establish a consistently stated early retirement eligibility for all of its plans, including retirement, health care and life insurance benefits. Also, this type of provision permits the plan sponsor to treat retirees and terminated vesteds differently in situations where the law permits it to do so. IRS regulations prevent an employer from imposing a significant detriment on a participant who fails to consent to an immediate distribution, however, and recent IRS audit guidelines indicate that restrictions on investment options and withdrawals before age 65 would be significant detriments.

Plans may also include a definition of deferred retirement to make it clear that employees will continue to make and receive contributions after normal retirement age (i.e., that they will continue to participate in the plan until they actually retire).

DISTRIBUTIONS ON TERMINATION OF EMPLOYMENT

The vested portion of an account balance is generally payable to or on behalf of an employee at termination of employment, whatever the reason. Actual payment of the employee's vested interest at the time of termination is not required, however, and the law permits the plan to withhold payment until the plan's normal retirement age.[2]

---

2. IRC Section 401(a)(14). This is not the case for ESOP distributions. Here, the employee can require that benefits be paid more rapidly. See page 117.

Nonetheless, most CODAs allow for payment of an employee's vested benefit at termination. Administrative considerations make it desirable to pay off the participant (or beneficiary) as quickly as possible and to terminate all further involvement. In many situations, however, this may not be the best course of action for the employee.

An employer cannot force an employee to take a distribution (other than at the plan's normal retirement age) if the value of the employee's account is greater than $3,500, however.[3] A participant must be given the option of leaving vested amounts in the plan for distribution at the later age of 62 or the plan's normal retirement age (or earlier, if the participant so elects under a plan provision).

Once participants reach normal retirement age, they typically have a choice of distribution options. One such option may be to defer distribution beyond normal retirement age and select from otherwise available options at a later date, so long as the minimum distribution rules are satisfied.

In general, a plan can provide that when distributions are made, they will be made in the form of a lump sum payment. A plan can also be designed to permit installment distributions— either for a fixed period not to exceed the participant's life expectancy or the joint life expectancy of the participant and his or her beneficiary, or on the basis of a recalculation of life expectancy on a yearly basis. A third option permits the distribution of an annuity contract. Still another option would be to permit the employee to transfer funds to the employer's defined benefit pension plan for the purchase of a QCOLA—to provide for inflation protection during retirement.[4]

The distribution itself can take several forms. As noted in Chapter 2, of the 596 companies in the EBIC database that sponsor defined contribution plans, 100 percent make distributions available as a lump sum, 55 percent permit installment distributions, and 25 percent permit the distribution of an annuity contract.

As with other provisions, the forms of payment offered under a plan should support employer objectives. For example, if the plan is to play a major role in meeting long-term or postretirement

---

3. IRC Section 411(a)(11).
4. See Chapter 3 and page 203.

health care needs, or protecting against the effects of inflation, the plan sponsor should consider the installment and/or QCOLA options discussed below, even though they add administrative burdens.

Another factor to consider is that to the extent funds are not needed to meet daily living expenses, leaving them invested under a tax shelter, with investment income compounding on a before-tax basis, can be very advantageous—to individuals at all income levels. Maximizing the tax-sheltering opportunities of a CODA is often an important employer objective. Making installment distributions available—and encouraging their use—is highly desirable when this objective is involved.

Deferred Distributions

While an immediate distribution of plan assets may be appealing at the time of retirement, economic considerations may make deferral the better choice for many participants, particularly those who are able to defer distribution for an extended period of time.

An employee who defers distribution usually preserves his or her options as to the form the distribution will ultimately take, that is, a lump sum or installment payments as described below. In the meantime, investment earnings are sheltered, and plan assets may be accessible via withdrawals, partial distributions, or loans. In addition, the responsibility for selecting and oversight of investment options—and some if not all investment management expenses—could remain in the company's hands. In short, deferrals often offer employees a highly flexible and economically efficient way to invest funds. (For an illustration of the economic impact of deferring distribution for as long as possible under the minimum distribution rules, see Exhibits 9–2 and 9–3 on pages 200 and 201.)

In some circumstances, however, the option of an immediate distribution could be attractive to a terminating employee. This could happen, for example, where the plan is structured such that employer contributions must be invested in company stock and where taking an immediate distribution is the only way in which investment of this part of the employee's account balance can be changed.

However, deferred distributions can create additional administrative effort and costs for the plan sponsor. For example, it is generally more difficult to communicate with former employees than it is with active employees. Further, the initiation and processing of various elections (investment changes, withdrawals, loans, beneficiary changes) will require special handling.

Lump Sum Payments

From the plan sponsor's perspective, lump sum distributions are an attractive option because they eliminate ongoing administrative involvement—no more recordkeeping, annual statements, election, and change processing—and end the employer's fiduciary obligations to the employee.

From an employee's perspective, a large cash payment may be a very appealing prospect. And, in some situations, being able to take money out of the plan (and away from perceived employer control) can be an important consideration. Also, for employees who participate in a plan requiring that employer contributions be invested in employer stock, this may be the only way this portion of their funds can be reinvested.

There are possible disadvantages to lump sums as well, however, including the following:

- Employees must take the market as they find it when they elect a lump sum. An employee can realize substantial profits if the market is up when his or her account is liquidated for distribution—or incur substantial losses if the market is down.[5] It should also be noted that the same effects could be achieved within the plan by making changes in investment options.

---

5. If the employee immediately reinvests in comparable investments, it is possible that this effect could be mitigated. This depends, to a great extent, on the investments selected as well as timing; in many instances the employee will not, as a practical matter, be able to recoup any losses suffered when plan holdings were liquidated.

- Lump sum payments may encourage unwise spending. While there is much to be said for using these funds to enrich the employee's lifestyle, there is also much to be said for using them, at least in part, to provide economic security—particularly when this is an important employer objective for the plan.

- The employee who receives a large amount of cash is faced with immediate problems of how this money should be invested. The average employee is not a sophisticated investor; while participating in the plan, he or she is given choices under funds that are selected and supervised by the employer. These choices are limited in number and, to some extent, are implicitly endorsed by an organization in which the employee generally has some degree of confidence. To this extent, the employee has made investment choices in a somewhat protected environment; once the funds are distributed, however, the employee must choose from among a vast array of investment vehicles and must often rely on investment advice and recommendations from individuals or firms that can be less than objective in the advice they give. This, in turn, could lead to inappropriate investment choices, and, ultimately, to investment losses that impair the values the plan has created. Allowing funds to remain in the plan for installment distribution could avoid or at least minimize these problems.[6]

- Investment choices made by the employee after funds have come into his or her possession will often involve some investment management expenses and/or sales fees that the employee must absorb. This represents a cost to the employee that could be avoided to the extent that it would be assumed by the employer (as is often the case), if funds were left in the plan.

- The employee who takes a lump sum distribution loses the advantages of the tax shelter. While this advantage might

---

6. It is possible, of course, that the plan investment options are not very attractive or well designed, for example, if the only investment choice available is a GIC. When this is so, the employee would probably do well to withdraw his or her funds and seek professional assistance in determining how they should be invested.

be preserved, to some extent, if the distribution is rolled over into an IRA, the employee who does this is still faced with the problems referred to above (i.e., making appropriate investments and possibly absorbing additional investment expenses).

Installment Distributions

Installment distribution options are less common than lump sum options because they require more administrative effort and expense. Further, some employers hesitate to offer installments because they believe the joint and survivor requirements will apply. In fact, these requirements apply only if an *annuity* is selected by the employee and if certain requirements are not met.[7] Installment distributions, even those calculated on a life expectancy basis, are not annuities, and the joint and survivor requirements will not apply if the employee's spouse is the automatic beneficiary (or the employee's spouse consents to another beneficiary) for 100 percent of the account balance.

Installment distributions include: (1) payments for a fixed period of time; (2) payments of a fixed amount until the proceeds are exhausted; (3) payments on an as needed basis; (4) payments over a period equal to the life expectancy of the employee or the joint life expectancies of the employee and his or her beneficiary; and (5) payments over the life expectancy of the employee or the joint life expectancies of the employee and his or her spouse with life expectancy recalculated each year.[8] These arrangements, which must satisfy the minimum distribution rules covered in Chapter 3, are described in more detail below.

Fixed Period/Amount Payments   The employee may choose to have payments made over a fixed period (such as 10 or 15 years) or in a fixed amount that will be paid periodically until the account balance is exhausted. The period of time involved cannot exceed

---

7. See Chapter 3.
8. Life expectancies for installment arrangements are determined under unisex tables in
   IRS regulations under Section 72 of the IRC.

the employee's life expectancy or the joint life expectancies of the employee and his or her beneficiary.

Payments over a fixed period are usually set in an amount that will exhaust the account balance by the end of the period based on future investment return assumptions; actual investment returns may require the employer to adjust payments upward or downward by dividing the current account balance by the number of remaining payments. Alternatively, the plan sponsor can terminate payments early if investment returns have been lower than assumed or make a final balloon payment if they have been higher.

The situation is much simpler when the employee elects to receive a fixed amount. The amount is paid on payment due dates until the account balance is exhausted. The employer may use some assumption as to future investment returns to estimate the length of the payment period; the actual period will depend on actual investment results.

As Needed Payments   This highly flexible but administratively complex arrangement permits the employee to draw down the account balance on a variable basis. The employee might elect to have a specified amount paid on regular payment dates for a fixed period of time such as one year, for example, renewing or changing the election at the end of the period. Another approach would permit the employee to elect the amount and timing of each payment; absent a specific election or request, the plan would pay nothing. Such an arrangement is, for all practical purposes, a system of unrestricted withdrawal rights.

Lifetime Payments   Once the employee's life expectancy or the joint life expectancies of the employee and his or her beneficiary are established pursuant to IRS regulations, this option operates like the fixed period option described above. It does not guarantee payments for life. Payments will cease when the period expires, even though the employee or beneficiary is still alive.

Payments can be made for life by recalculating life expectancy each year, however. The employee's life expectancy (or the joint life expectancies of the employee and/or his or her spouse) at the beginning of the payment period is divided into the employee's account balance to determine the payment for the first year. At the beginning of the second year, this life expectancy is recalculated— and, because the employee and/or spouse is a year older, it will have changed. This new life expectancy is then divided into the new account balance (last year's account balance minus the first year's payment plus investment income) to determine the payment for the second year. This process is repeated each year, and payments are, in fact, made over the employee's (and spouse's) lifetime, regardless of whether it is longer or shorter than originally expected.

An example will illustrate how this arrangement works. Under the Section 72 regulations, the single life expectancy for a 65-year-old is 20 years. An initial account balance of $300,000 would produce a first-year payment of $15,000 ($300,000 divided by 20). If the payment were made in monthly installments, and the unpaid balance earned 8 percent interest during the year, the account balance at the beginning of the second year would be $308,458. At that point, the individual's life expectancy would be 19.2 years. Dividing 19.2 into $308,458 would yield a second-year payment of $16,066. This process would be repeated each year until death.

This installment arrangement allows the employee to keep the maximum amount in the plan, earning investment income under a tax shelter for the maximum period of time. If coupled with the deferral of all payments until age 70-1/2 (when payments must commence under the minimum distribution rules), substantial assets can be accumulated. The combined effect of these two techniques is demonstrated in Exhibits 9–2 and 9–3 on the following pages. These exhibits assume that an individual retires in 1995 at age 62 with an initial account balance of $500,000 and elects to defer payments until age 70-1/2; investment income of 8 percent a year is also assumed. When payments commence, at age 70-1/2, they are made on the basis of the employee's then life expectancy and are recalculated each year based on the employee's changing life expectancy. Annual payments are shown in Exhibit 9-2.

Exhibit 9–3 shows how the employee's account balance would grow throughout his entire lifetime. From 1995 until age 70-1/2, when payments begin, the initial $500,000 almost doubles.

E X H I B I T   9–2

Annual Minimum Distribution (Account Balance $500,000 at Age 62; 8 percent interest/single life expectancy)

Age	Annual Distribution	Age	Annual Distribution
62	$ 0	79	$ 95,271
63	0	80	98,279
64	0	81	102,254
65	0	82	104,835
66	0	83	107,118
67	0	84	109,028
68	0	85	110,482
69	0	86	109,666
70	57,842*	87	108,228
71	61,546	88	106,101
72	65,523	89	103,218
73	69,615	90	97,521
74	73,897	91	91,296
75	78,366	92	84,573
76	82,318	93	77,395
77	87,110	94	68,028
78	91,186	95	59,056

*Amount paid out in following year—first payout due April 1 after age 70-1/2.

The account balance continues to grow, even though payments are being made, until it reaches a projected maximum of almost $1,000,000 at age 71—and does not drop below its original level until age 90.

The initial annual payment, at age 70-1/2, is estimated to be $57,842. This amount, too, continues to increase until it reaches a projected level of $110,482 when the employee is age 85. Thereafter, it reduces but, even at age 95, is slightly more than the initial amount.

Designing Installment Provisions   Employers who decide to make installment distributions available must make a number of decisions:

EXHIBIT 9–3

Account Balances (Under Minimum Distribution; 8 percent interest/single life expectancy)

Age	Beginning of Year Balance	Age	Beginning of Year Balance
62	$500,000	79	$952,707
63	540,000	80	933,652
64	583,200	81	910,065
65	629,856	82	880,615
66	680,244	83	846,229
67	734,664	84	806,809
68	793,437	85	762,325
69	856,912	86	712,829
70	925,465	87	660,189
71	999,502	88	604,776
72	956,637	89	547,057
73	967,645	90	487,603
74	975,441	91	429,091
75	979,579	92	372,122
76	979,579	93	317,318
77	975,627	94	265,309
78	966,567	95	218,506

- Should the installment option be offered to employees who terminate employment before meeting early retirement eligibility requirements—either at the time of termination and / or at a later time if they elect to defer payments?

- Should installment payments be made on a monthly, quarterly, or annual basis? Will payment frequency be at the employee's election? Will employees be permitted to change the frequency once payments have begun?

- What installment arrangements, if any, will be made available to a beneficiary upon the death of an active employee or terminated employee who has not yet begun to receive installments?[9]

- Once installment payments have begun, will employees be able to withdraw all or any part of their remaining funds or change the terms of the arrangement? Should they be able to make plan loans using the unpaid balance as security?

- If an employee dies before receiving the full account balance, should the remaining amount be paid in a lump sum to the beneficiary, or will payments continue under the same conditions that applied to the employee?

Annuities

When a plan provides for the distribution of annuity contracts, the joint and survivor provisions apply with respect to participants who elect the annuity. These requirements have undoubtedly discouraged employers from including an annuity option, particularly when an employee can roll over all or part of a lump sum distribution into an annuity that satisfies the IRA requirements.

Fiduciary issues also tend to discourage employers from offering annuities. The annuity marketplace is quite competitive, and obtaining the best rate—from an insurance company that is financially secure—is an important responsibility. But an employer is usually in a better position to make an appropriate selection than is an employee, and employers may feel they should assume this responsibility.

Some employers arrange for competitive bidding each time they purchase an annuity. Others enter into open-ended group annuity contracts with one or more insurers and make annuity purchases under these arrangements, relying on periodic bidding and analysis to ensure that purchase rates remain competitive.

---

9. The minimum distribution rules generally require that death benefits be fully distributed within five years of the employee's death. There is an exception if the employee's interest is payable for the beneficiary's lifetime (or a period equal to life expectancy). Under this exception, distributions must begin within one year after the employee's death, except that the employee's spouse can delay payments until the time the employee would have attained age 70-1/2.

Annuity purchases require considerable administrative effort. Apart from insurance carrier selection, employers must explain the various annuity forms that are available along with their financial implications, process the actual annuity purchase, and arrange for such items as birth-date evidence for the employee and/or any joint annuitant.

Overall, an annuity option can create administrative complexities without offering any significant advantages over lump sum and installment distributions.

QCOLAs

Chapter 2 included a brief description of the qualified cost-of-living arrangement (QCOLA), a mechanism that permits employees to purchase inflation protection for their pension benefits in the form of automatic cost-of-living adjustments.[10] Because the opportunity to purchase a QCOLA typically arises when defined contribution assets become available for distribution, the concept is explained in more detail below.

An employee can purchase a QCOLA by transferring defined contribution funds attributable to employer contributions (which includes employee elective deferrals under a CODA) to the defined benefit plan. The plan sponsor can set the price for the QCOLA in an amount that should not result in a gain or loss to the defined benefit plan, or it can set the price to include an employer subsidy.

As noted in Chapter 2, a QCOLA provides lifelong inflation protection, and it can be an attractive investment opportunity for retirees. If defined contribution assets are expected to earn 8-1/2 percent over the long term and defined benefit plan assets are expected to earn 10 percent, for example, the plan sponsor can pass the difference along to the employee at no cost to the pension plan (absent timing differences).

To illustrate, assume a 65-year-old employee is entitled to a $1,000 per month pension from the defined benefit plan. Based on the 1983-GAM mortality table and a 10 percent interest

---

10. IRC Section 415(k).

return, he or she could purchase a QCOLA equal to the CPI (limited to a maximum of 3 percent per year, as explained below, and without death benefits) for approximately $20,700. At the assumed defined contribution plan return of 8-1/2 percent, a principal sum of $24,000 would be needed to provide the same protection.

The transfer of the QCOLA purchase price into the defined benefit plan will not be subject to the annual addition limit under Section 415 if the arrangement meets certain requirements. The QCOLA:

- Must be elective, and the participant must be able to elect the QCOLA no later than the year he or she attains early retirement eligibility under the defined benefit plan or separates from service.

- Must be available to all participants on the same terms.

- May not discriminate in favor of highly compensated employees; further, key employees, as defined for the top-heavy rules, generally may not participate.[11]

- Must be based on actual cost-of-living increases after benefits commence and cannot exceed average increases determined by reference to one or more indices prescribed by the Treasury Department. (Presumably, any reasonable index may be used since the Treasury has not yet prescribed any indices.)

There can be a minimum QCOLA increase of 3 percent per year; plan sponsors can also cap the increase, for example, providing increases equal to the CPI rate, not to exceed 3 percent.

Because the QCOLA is a relatively new concept, few employers offer this option under their plans.[12] QCOLAs offer unique opportunities both for employers and employees, however, and should not be overlooked in the planning process.

---

11. See page 64 for a definition of key employees and the top-heavy rules.
12. While it is the defined benefit plan that actually offers the QCOLA option, the defined contribution plan should include a provision describing the option and authorizing the transfer of funds.

IN-SERVICE WITHDRAWALS

Legal requirements governing in-service withdrawals are summarized in Chapter 4. In the plan design context, two points are worth repeating: different tax law requirements govern withdrawals of different types of contributions, and in-service distributions before age 59-1/2 may be subject to the 10 percent early distribution tax.

The first question a plan sponsor needs to address in considering in-service withdrawal provisions is whether such withdrawals should be permitted at all. If the accumulation of funds for retirement is a primary plan objective, withdrawal provisions could be counterproductive. On the other hand, employees may choose not to participate in the plan if they have no access to their money. A loan provision could solve the latter problem and may even obviate the need for a withdrawal provision.

As a practical matter, withdrawals from a plan that permits only elective deferrals and QMACs or safe harbor contributions would be so restricted that there would be little or no value in permitting them. When a plan permits aftertax employee contributions, and when matching employer contributions are not safe harbor contributions or are not converted to QMACs, the plan sponsor has a fair amount of flexibility in structuring withdrawal provisions.

If hardship withdrawals of elective deferrals are to be permitted, the plan sponsor must decide whether to require that withdrawals meet the safe harbor requirements, facts and circumstances, or a combination of the two.[13] Reliance on the safe harbors will still require the plan sponsor to make reasonable efforts to ascertain that employee representations are accurate. Withdrawals that fall outside the safe harbors will require careful evaluation and documentation to assure that distributions are made only in the case of true hardships.

Employers must also take two other factors into account: the basis recovery rules that apply to aftertax employee contributions and possible grandfather protection for pre-1987 contributions.[14]

---

13. See Chapter 4. Hardship withdrawals of aftertax employee contributions and matching employer contributions are not subject to the same stringent requirements.
14. These rules are discussed in Chapter 6.

The issue of whether to establish separate contracts for basis recovery purposes can have a significant impact on plan accounting and reporting procedures and on the incidence and amount of taxes paid by employees.

Establishing Contracts

As noted in Chapter 6, the IRC permits employee contributions (and earnings) to be treated as held under a separate contract from other contributions held under the plan (e.g., as employer contributions). If established, such a separate contract may consist of all aftertax contributions or only post-1986 aftertax contributions.[15] This gives plan sponsors three general options for establishing contracts in a plan:

- **Option 1: One contract.** There is no separate contract for employee contributions; the plan consists of only a single contract in which all contributions and associated earnings are held.

- **Option 2: Two contracts.** Pre-1987 and post-1986 employee aftertax contributions and associated earnings are held in a separate contract; all other plan contributions and earnings are held in the other contract.

- **Option 3: Two contracts.** There is a separate contract for only post-1986 aftertax employee contributions and earnings; the other contract contains all other plan contributions and earnings, including pre-1987 employee contributions and earnings. This option has been called the fresh start approach.

The following example shows how taxation would be determined under each of the three options.

Assume that an employee begins participating in a CODA on January 1, 1986. The plan permits the withdrawal of aftertax contributions as of May 6, 1986; employer contributions are fully vested. The employee withdraws $2,500 at a time when his account balance consists of the following:

---

15. IRS Notices 87-13 and 89-25.

Year	Employee Contributions	Earnings	Employer Contributions	Earnings	Total
Pre-87	$1,000	$200	$2,000	$400	$ 3,600
Post-86	5,000	500	2,000	200	7,700
Total	6,000	700	4,000	600	11,300

Under Option 1, all contributions and earnings are contained in a single contract. Because that contract holds pre-1987 aftertax contributions, the $2,500 withdrawal request would first be satisfied by the return of the $1,000 (grandfathered) aftertax contributions. Of the remaining $1,500, $728 would be treated as a return of post-1986 aftertax contributions based on the following calculation:

$$\$1,500 \times \frac{\$5,000 \text{ (post-1986 employee contributions)}}{\$10,000 \text{ (total contract vested value)}}$$

Under Option 2, aftertax contributions—both pre-1987 and post-1986—are contained in a separate contract; employer contributions and their earnings are in the other contract. The plan would provide that withdrawals would first be charged against that separate contract. Thus, the $2,500 withdrawal request would first be satisfied by the return of the $1,000 (grandfathered) aftertax contributions. Of the remaining $1,500, $1,316 would be treated as a return of post-1986 aftertax contributions based on the following calculation:

$$\$1,500 \times \frac{\$5,000 \text{ (post-1986 employee contributions)}}{\$5,700 \text{ (total separate contract vested value)}}$$

Under Option 3—the fresh start approach—a separate contract is established for post-1986 aftertax contributions and earnings only (Contract A); the other contract (Contract B) contains all other contributions and earnings, including the pre-87 aftertax contributions. Under this approach, the plan provides that a withdrawal will be charged against the plan contracts in the following order:

- First from Contract B (containing the grandfathered pre-1987 employee contributions), up to the amount of such contributions. This amount will be entirely tax-free.

- Next from Contract A (containing post-1986 employee contributions and earnings), up to the full value of the contract. A portion of this amount will be tax-free.

- Then back to Contract B for the remainder of the withdrawal request. This amount will be fully taxable.

Following this order—as with Options 1 and 2—the $2,500 withdrawal is first satisfied by the return of $1,000 of pre-1987 aftertax contributions. Of the $1,500 that remains, $1,364 would be treated as a return of post-1986 aftertax contributions based on the following calculation:

$$\$1,500 \times \frac{\$5,000 \text{ (post-1986 employee contributions)}}{\$5,500 \text{ (total separate contract vested value)}}$$

As can be seen from this example, the fresh start approach produces the best short-term tax result; the participant pays the least amount of taxes on the $2,500 withdrawal.

Because of the basis recovery rules, the way a distribution will be treated for tax purposes may be at odds with employee perceptions and expectations. For example, if a plan permits withdrawals of aftertax employee contributions only, without investment earnings, employees might think they are receiving amounts on which they have already paid tax, and that no further taxes are due. Some part of such a distribution could be taxable, however, so careful employee communications are essential.

Additional issues in designing withdrawal provisions include the following:

- When should employees be permitted to make withdrawals? As of any valuation date in the year? As of only one valuation date?

- How frequently should withdrawals be permitted? Once in a plan year? At any time, but only once in a specific period such as 12 or 24 months?

- If the withdrawal provision calls for more frequent valuation dates for plan investments than would otherwise be necessary, are the additional valuation costs acceptable?
- Should there be a minimum withdrawal such as $500? A maximum?
- Should some penalty be imposed on employees who make withdrawals—for example, suspension from participation for a period of time such as six months?[16] (Such penalties could discourage employees from making withdrawals—particularly if loans are available.)

In general, the more flexible the withdrawal provision, the more attractive it will be to employees and the more complex it will be to administer.

Exhibit 9–4 summarizes withdrawal provisions in 596 savings plan CODAs in the EBIC database.

E X H I B I T   9–4

Summary of Withdrawal Provisions

| | | Number of Plans Permitting Withdrawals for Reasons Shown | | |
Source of Funds	Plans With These Funds	Hardship	Age 59-1/2	Regular In-Service Withdrawals
Aftertax contributions	356	347	350	341
Elective deferrals	596	550	573	N/A
Matching contributions	526	363	396	281

---

16. Such penalties are commonly found in savings plans that have been in existence for many years. At one time, the doctrine of constructive receipt applied to qualified plans. Under this doctrine, if an employee could freely withdraw taxable funds and without penalty, he or she could be in constructive receipt of the total amount available. To avoid this result, penalties were imposed, the most common one being a suspension of participation. This doctrine no longer applies to qualified plans and suspensions of this type are no longer necessary to avoid constructive receipt.

LOANS

Because of the restrictions and complexities associated with withdrawals, and the fact that withdrawals may defeat long-term employer objectives, many plans make funds available to employees through plan loans. Loans are permitted in 466 of the 596 savings plan CODAs in the Towers Perrin Employee Benefit Information Center.

As noted in Chapter 3, both the IRC and ERISA exempt loans from the prohibited transaction rules and antiassignment and alienation prohibitions if certain conditions are met.[17] These and the other legal requirements that govern the design of plan loan provisions are summarized below.

Loan Availability

In general, loans must be available to participants and beneficiaries on a reasonably equivalent basis. To satisfy this requirement: (1) loans must be available without regard to race, color, religion, sex, age, or national origin; (2) only factors that would be considered by a commercial lender making similar types of loans may be taken into account; and (3) loans may not be unreasonably withheld from any applicant in actual practice.

In addition, loans cannot be made available to HCEs in an amount greater than the amount made available to NHCEs, and they must be made in accordance with specific plan provisions.

Overall, the loan must create a bona fide debtor-creditor relationship between the plan and the borrower. This requires, among other things, a complete set of documents, including an application, a promissory note, a security agreement, an amortization schedule, and a truth-in-lending statement.

Plan sponsors have several decisions to make in structuring plan loan provisions. As a threshold matter, they must decide how they will characterize loans. Some companies consider loans to be investments made by the plan's fixed income fund and treat interest paid by employees as part of that fund's overall interest income. The more common approach is to view the loan as having been made from the employee's own account and to credit interest

---

17. IRC Section 4975(d)(1) and ERISA Section 408(b)(1) DOL Reg. Section 2550.408b-1 applies for purposes of the Code and ERISA.

to that account. In the latter case, the sponsor must decide whether the loan may be made from one investment account only or on a pro rata basis from all accounts in which the employee's funds are invested or on some other basis, such as a hierarchy of funds. If loans are made from a single account, the sponsor must also decide whether the employee may choose the account and/or whether the employee must transfer funds from other accounts to the account from which the loan is to be made.

Another consideration is whether to set a minimum loan amount. (Maximum loan amounts are discussed in Tax Constraints, below.) The law permits plans to set a minimum loan amount of $1,000, to charge a service fee to an employee who applies for a loan and—as noted above—to restrict the accounts from which loans are made. Minimum loan amounts and service fees are often used in an effort to reduce administrative involvement and expenses.

Provisions of this kind will not be allowed if they result in loans being made on a discriminatory basis, however.

The plan loan provision should also consider the question of how often loans can be made and the number of loans that a participant may have outstanding at any one time. Some plans limit employees to one loan outstanding at any one time. Others limit employees to making one loan in any plan year or in any 12-month period. Some plans permit loans at any time, but limit the number of outstanding loans to some number such as two or three. Still other plans use both limitations—not more than a given number of loans in a specified period and not more than a specified number outstanding at any one time. And some plans have no restrictions at all other than those that are imposed by law (e.g., the maximum amount that can be borrowed and outstanding at any time). The decision as to how this provision is to be structured will be influenced by administrative considerations. And, of course, any provision of this type should not result in loans being made on a discriminatory basis.

Some plans also limit the amount of a loan with reference to the participant's compensation and his or her ability to make repayments. The reason for such a provision, of course, is that the probabilities (and problems) of defaults are increased if loans are allowed on a basis that requires repayments the participant might find burdensome. If such a provision is included in a plan, particular care must be taken to assure that it is applied in a non-discriminatory fashion.

The DOL has taken the position that loans must be offered to parties in interest, including inactive as well as active employees—for example, employees on disability, layoff, or leave of absence, whether paid or unpaid. DOL regulations permit loans to inactive employees to be made on terms and conditions that are different from those offered to active employees, however, provided those terms and conditions are based solely on factors considered by commercial lenders (e.g., a higher application fee to cover the additional costs associated with approving applications and collecting repayments from inactive employees.)[18]

Tax Constraints

The IRC considers loans to be taxable distributions unless they meet four basic requirements.[19] The first is a limit on the amount that may be borrowed and outstanding at any time. As a general rule, a loan cannot exceed the *lesser* of these two amounts:

- $50,000, reduced by the excess, if any, of the highest outstanding loan balance that the employee had during the 12-month period ending on the day before the loan was made over his or her actual outstanding loan balance on the day the loan was made, or
- The greater of 50 percent of the employee's vested account balance or $10,000.

The $10,000 limit is not workable in practice, because it comes into play only if it exceeds 50 percent of the individual's vested account balance; in such cases the loan would not be adequately

---

18. To satisfy fiduciary obligations, the plan administrator should, at a minimum, establish procedures to ensure that inactive employees have a source of income from which to repay a loan. Special repayment and monitoring procedures may also be necessary because the potential for default could be far greater for this group.
19. IRC Section 72(p)(1); IRS Prop. Reg. 1.72(p)-1.

secured (see below) and would be a prohibited transaction (unless the plan takes outside collateral).[20]

The second requirement limits the loan repayment period to five years unless loan proceeds are used to purchase the employee's primary residence. If the original term of the loan is more than five years (except for certain home loans), the loan will be treated as a taxable distribution even though it is in fact repaid in less than five years. If the repayment period is extended beyond five years, the outstanding balance at the time of extension will be treated as a distribution at that time. If the loan is not repaid by the end of the five-year period, the outstanding balance will be treated as a distribution.

The five-year requirement does not apply to a loan used to acquire any dwelling that is to be used within a reasonable time as the participant's principal residence. Plan loans to improve an existing residence, purchase a second home, or finance the purchase of a home or home improvements for other members of the participant's family are subject to the five-year rule.

Under the third requirement, the loan must be repaid in substantially level payments, no less frequently than quarterly.

Level amortization is not required when an employee is on an unpaid leave of up to one year. Upon resumption of employment, the loan must be repaid over the remaining loan period, either with increased amortization or at the old amortization rates with a final payment that liquidates the loan at the end of the period. Further, the requirement does not preclude prepayments or acceleration or the use of a variable interest rate.

The fourth requirement is that the loan be evidenced by a legally enforceable agreement setting forth the amount, term, and repayment schedule of the loan.

A taxable distribution is deemed to have occurred if any of these requirements are not met. If the loan exceeds the statutory maximum, the amount of the loan that is considered to be taxable is the excess of the actual loan over the maximum permissible amount, and this will be considered to have occurred on the date

---

20. The DOL has taken the position that the loan cannot exceed 50 percent of the employee's vested account balance. Because of this conflict between the DOL and the IRS, most plans have limited the available amount to 50 percent of the employee's account balance and no longer include the $10,000 minimum. Note, however, that the loan could be secured by outside collateral, in which case the IRS maximums could be used.

the loan is made. Failure to meet any of the other requirements results in the full amount of the loan being deemed a taxable distribution at the time the loan is made.

Even if all of these requirements have been met, failure to make repayments in accordance with the terms of the loan could result in the outstanding balance of the loan being considered a taxable distribution at the time of repayment failure. The plan may allow a grace period for making up missed payments before this penalty is invoked; this grace period may extend until the end of the calendar quarter following the quarter in the payment was missed.

Interest Rates

DOL regulations state that the interest rate on plan loans must provide the plan with a return commensurate with the prevailing rate charged on similar loans by persons in the business of lending money. This has proven somewhat controversial. The DOL believes loans are plan investments and as such are subject to the same fiduciary standards as any other investments made by the plan. Most loan programs are structured so that the employee borrows directly from his or her own account and repays principal and interest directly back to that account, however; thus, in practice, the employee is the only one affected by a lower-than-prevailing interest rate.

The regulations recognize a difference between national and regional plans. If a plan is administered on a nationwide basis, the employer can choose between a national rate and regional rates. Regional plans must use regional rates.

One possible approach is use of a passbook interest plus rate that many banks offer to their savings account or certificate of deposit (CD) customers—the passbook or CD rate plus additional points, with the loans secured by the savings account or CD. Because these loans can be immediately foreclosed on default, however, they are not similar to all loans made under a CODA (e.g., CODA loans secured by elective deferrals). Thus, a passbook rate may not be acceptable in all situations.

Many employers use either the prime rate, or the prime rate plus one or two percentage points, as a benchmark. But employers should consult with a commercial lender before establishing a rate, taking into account all factors that would be considered in a commercial lending context. These would include, for example, whether different rates should be set for loans of differing durations, whether the rate will be fixed for the entire period of the loan and, if so, how this would affect the rate as compared with the rate for variable interest loans. Exhibit 9–5 summarizes the interest rate provisions of the 466 savings plan CODAs in the Towers Perrin Employee Benefit Information Center that include loan provisions.

The interest rate charged must be reasonable at the time the loan is made or renewed. Thus, the employer should review and, if necessary, adjust the rate as often as loans are made—quarterly or monthly, for example.

Adequate Security

All plan loans must be adequately secured. This will be the case if the security is something in addition to and supporting the promise to pay and has value and liquidity such that it may be reasonably anticipated that no loss of interest or principal will result. In this regard, the employee is generally required to execute a promissory note and collateral security agreement.

When a participant's vested accrued benefit is used as security, as is usually the case, no more than 50 percent of the value of such benefit can be considered as security for the outstanding balance of all plan loans.

EXHIBIT 9–5

Loan Interest Rate Provisions

Interest Rate Charged	Number of Plans Reporting
Prime rate	121
Prime rate + .5%	13
Prime rate + 1%	195
Prime rate + 2%	41
Fixed rate	21
Local commercial lending rates	36
Credit union rate	8
Other	31

DOL regulations do not require enforcement of the plan's security interest at any particular time after a loan default, provided that no loss of principal or income will occur due to a delay in enforcement. Thus, loans secured by elective deferrals (which generally cannot be distributed prior to termination of employment) are permissible.

Default and Collection

Loan default conditions that require immediate repayment in full typically include: (1) failure to make any repayment when due; (2) bankruptcy or insolvency; and (3) termination of employment.

Plan fiduciaries generally have the same duty of collection for participant loans as they do for other plan assets. Thus, plan sponsors must decide what action the plan will take in the event of a default resulting from missed payments. (Requiring repayments through payroll deduction should minimize the likelihood of in-service defaults.) They also need to establish the circumstances in which a participant who has defaulted will be allowed to make up the missed payments. If the plan is intended to provide postretirement benefits, make-up procedures are probably in order.

The distribution of a participant's account balance in the event of a default may not be made a matter of discretion. Plans should include express provisions specifying when distributions arising from the execution of the plan's security interest in the participant's account will occur. A defaulted loan cannot be charged directly to the participant's vested account unless funds could be made available to the participant while employed; that is, the loan cannot be charged to amounts subject to in-service withdrawal restrictions. To do otherwise would constitute a premature distribution and could cause plan and/or CODA disqualification.

Plan Provisions

The DOL regulations set forth seven items that must be included either in the plan document or a written document forming part of the plan. These are:

- The identity of the person or positions authorized to administer the loan program.

- The loan application procedure.
- The basis for approving or denying loans.
- Any limitations on the types or amounts of loans.
- The procedure for determining a reasonable interest rate.
- The types of collateral that may be used as security.
- The events constituting a default and the steps that will be taken to preserve plan assets in the event of a default.

In many cases, employers will opt to include these provisions in a separate document such as an SPD. Additional information may have to be included as necessary to provide an adequate description.

Truth in Lending

Plans may be subject to the Federal Truth-in-Lending Act and Regulation Z if loans:[21]

- Are offered or extended to consumers.
- Are made regularly (i.e., more than 25 times in the preceding or current calendar year).
- Bear interest and are payable by written agreement in more than four installments.
- Are primarily for personal, family, or household purposes.

Loans in excess of $25,000 are not covered unless secured by a home.

If a plan is subject to these requirements, participants must be provided with a disclosure statement setting forth, among other things: (1) the amount of the loan; (2) the number and amount of payments; (3) the cost of credit as a yearly percentage rate; (4) the amount of interest and any other charges; and (5) the total amount paid after all scheduled payments have been made.

The Act also requires that borrowers be notified of their right to cancel transactions without penalty under certain circumstances. Violators are subject to criminal penalties and civil liability.

---

21. 15 U.S.C., Section 1601, et seq., and 12 C.F.R., Section 226.1 et seq.

Equal Credit Opportunity

Plan loans are potentially subject to the Equal Credit Opportunity Act and Regulation B, which prohibit discrimination in the granting of credit on the basis of, among other things, age, marital status, religion, sex, race, or national origin.[22] These requirements are consistent with the reasonably equivalent basis requirements of the DOL regulations.

State Laws

ERISA generally supersedes laws insofar as they relate to employee benefit plans. State insurance, banking, and securities laws are not preempted, however. Thus, even though a benefit plan is not deemed to be a bank, insurer, trust company, or investment company, it could be subject to such laws to the extent they are applicable to other persons.

In addition, ERISA does not preempt generally applicable state criminal laws. Thus, some state usury laws, confession of judgment restrictions, wage payment laws (e.g., laws that prohibit the deduction of loan repayments from wages without the employee's consent), and plain language document requirements may apply to a plan's loan program. Such determinations must be made on a case-by-case, state-by-state basis.

---

22. 15 U.S.C., Section 1691-1691f, and 12 C.F.R., Section 202.1 et seq.

CHAPTER 10

Plan Design— Miscellaneous Plan Provisions

This chapter includes a brief discussion of provisions relating to: (1) determination of service; (2) minimum participation requirements; (3) the plan committee and trustee; (4) fiduciary requirements; (5) amendment and termination of the plan; (6) additional tax requirements; and (7) miscellaneous administrative provisions such as facility of payment authority and treatment of leaves of absence.

DETERMINATION OF SERVICE

The rules for determining an employee's service for various purposes are described in Chapter 3.[1] In brief, the law specifies how service is to be determined for purposes of eligibility to participate, vesting, and eligibility for a benefit accrual. An employer can determine service for other purposes, such as eligibility for early retirement, on any basis it chooses, so long as it does not discriminate in favor of HCEs. As a practical matter, most employers choose to use the same definition of service for all plan purposes.

The first decision an employer must make is which compliance method to use—actual hours counting, an equivalency, or elapsed time—and whether the same method will be used for all

---

1. See discussion beginning on page 58.

employees and for all plan purposes. Actual hours counting works well for hourly, nonexempt employees and part-time employees. The same cannot be said for exempt employees; because they do not normally keep records of actual hours worked, the plan sponsor will need to establish special recordkeeping systems or procedures if it wants to use actual hours counting.

Many employers use either elapsed time or one of the time-period equivalencies for all employees, monthly or weekly time periods being the most common. Elapsed time is the simplest method to administer and the easiest to explain and communicate to employees. Alternatively, some employers will decouple their service counting methods, using hours counting for those employees whose hours are recorded and using an elapsed time or equivalency method for everyone else.

A plan's service counting provisions should define what constitutes an hour of service, establish the computation periods that will be used for all plan purposes, and address breaks in service, including maternity/paternity, family and military leaves. A plan that does not provide for full and immediate vesting must define the extent to which service will *not* be counted for vesting, such as service before age 18 or before the plan was in effect.

MINIMUM PARTICIPATION REQUIREMENTS

A plan sponsor must also determine whether to require that employees reach a minimum age and/or complete some period of service before they can participate in the plan. Such requirements cut down on the administrative costs associated with terminations that occur during the first year or so of employment and at younger ages. Further, additional benefit costs associated with full or partial vesting of employer contributions can be reduced if employees are required to complete at least one year of service and/or attain age 21 before they are eligible to participate.

Participation requirements may also help the plan pass the ADP/ACP tests. If very young and short-service employees do not make elective deferrals to the same extent as older employees, which is usually the case, the younger group will pull down the ADP for the NHCE group. (Remember, however, that beginning with the 1999 plan year, the ADP test can be performed by excluding NHCEs who participate in the plan before attaining age 21 and completing one year of service, provided this group separately satisfies the section 410(b) minimum coverage requirements.) On the other hand, if there is reason to believe participation rates will be high, allowing them to participate as soon as possible may have a beneficial effect on test results.

An eligible employee can usually begin participation at the beginning of any pay period that coincides with or follows the date on which participation requirements have been met, although some plans have limited entry dates (e.g., quarterly or semiannually). The combination of participation requirements and entry dates cannot result in deferring participation more than six months beyond the date that service and/or age requirements are met, or later than the first day of the plan year following such date, whichever is earlier.

COMMITTEE PROVISIONS

The CODA plan document should specify the administrative powers, responsibilities, and composition of the plan committee, including the number of members, how they are appointed and removed (e.g., by action of the board of directors), and their term of office.

The committee is usually given the full power to administer the plan and to construe and apply all of its provisions. More specifically, its powers typically include the following: (1) appointing agents; (2) resolving disputes with regard to the rights of employees, participants, and beneficiaries; (3) compiling and maintaining all plan records; (4) authorizing the trustee to make benefit payments; (5) retaining legal, administrative, consulting, investment, accounting, and other professional services; (6) adopting and promulgating rules for plan administration; and (7) interpreting and approving QDROs.

The plan document should spell out how the committee takes action (e.g., by majority vote at a meeting at which a quorum is present) and should give the committee the authority to designate one of its members to sign on behalf of all members in ministerial matters. Plans typically bar a member from voting or in any way acting on matters that solely involve his or her own participation.

A common provision states that committee members will not receive compensation for their services, but that the employer will pay all committee expenses such as legal and other fees. Another common provision states that the employer will indemnify the committee members from liability unless liability arises from their own willful misconduct or gross negligence.

TRUSTEE PROVISIONS

Most plan sponsors establish a trust to receive, hold, and invest funds, and to disburse benefit payments from a CODA.[2] The plan document is usually separate from the trust agreement and makes only limited references to the trustee and the trust arrangement. The trust agreement is between the employer and trustee and usually contains provisions regarding: (1) the irrevocable nature of employer contributions and the nondiversion of plan assets; (2) the investment powers of the trustee; (3) the duties and responsibilities of the trustee with respect to directions received by appointed investment managers; (4) the allocation of fiduciary responsibilities; (5) the payment of legal, trustee, and other fees; (6) periodic reports to the employer to be prepared by the trustee; (7) the records and accounts to be maintained by the trustee; (8) the conditions for the removal or resignation of a trustee and the appointment of a successor; (9) the payment of benefits under the plan; (10) the rights and duties of the trustee in case of amendment or termination of the plan; and (11) the right of the trustee to rely on directions and information from the committee.

FIDUCIARY PROVISIONS

Both the plan document and the trust agreement should clearly specify how fiduciary duties are to be allocated among the employer, the committee, the trustee, and any other fiduciary involved (e.g., an insurance company). The plan should also specify a named fiduciary (usually the employer and the committee), a procedure for establishing and carrying out a funding policy, and

---

2. Fully insured plans, where all funds are held by an insurance company, need not be trusteed.

the way payments are to be made to and from the plan. Further, it is generally desirable to include a specific provision permitting the delegation of fiduciary responsibilities to the extent permitted by law.

PLAN TERMINATION

The law requires that a plan be permanent (i.e., established with the intention that it continue on an indefinite basis). This does not preclude plan termination if termination is warranted for a reason such as business necessity.

A well-constructed plan will clearly reserve the employer's right to terminate the plan—usually by action of its board of directors for any reason whatsoever. A termination provision should also make it clear that:

- The rights of participants to their account balances will in no way be adversely affected by the termination.

- All benefits accrued up to the time of termination will be fully vested in all participants, regardless of length of service.

- Benefits will be distributed or made available to participants in accordance with the provisions of the law.

PLAN AMENDMENTS

Another important plan provision gives the employer the right to amend the plan at any time and for any reason. Amendments are usually made by action of the board of directors, though some plans empower the committee (or officers of the employer) to make amendments of a nonsubstantive nature.

The plan should clearly state that no amendment will deprive an employee of his or her rights to the extent protected by the law. Further, if the plan's vesting provisions are made less liberal, the vesting rights of any employee with at least three years of service must be protected under the prior vesting arrangement—for both prior and future accruals.

TAX REQUIREMENTS: A CHECKLIST

Tax law requirements have been covered in detail in earlier chapters. The following summary will serve as a checklist in the context of the plan document:

- Nondiversion/Exclusive Benefit Rules: The document should make it clear that the plan is for the exclusive benefit of employees and their beneficiaries, and that no part of the funds may be diverted to or recaptured by the employer prior to the satisfaction of all plan liabilities. The plan document should also cover the circumstances permitting the return of employer contributions described in Chapter 3.

- Definition of HCEs: The plan should define who is an HCE.

- Joint and Survivor Requirements: The plan should include joint and survivor provisions if it offers an annuity option, if it does not provide that an employee's spouse is the automatic beneficiary of 100 percent of the employee's account balance unless another beneficiary is designated with spousal consent, or if it is a transferee of monies that are subject to the joint and survivor annuity rules.

- Separate Accounts: Defined contribution plans must establish and maintain individual accounts for each participant, as well as subaccounts for different types of contributions. Separate accounts may also be necessary in special situations, as when the employer wants to deduct dividends passed through a leveraged ESOP.

- ADP/ACP Tests: Plan documentation should spell out how these tests will be applied, how ADPs and ACPs for HCEs will be adjusted if necessary to pass the tests, and how excess contributions will be handled.

- Individual Limits: The Section 415 limit, the compensation limit, and the elective deferral limit should be included as plan provisions, although the plan may incorporate the Section 415 limit by reference. The plan should also specify how contributions that exceed the elective deferral limit are to be treated.

- Leased Employees: The definition of employee should include leased employees and their treatment, for example, how service is to be counted for vesting.

- Section 72 Contracts: Plans that include aftertax employee contributions and permit in-service withdrawals must specify how many contracts will be established for purposes of the basis recovery rules under Section 72 of the IRC.

- Top-Heavy Provisions: Even though a plan may never become top-heavy, it should include provisions to cover this contingency. These provisions should describe the conditions that might make the plan top-heavy, define key employees, and specify the consequences of top-heavy status, that is, minimum contributions for nonkey employees, more rapid vesting, and (possibly) lower combined limits under Section 415.

- ESOPs: If part of the plan is an ESOP, the plan must so state. In addition, the document should include the special rules applicable to ESOPs (e.g., the participant's right to diversify investments and pass-through voting rights).

- Distributions: The plan should spell out the distribution rules described in Chapter 3. It should also include provisions on when distributions will commence absent a specific participant election, the forms of distribution that are available, and the right of a participant to defer distribution. In the case of an ESOP, the employee's right to demand payments must also be included.

- Assignments/QDROs: The plan must state that an employee's interests are not assignable. Exceptions are permitted for: (1) revocable assignments of up to 10 percent of benefit payments; (2) use of up to 50 percent of an employee's account balance as collateral security for a plan loan; and (3) qualified domestic relations orders (QDROs). The plan should include a provision stating that it will comply with the terms of a QDRO.

- Rollovers/Direct Transfers: The plan must provide that if a distributee so requests, a plan distribution otherwise eligible for rollover treatment will be transferred directly to an IRA or to another employer's qualified plan.

MISCELLANEOUS ADMINISTRATIVE PROVISIONS

Administrative provisions should also be incorporated into the plan document. A brief discussion of some of the more important of these provisions follows.

Valuation Dates

The plan (and the trust agreement) should identify specific dates during the plan year on which plan assets will be valued.[3] These dates are important for determining the value of a participant's account for such purposes as in-service withdrawals, loans, distributions on severance of employment, and investment changes. Frequent valuation dates permit more flexibility in plan design, but they also increase administrative costs unless assets are held under some easily valued arrangement such as a mutual fund. Monthly valuation dates are common, though some large plans use daily valuations.

Voting Rights/Tender Offers

When employer stock is a plan investment option, employees typically have pass-through voting rights and the right to vote on tender offers; pass-through voting is mandatory in an ESOP. A typical voting provision allows employees to direct the trustee to vote the total number of shares allocated to their accounts. The plan should also specify how shares are to be voted in the absence of participant direction and, in the case of an ESOP, when shares are unallocated. These shares are typically voted in the same proportion as the shares for which directions have been received.

Leaves of Absence

A well-designed plan will include a provision governing leaves of absence for disability, military service, maternity/paternity, or personal reasons. The provision must comply with any legal requirements such as the minimum number of hours credited for maternity/paternity leaves or the service spanning rules under the elapsed time method of crediting service. Leaves that come within

---

3. See Chapter 12.

the purview of the Family and Medical Leave Act (FMLA) must be treated by the plan in the same way as other forms of leave. Military leaves must be handled in a fashion that complies with the Uniformed Employment and Reemployment Rights Act of 1996 (USERRA).[4]

Additional issues include the following:

- Will paid and unpaid leaves be treated differently for plan purposes?
- Should the plan permit mandatory and/or voluntary contributions during a paid leave? Should aftertax contributions be permitted during an unpaid leave? If so, how will they be collected?
- Will any employer contributions be made on behalf of an employee who is on leave? If mandatory contributions are permitted, will the employer matching contribution be made? In a profit-sharing CODA, will an employee on leave be entitled to a contribution for the period he or she is absent?
- How will the leave be treated (over and above any legal requirements) for crediting service for vesting and other plan purposes?
- Will the leave be treated as an event permitting distribution of the employee's account (e.g., if the employee is on disability leave)?
- Should the employee be allowed to withdraw funds or change investment options while on leave?[5]

Certain qualification requirements (e.g., the Section 415 limits and nondiscrimination requirements) and other legal requirements (e.g., FMLA and USERRA) must be considered when determining how the leave of absence provision will be structured. Other major factors to be taken into account are administrative considerations and the employer's overall human resource policies.

Facility of Payment Provision

A provision that permits the committee or plan administrator to distribute an individual's account when the payee is legally incom-

---

4. See discussion beginning on page 162.
5. Plans with loan provisions must permit employees who are on leave to make loans.

petent to receive payment (e.g., a minor or a person who is physically or mentally disabled) facilitates plan administration. The customary provision allows payment to the payee's guardian or committee or, in the absence of any guardian or committee, to any person or institution that is maintaining or has custody of the individual. A provision protecting the plan committee or administrator in making a good faith payment under these circumstances is advisable.

Missing Persons

Another helpful provision provides for the forfeiture of a benefit if the committee or plan administrator cannot locate the participant or beneficiary after reasonable and diligent efforts. A typical provision would provide for forfeiture after five years and would provide for reinstatement, without interest, if the payee later appears and files a claim.

Claims Procedures

The plan should set forth specific claims procedures, including an appeal process.[6]

Beneficiary Provisions

The plan should provide that the employee's spouse is the beneficiary for the full amount of the employee's account balance unless the spouse consents in writing to another designation or unless the plan is made subject to the joint and survivor requirements. Otherwise, the plan should spell out how a beneficiary is named or changed, and when a designation or change becomes effective (e.g., when filed with the plan committee at a specific location). It should also specify what will happen if the employee dies before the change has been properly filed (i.e., that the change will be effective even though it is filed after the employee's death). But the plan should also be protected if it has made any good faith payment to a previously designated beneficiary before the change was received. In the absence of a valid designation, the plan should

---

6. See Chapter 7, page 152.

provide that payment may be made to the employee's estate or to one or more of a designated class of survivors (e.g., the employee's spouse, children, parents).

Rollover Contributions

Many plans permit employees to roll amounts over into the plan from other qualified plans. A common provision allows such transfers if made directly from the plan of the employee's former employer. If the rollover contribution is made by the employee or is transferred from an IRA, the customary plan provisions require that these conditions be met:

- The rollover is in cash.
- The rollover does not include any employee contributions.
- The former employer provides a letter stating that the distribution that gave rise to the rollover was from a plan qualified under Section 401(a) of the IRC and that the distribution was made on account of severance of employment.
- The employee states in writing that the contribution was or will be made within the time allowed under the law (60 days), and that to the best of his or her knowledge, it meets all IRC requirements for rollover treatment.

These requirements are important because the employer's plan risks disqualification in certain circumstances if the rollover contribution is not properly made. The plan will have to account for rollover contributions separately, and rollovers will, of course, be fully vested at all times.

Voluntary Plan

A commonly used plan provision states that the plan is a voluntary undertaking on the part of the employer and that the creation of the plan or any benefit thereunder does not give the employee or any other person: (1) any legal or equitable right against the employer or any other fiduciary (other than those rights specifically conferred by the plan), and (2) any right to be retained in the employment of the employer. The provision usually includes a further statement to the effect that the existence of the plan does not interfere with the employer's rights to discharge employees for any legally acceptable reason.

Governing State

It is customary to provide that a plan will be construed and interpreted according to the laws of a specific state—usually the state where the employer has its primary location—except to the extent preempted by ERISA.

Investing Plan Assets–
Basic Principles

Both employers and employees have a vital stake in plan investment provisions. The employer is responsible for structuring appropriate investment programs, selecting suitable investment managers, monitoring manager performance and communicating crucial investment information to employees. In the typical plan, employees are responsible for deciding how to invest their account balances and they assume all of the risks associated with investment performance. Both employers and employees must have a sound understanding of basic investment principles if they are to succeed in fulfilling their respective responsibilities.

The benefits of a successful investment program include, for the employer, low cost fees and ease of administration, flexibility to make needed changes to investment provisions, and improved recognition of the company as a source of valuable benefits. For employees, a well-executed investment program maximizes capital accumulation through increased participation, improved returns, and lower costs.

This chapter begins with a brief discussion of the basic investment concepts of risk and return, followed by a summary of the most common investment options available today.

RISK AND RETURN

It is a fundamental assumption in investment literature that investors are basically risk averse—if two investment alternatives offer the same expected rate of return, the investor will choose the less risky of the two options. In reality, there is little likelihood that a less risky asset will offer the same return as a more risky asset; the market will price the two options relative to their perceived risk—willing to pay more for the less risky asset and thus driving down the expected returns. Thus, an investor is continually compelled to evaluate the trade-offs between risk and return when making investment choices. These trade-offs are graphically portrayed by arraying options along an efficient frontier.[1] In its simplest format, the efficient frontier can be portrayed, as illustrated in Exhibit 11–1, as various combinations of stocks and bonds along a continuum from 100% bonds to 100% stocks. Moving along the curve from the left to the right, each portfolio offers a higher potential rate of return, consistent with the higher commitment to stocks. These portfolios also entail successively higher degrees of risk, however.

E X H I B I T   11–1

Efficient Frontier

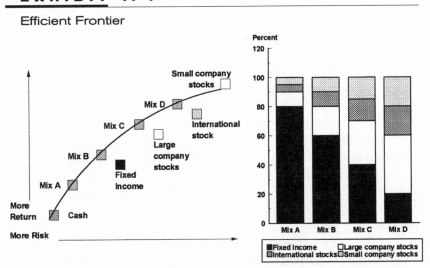

1. The efficient frontier represents sets of portfolios such that, at any point along the frontier, there is no other combination of assets that can be expected to generate a higher return without correspondingly higher risk. Each efficient portfolio has been constructed in such a way as to maximize the diversification benefits of assets that have different patterns of returns.

It should be kept in mind that more risk is not necessarily a situation to be avoided; each investor will have his or her own tolerance for risk.

Return

There are various measures of return in financial assets. For example, in bond investments, there is both the current yield and the yield to maturity, while in stock investments there is the dividend yield and the earnings yield. In order to express returns consistently across time periods and across asset classes, a total rate of return measure is commonly used. Total rate of return accounts for return derived not only from dividend or interest received during the investment period (current yield or dividend yield) but also the growth or decline in value of the underlying assets. The simplest expression of the total rate of return measure is:

$$R = \frac{\text{income payments received during the period} + }{\text{value of the portfolio at the beginning of the period}} \frac{\text{value of the portfolio at the end of the period}}{} - 1$$

References to returns that are made in the following sections, mean total rates of return.

Risk

In the professional investment community, risk is defined as the probability that a given outcome will be *different* than the expected outcome. It does not matter whether the outcome is better or worse than originally anticipated; *risk is measured as the deviation from the expectation.* To more fully understand and manage risk, professionals have divided it into two broad categories: systematic and unsystematic. These classifications help an investor understand which risks are avoidable and which are not. Systematic risks are risks common to all assets which must be endured by anyone who chooses to make investments. Examples of systematic risk include:

- **Inflation risk:** The probability that realized real rates of return will be worse (or better) than expected due to the corrosive (beneficial) effects of price inflation (deflation)

- **Interest rate risk:** The probability that returns will be better or worse than expected due to changes in the level of interest rates. For example, a rise in the general level of interest rates serves to drive bond prices lower and to raise the discount rate applied to future equity earnings, thus driving stock prices lower.
- **Market risk:** The probability that returns will be better or worse than expected because of changes in the overall levels of the markets. (When the broad stock market averages move higher, most stocks generally move higher in tandem.)

Unsystematic risks are those which are unique to the specific security to be purchased and can be categorized as follows:

- **Company risk:** Risks that are unique to the security due to management or financial structure. For example, weak sales and profits lead to a downgrading of the company's debt securities, making new financing more expensive and reducing the value of outstanding debt securities.
- **Industry risk:** Risks that are unique to a specific sector of the economy. For example, governmental initiatives on health care reform will affect all health care stocks to some degree.

Investment risk is commonly expressed as the standard deviation of return over some period of time. This statistical measure provides a gauge of the potential volatility of returns on a given investment relative to the expected, or mean, return. Exhibit 11–2 shows the standard deviations and the total range of returns to various asset classes over the past 70 years. The standard deviations reflected in the Exhibit demonstrate the relative level of systematic risk for each asset class. A different measurement period would result in different volatility and return measures, although relative rankings would not change.

Diversification

An investor will not be compensated for taking on unsystematic risk. By combining one or more assets within each asset class, the level of unsystematic risk in a portfolio can be driven close to zero.

E X H I B I T   11–2

Risk/Return Spectrum for Some Common Asset Classes
(1926–1995)*

	Average Annual Rate of Return	Standard Deviation	Range of Returns	
			Low	High
U.S. common stocks	12.5%	20.4%	-43.3%	54.0%
U.S. small company stocks	17.1%	34.4%	-58.0%	142.9%
Long-term corporate bonds	6.0%	8.7%	-8.1%	42.6%
Long-term government bonds	5.5%	9.2%	-9.2%	40.4%
Intermeditate government bonds	5.4%	5.8%	-5.1%	29.1%
U.S. Treasury bills	3.8%	3.3%	0.0%	14.7%
International stocks	15.9%	17.3%	-23.2%	69.9%

*Stocks, Bonds, Bills and Inflation (Chicago, Illinois: Ibbotson Associates, 1996).

Various studies have shown that combining as few as ten or twelve individual stocks can nearly eliminate unsystematic risk within the equity markets—where a large part of the risk is, in fact, unsystematic. This result is illustrated in Exhibit 11–3 on page 236.

In the fixed income markets, risk is largely systematic, with interest rate changes being the key determinant of returns. Thus, the benefits of adding additional securities to a fixed income portfolio are not nearly as strong as in the equity markets. By combining different asset classes (stocks and bonds, for example) with different patterns of returns and different levels of systematic risk, however, *total* portfolio risk can be further reduced.

There are other factors which an investor must consider in managing the risk of his or her portfolio. A long investment horizon has the benefit of dampening the volatility of the highest risk/ highest return asset classes. While on a quarter-to-quarter or year-to-year basis, small-capitalization equities demonstrate high volatility, those ups and downs tend to cancel each other out over longer time periods. Exhibit 11–4 (page 236) illustrates this effect on an asset with a 10 percent expected return and a 20 percent annual standard deviation over a 15-year time horizon. The upper and lower lines represent the expected annualized return of 10 percent,

Diversification of Unsystematic Risk

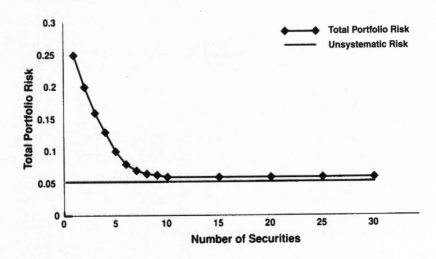

Time Horizon Effects on Volatility

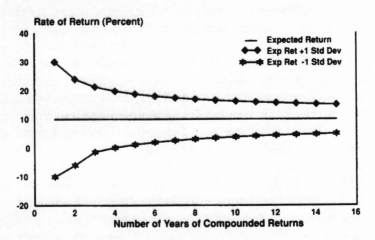

plus or minus one standard deviation. As time passes, the volatility of the compounded investment return decreases, and the likelihood of achieving a compounded return that is significantly different from the 10 percent expected return also decreases.

Tied to the issue of the available investment horizon are the liquidity constraints of the investor. Where the investor has a high probability of needing to deplete the portfolio for cash expenditures, such as with an employee nearing retirement, the risk-reducing power of compounding returns over time is diminished. Investors who need ready access to cash tend to concentrate their investments in various money market instruments, assets which are highly liquid but with lower long-term rates of return. By contrast, investors focussed on the long term growth of the portfolio are in a position to sacrifice some liquidity and invest more heavily in equity securities, seeking to maximize long-term returns.

ASSET CLASSES

Most public market assets can be classified as either debt or equity. There are certain other asset classes, such as real estate, venture capital, futures, and commodities, which do not fit cleanly within this classification scheme, but their use within the defined contribution arena is limited at best and beyond the scope of this discussion.

Equity Investments

The most prevalent types of equity investments are depicted in Exhibit 11–5.

The most prevalent equity securities are the common stocks of U.S. and international corporations. (Other equity instruments, such as warrants and appreciation rights, have a very small representation in the investment marketplace and will not be addressed in this discussion.) A share of common stock represents an ownership interest in the company, and, in the event of bankruptcy, stockholders are entitled to company assets and earnings that remain after all liabilities and debts have been satisfied. As owners, stockholders bear the main business risk—and enjoy most of the financial success over time—of the organization.

A company that issues common stock may or may not pay periodic dividends to shareholders, depending on whether the company is profitable, and whether it decides to distribute profits or to reinvest them in the business. Small, emerging companies

EXHIBIT 11-5

Types of Equity Investments

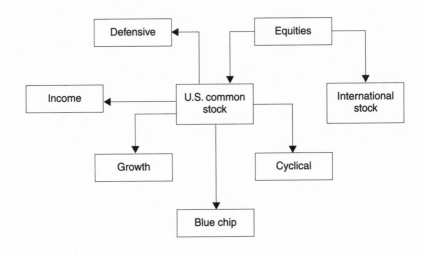

usually pay no dividends, while larger, well-established companies typically pay regular dividends.

Common stocks can also be classified as either large-cap or
small-cap stocks, depending on their market capitalization—the
number of shares outstanding multiplied by the current market
price. The most common breakpoint between large- and small-cap
stocks is a market capitalization of $1 billion, though some invest-
ment professionals use a $500 million or $250 million breakpoint.
Common stocks are either traded on established stock exchanges,
such as the New York, American, or Tokyo exchanges, or on an
electronic trading system known as the over-the-counter market.
Millions of shares of stock in large companies will typically be
traded every day, while only a few hundred shares of a small company may change hands during the same period. The prices at
which these stock trades occur are very fluid and are influenced by
a variety of factors, including the overall economic environment,
investor expectations, company-specific conditions such as earnings levels, and general stock market conditions.

U.S. common stocks may be classified as follows:

- **Blue Chip:** Stocks of well-established, market-dominating companies with a long record of dividend and earnings growth through both good and bad economic conditions.
- **Cyclical:** Stocks of companies whose business activity tends to mirror the overall fortunes of the economy. Earnings of these companies can fluctuate sharply with the business cycle. Automobile, machine tool, and heavy equipment manufacturers are examples of cyclical industries.
- **Defensive:** Stocks of companies that are viewed as relatively safe and stable, even during economic downturns. Stocks of utilities, food, and drug companies are usually considered defensive, since they are tied to products or services that are essential regardless of economic conditions.
- **Growth:** Stocks of companies whose sales and earnings are expanding faster than the economy as a whole, typically in growth industries such as drugs, biotechnology, electronics, and pollution.
- **Income:** Stocks that are primarily seen as good sources of steady and high levels of dividend income. These are typically stocks of mature companies in stable industries that pay out most of their earnings in dividends. Utility stocks fall into this category.

International common stocks usually share the basic characteristics and features of U.S. common stocks, though—for the U.S. investor in these stocks—currency fluctuations can have an impact on investment returns. Investors in international common stocks also face possible political risk, illiquidity, and higher transaction costs.

Fixed Income Investments

In simple terms, fixed income securities promise investors a stated amount of income on a regular, periodic basis. They represent a contract between the buyer and the issuer whereby the issuer agrees to pay a certain amount of money on a stated schedule to the buyer, and to refund the face value of the security to the buyer at a certain maturity date. Fixed income investors generally have no ownership stake in the issuing company. They are technically viewed as creditors of the company, and the securities are viewed as debt obligations of the issuer.

Fixed income securities are issued at face, or par, value—typically $1,000 in the U.S.—with a fixed interest rate representing the percentage of par value that will be paid to the security holder on an annual basis. Payments are usually made twice a year; thus, a 9 percent bond would pay $45 to the holder every six months.

The initial interest rate on a fixed income investment depends on the type of security (see below), the company's financial strength, the use it intends to make of the proceeds, the term or time to maturity of the instrument, and the level of interest rates in the overall economy.

Once issued, most fixed income instruments are freely traded on electronic secondary markets, where billions of dollars worth of such securities—especially U.S. government bonds—change hands every day. The market price of most fixed income securities is quoted as a percentage of par value and changes daily based on interest rate movements, the financial performance of the issuing entity, and general market conditions. Thus, most securities trade at some premium over or discount from the original issue price. This, in turn, affects an investor's current yield. A 9 percent, $1,000 par bond bought at 90—or $900—has a current yield of 10 percent. The same bond purchased at 110—$1,100—produces an 8.2 percent yield.

Several organizations, including Moody's Investors Service, Standard & Poor's, and Duff & Phelps, rate fixed income securities to give investors an indication of the financial strength of the issuing organization. Ratings range from AAA (the highest) to D (for securities of an insolvent or bankrupt issuer). U.S. government securities have an implied rating of AAA. All securities rated AAA, AA, A, or BBB are classified as investment-grade securities. Anything below BBB is usually considered non-investment-grade.

Fixed income securities vary by maturity, issuer, and payment terms. They can generally be classified as illustrated in Exhibit 11–6 and are explained in more detail below.

Cash Equivalents In general, these securities have a maturity of less than one year; maturities may be as short as one day.

Types of Fixed Income Investments

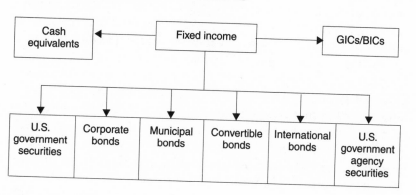

Cash equivalents are usually issued to meet short-term cash needs and are usually purchased by investors who do not want to tie up their money for long. Overall, these securities comprise what is called the money market. Interest rates can be fixed or floating, varying on a daily, weekly, monthly, or quarterly basis. Examples include:

- Certificates of deposit.
- Money market funds.
- U.S. Treasury bills.
- Commercial paper.
- Short-term corporate bonds.

U.S. Government Securities   These securities are issued by the U.S. government and are backed by its full faith and credit; while not explicitly rated by the rating agencies, they are generally considered the safest possible investments. This investment category includes U.S. Treasury bills (maturing in less than one year), U.S. Treasury notes (maturing in 1 to 10 years), and U.S. Treasury bonds (maturing in 10 to 30 years).

U.S. Government Agency Securities   Securities issued by agencies of the U.S. government are either directly guaranteed by the federal government, as with Ginny Mae's (GNMA), or have the implicit backing of the federal government. Maturities can range from less than 1 year to 40 years. Issuing agencies include the Government National Mortgage Agency (GNMA), the Federal Housing Authority (FHA), the Federal National Mortgage Association (FNMA), the Tennessee Valley Authority (TVA), and the Federal Home Loan Mortgage Corporation (FHLMC).

U.S. Corporate Bonds   Securities issued by U.S. corporations can have maturities ranging from less than 1 year to 30 years. Features of corporate bonds—including sinking fund provisions, put and call provisions and interest payment—can vary. Further, these bonds may be secured (backed by a pledge of specific assets) or unsecured (backed by the creditworthiness of the corporation). Quality ratings are assigned to most issues by one of the rating agencies.

Municipal Bonds   Proceeds from the sale of securities issued by state, county, and local governmental entities are commonly used to meet short-term cash flow needs, to build housing or public works projects, or to subsidize industrial projects. In most cases, interest on these municipal bonds is free from federal taxation and from state taxation if the buyer is a resident of the state in which the issuer is located. This feature allows state and local governments to pay a lower interest rate on their borrowings. Municipal bonds are generally not attractive investments for qualified plans since these plans already enjoy a tax exemption for their investment income.

Convertible Bonds   These securities are corporate debt instruments that may be exchanged at some future date for a specified number of shares of the common stock of the company. Convertible debt has the same basic interest and principal repayment characteristics of straight corporate debt. Because the investor has some claim on the common stock of the issuer, however, the price of convertible debt will fluctuate more than that of straight debt; as the price of the common stock moves, the change in the value of the shares into which the debt is convertible will cause the bond price to move. As with straight corporate debt, maturities and credit quality will vary from issue to issue.

International Bonds   The maturities and credit ratings of securities issued by foreign corporations or governmental entities are very similar to U.S. fixed income securities; certain provisions, such as par value and repayment schedules, can be quite different, however. International bonds can be denominated in either U.S. dollars or a foreign currency. Investment in these instruments exposes the investor to additional risks, such as currency fluctuations and political risk, not associated with U.S. domestic bonds.

GICs and BICs   Guaranteed investment contracts (GICs) are fixed dollar funding arrangements offered by insurance companies, usually to large, tax-qualified retirement and profit-sharing plans. BICs, or bank investment contracts, are similar but are issued by banking organizations. GICs are offered in exchange for a deposit of funds into the general account of the insurance carrier. Deposits can be made as a lump sum or over a fixed period of time; the interest rate may be fixed or allowed to float with some guaranteed floor rate. Repayment of the principal on deposit is scheduled for some future date, either as a lump sum or over a prescribed time period. While GICs have many of the characteristics of corporate or government bonds, they are in fact closer to annuity contracts, and there is no secondary market for these investments.

In recent years, concern over the ability of insurance carriers to meet their obligations under existing GIC contracts has increased investor interest in BICs and synthetic GICs. A synthetic GIC is an investment in an underlying portfolio of bonds, usually U.S. government bonds, with an insurance company agreeing to pay interest and principal if the portfolio is unable to meet its stated obligations. Synthetic GICs give investors the protection of investing in a known and segregated portfolio of bonds, rather than the general fund of the insurance carrier, and may enable them to achieve higher returns through active management of the portfolio by an independent investment manager.

Compared to other fixed income instruments, GICs and BICs have less liquidity than bonds or cash equivalents and generally have a yield that is 0.5 percent to 1.0 percent higher than comparable maturity for U.S. government bonds. There is no fluctuation in the value of the contracts, and under current accounting rules they are carried at book value by the plan sponsor.

Preferred Stock

Preferred stock, like common stock, represents an ownership interest in the issuing corporation. It differs from common stock in three significant ways, however:

- Preferred stockholders have a higher claim on company assets. Upon liquidation of an organization, the debt or bondholders have the first claim on the assets, followed by preferred stockholders and then by common stockholders.
- Preferred stock normally pays dividends at a fixed rate, set at issuance as a percentage of the par value of the preferred shares. Preferred dividends remain constant over the life of the issue and usually must be paid in full each quarter before any dividends can be declared on common stock.
- Preferred stockholders may or may not have voting rights for electing directors, amending bylaws, or any other such matters.

Because preferred stock has features of both common stock (ownership) and fixed income securities (liquidation rights, set payment stream), it is usually considered a hybrid security.

Some preferred stock issues are convertible and may be exchanged at some future date for a specified number of shares of common stock. Other features of preferred stock that can vary from issue to issue include the following:

- The use of sinking fund provisions to retire the issue over time.
- Cumulative dividend rights, whereby any missed dividends must be paid in full before dividends can be paid on the common stock.
- The inclusion of put and/or call provisions.
- The use of a floating-rate structure, with dividends reset based on a specified formula.
- Limitations on the corporation's right to repurchase or issue additional shares of its common stock.

SHARED RESPONSIBILITIES

As noted in the introduction to this chapter, both employers and employees must understand the basic principles of investing if they are to make effective use of their defined contribution plans. While it is the employee who makes the ultimate investment decision, it is the plan sponsor who is responsible for providing a suitable investment framework. The issues involved in constructing such a framework are the subject of the next chapter.

Investing Plan Assets–
Plan Provisions And
Operation

The investment framework employers construct for their CODAs and other defined contribution plans can have a significant impact on ultimate plan values. This chapter begins with a review of past and present practice in defined contribution investing. It then focuses on key plan design issues, including employer fiduciary responsibilities, and concludes with a discussion of investment planning, operations, and control.

HISTORICAL DEVELOPMENT

The initial era of defined contribution investing was driven, to a large extent, by expediency. Ease of administration—particularly participant record keeping—often dictated the number and types of investment choices that plan sponsors made available. Some plans provided no choice at all, simply investing plan assets as a single fund. Others offered two investment funds—one a fixed income fund such as a GIC, in which all employee contributions were invested, and the other an employer stock fund in which all employer contributions were invested. Still others allowed true but relatively limited choice—between a fixed income fund and an equity fund, for example.

Another factor that tended to limit investment options was employer concern about potential legal liability for giving employees any kind of financial advice. Restricting investment choice obviously limited the need for such counsel.

Most important, however, was the fact that few employers had articulated specific investment objectives for their defined contribution plans. In many situations, this reflected the fact that investment results in these plans do not affect the employers' financial statements; thus, this pressure to improve financial performance does not exist. Most employers designed their defined benefit plans to replace specified levels of preretirement income and viewed their defined contribution plans as simply providing supplemental funds. Thus, little thought was given to defined contribution investment choices—and investment performance. While the need to diversify is a staple of modern investment theory, for example, many plans gave employees little or no opportunity to diversify, either among or within various investment classes. Further, employers tended to do little in the way of providing useful investment information to their employees—either about the options available to them or about basic principles of investing.

In short, the early age of defined contribution asset management was characterized by limited employee choice and by the lack of well-defined plan and investment objectives.

The last fifteen years have seen a definite shift—at least in terms of the investment opportunities made available to employees. Many factors have contributed to this change: a growing public awareness of the role of defined contribution plans in providing economic security and the importance of saving and investing wisely, an increased recognition on the part of employers of the need to provide flexibility of choice and investment education, improved and more efficient administrative capabilities, and the aggressive marketing efforts of the leading mutual funds, to name but a few. Exhibit 12–1 shows the prevalence of investment options in the 596 CODAs included in the Towers Perrin EBIC data base. Of these plans, 574 (96 percent) provide employees with a choice of three or more funds for investing their own contributions; 376 provide a choice of five or more funds for these amounts. The options for investing employer contributions are not as great, reflecting the fact that many plans automatically invest these amounts in employer stock. Nevertheless, 333 of these plans (or 60 percent) provide a choice of three or more funds for employer contributions.

Number of Funds Available for Investment

	Employee Contributions	Employer Contributions*
1 Fund	8	206
2 Funds	14	13
3 Funds	61	36
4 Funds	137	70
5 Funds	118	66
6 Funds	99	59
7 Funds	76	53
8 Funds	38	23
9 Funds	18	9
10 or More Funds	25	14
Other	2	3

*44 plans do not provide for employer contributions.

Exhibit 12–2 depicts the investment choices offered by the plans in Towers Perrin's EBIC data base. Clearly, most of these plans provide a wide variety of investment funds for their participants. The number of choices now available in these plans underscores the need for educating employees to become better investors, however. The fact that employees have more investment choices does not mean that they are making the most of what their plans have to offer. Overall, billions of dollars in CODA and other defined contribution plan assets are still being invested very conservatively and with little diversification. While this reflects the fact that employees need to know more about investments and financial planning, it also reflects the fact that many employers still not have focused on managing their plans as effectively as possible.

This situation is changing, however. As costs continue to rise, employers are taking a closer look at plan objectives and plan performance, and are recognizing that more effective plan management can improve plan values with no additional company contributions to the plan. The components of effective plan management—including the design of investment structures and overall investment operations considerations—are discussed below.

E X H I B I T   12–2

Types of Investment Funds Available

Fund	Employee Contributions	Employer Contributions
Employer stock	353	375
Domestic balanced	404	241
Fixed income	314	183
Growth equity	264	160
Diversified equity	233	146
Equity index	267	147
GIC/BIC	244	154
Money market	257	148
International equity	169	104
Small cap equity	131	72
Equity income	101	60
U.S. Government obligations	92	55
Short-term fixed income	80	38
Global balanced	25	11
Fixed income indexed	26	14
Other	34	26
No choice	1	45

PLAN DESIGN CONSIDERATIONS

The investment provisions of a defined contribution plan must be compatible with the objectives articulated by the plan sponsor in creating the plan. Three major areas to be considered are: the plan sponsor's fiduciary responsibilities, the role employer stock will play, and administrative issues.

Fiduciary Considerations

As noted in Chapter 7, a fiduciary must discharge its duties solely in the interests of plan participants and their beneficiaries and for the exclusive purpose of providing plan benefits and meeting administrative expenses. Further, a fiduciary is held to a prudent expert standard[1] in the discharge of its duties.

It is not uncommon for plans to be structured so that trustees and external investment managers, rather than the employer, are responsible for the investment of plan assets. In this way, the plan sponsor has delegated specific investment authority to outside professionals, limiting their own fiduciary responsibility to the selection and retention of these external fiduciaries. A plan sponsor can further limit its fiduciary liability by permitting employees to make their own allocations among the various investment options, provided a certain minimum number of options, spanning a range of investment classes, is offered and that the employee may make changes to their allocations no less frequently than quarterly. The employer must also provide employees with information sufficient for them to make an informed choice among the various options available. These provisions, contained in section 404(c) of ERISA, are covered in more detail in Chapter 7, and are commonly referred to as "safe harbor provisions." In general, the safe harbor provisions require that a plan offer at least three diversified categories of investment with materially different risk and return characteristics.

Compliance with these guidelines does *not* relieve the employer of the responsibility for ensuring that the investment options offered under the plan are prudent and properly diversified and it does not relieve the employer of fiduciary responsibility for investments over which the employee has no control, such as employer contributions which are automatically directed to one of the investment options.

Offering Employee Stock as an Investment Option

The safe harbor provisions of Section 404(c) permit the company to offer employee stock as one of the investment options, provided the plan also offers the three required options, and the employer's shares are publicly traded in a recognized market. In addition, all

---

1. See page 153 for a description of the prudent expert rule. It should be noted that fiduciary responsibilities, in the context of an ERISA plan, apply the concept of portfolio diversification to the total portfolio and not on an asset by asset basis.

purchases, sales, voting, and related share activities must be implemented on a confidential basis. If the employer stock investment option meets these criteria, the fiduciary liability protection afforded plan sponsors under section 404(c) is extended to the employer stock option.

Employer stock is a common investment option in many defined contribution plans. Some employers believe that stock ownership strengthens the link between employee and corporate interests. Others seek to create or expand a friendly group of shareholders as a barrier to hostile takeover attempts.

However, there are several arguments against the use of employer stock as an investment option:

- Employer stock is a completely undiversified investment option and may be inappropriate from a financial perspective.
- Employer contributions invested in company stock at the employer's direction are not eligible for the safe harbor provisions of 404(c).
- Plan sponsors who permit employee contributions to be invested in company stock must comply with SEC registration and reporting requirements (covered in Chapter 7).
- Employee relations problems may surface if the value of the employer's stock declines.
- If significant balances are built up in the company stock option, employees have not only their livelihood but also a sizeable block of their savings tied to the well-being of the company.
- Any investment in employer stock, while not subject to the requirement for a diversified investment alternative, must be shown to satisfy the requirement that plan assets be "expended for the exclusive benefit of the employees," and must satisfy the requirement for prudence.

If employer stock is offered as one of the investment options, the plan sponsor must also consider what opportunities the employee will be offered to diversify out of the employer stock as they approach retirement.[2]

---

2. Such a diversification right is required if the plan is an ESOP. See the discussion beginning on page 116.

If the plan is an ESOP or KSOP, yet another issue to be considered is whether dividends will be passed through to employees and, if so, how frequently (e.g., quarterly or annually). And employers whose stock is not publicly traded must also deal with such issues as the inclusion of rights of first refusal and put options.

Administrative Concerns

The administrative issues which need to be addressed in structuring the investment provisions of a defined contribution investment program can be grouped into several broad categories:

Frequency of valuation   How often will plan assets and account balances be valued for purposes of processing loans, distributions, withdrawals and investment election changes? If monthly or daily valuations are preferred to quarterly valuations, what will be the additional expense? How long will it take to process a requested transaction subsequent to the valuation date? How does the choice of valuation frequency affect other plan provisions, such as the availability and repayment of plan loans?

Frequency of change   How often will employees be permitted to change their investment elections? The safe harbor provisions of section 404(c) require that employees must be permitted to make changes at least quarterly, and more often for more volatile investment options. An employer may choose not to comply with these safe harbor provisions. Plans generally permit employees to make changes to the investment elections on either a quarterly, monthly, or daily basis. Some plans differentiate between changes intended to accommodate new contributions and those that affect existing plan balances. Others place limits on the total number of changes an employee may make in any one year; however, this provision may inadvertently violate the safe harbor provisions of 404(c) if the employee has used up all of his change options by the third quarter of the year.

Allowing employees to change their investment elections frequently—for example, on a daily basis—may send them mixed signals. On the one hand, the focus in educating employees to save wisely for their futures requires an emphasis on setting and achieving long-term goals. Permitting frequent changes to investment elections may appear to be inconsistent and may potentially thwart the long-term focus of defined contribution plan investing.

Default Provisions   Employers must provide some sort of default option in the event the employee fails to make an investment election for contributions. The employer may opt for the most conservative option—an investment in GIC's for example, or may choose to have contributions invested in proportion to the employee's existing account balances. In setting this provision, the employer must consider the trade-offs between fiduciary liability and investment responsibility.

Employee Communications   Employee communication is a critical link in the long term success of defined contribution plans. The Department of Labor now requires that the employer offer participants sufficient information to enable them to make an intelligent choice among the investment options available to them. This information should encompass such investment basics as the importance of diversification, the relationship between risk and reward, and the influence of the investment time horizon on the potential outcome of plan investments.

Special Rights   In plans that provide for the automatic investment of contributions in certain funds (e.g., employer contributions in employer stock), plan sponsors need to consider whether employees should be given special rights of diversification as they near retirement age. (This issue also arises in ESOPs, where a diversification right is mandatory under certain circumstances).[3] Employers who decide to include special rights will have to establish eligibility requirements; these requirements will typically be tied to early retirement eligibility requirements (e.g., attainment of age 55 and, possibly, the completion of 10 years of service).

---

3. See page 116.

DESIGN, IMPLEMENTATION, AND MONITORING OF PLAN INVESTMENTS

There are three continuing stages to the development of plan investment provisions: design, implementation, and monitoring.

Design   In the design phase, the plan sponsor must make a series of decisions about plan assets. The first is to consider what asset classes will be offered. This decision will be influenced by administrative costs, risk and return characteristics, plan objectives, and participant needs. The range of asset classes to be considered include: cash equivalents, GICs (BICs), bonds, large-capitalization stocks, small-capitalization stocks, international stocks and bonds, emerging markets, and employer stock. Some plans may wish to consider the use of real estate, energy, and private equity (venture capital) investments. These asset classes are somewhat more cumbersome to include given the private nature of the markets in which they exist and the liquidity constraints this imposes.

The next issue in the design phase is whether to offer these asset classes as distinct investment options from which the employee will choose their own mix, or to combine them into predetermined sets of diversified portfolios reflecting different risk and return characteristics. This issue will be discussed in more detail in the section that follows.

Each asset class in and of itself can also be diversified, combining different management styles such as growth and value in the equity portfolio, long-term and short-term fixed income strategies, and a stable of GIC providers in a GIC portfolio. Employers who offer company stock as an investment option may want to consider an alternative equity option specifically designed to complement the company stock. For example, an energy company, whose economic fortunes are closely tied to the rise and fall of the energy markets, may want to ensure that an equity option with less-than-market exposure to energy stocks is among the offerings.

In the past, employee contributions have been heavily invested in the most conservative investment choices such as the GIC (or BIC) option. Where the employee's investment horizon spans ten or twenty years, these seemingly risk-free investments can actually result in unintended risks—erosion of purchasing power or insufficient retirement income, for example.

Combining Asset Classes into Predetermined Portfolios

Different employees will have different degrees of risk tolerance, depending not only on their investment horizon (relative proximity to retirement) but also based on their own psychological preferences. It is quite difficult for a professional investor to gauge the relative merits of the trade-offs between risk and return of the various potential combinations of assets, even with the benefit of years of education and experience. If plan participants are to make an intelligent allocation of their investment dollars, then substantial guidance is required from the plan sponsor.

One approach is to combine the asset classes in varying degrees into a series of portfolios lying along the efficient frontier, which express successively higher risk/reward expectations. One company, for example, combined the five basic asset classes (Money Market, Bond, Large Company Domestic Stocks, Intermediate and Small Company Domestic Stocks, and International Stocks) into six different portfolio options, as illustrated in Exhibit 12–3.

Mix A is the most conservative, but still diversified, portfolio option available to participants. Moving from left to right, the portfolios get progressively more aggressive, with mix D have the minimum allocation to fixed income, at 20 percent, and Mix E being the most aggressive, invested 100 percent in stocks. Each of these portfolios is regularly rebalanced to the original allocation in order to retain the same risk/reward characteristics that were established at the outset. For those employees who believe themselves to be more conservative or more aggressive than any of the predetermined mixes, a sixth Mix (F) is offered, in which a participant is free to allocate his or her contributions among any of the five asset classes in any proportion. Mix F is also beneficial to participants who are attempting to coordinate their defined contribution plan investments with other savings programs, either their own or a spouse's.

This company's experience with the introduction of these preselected mixes was quite striking. Prior to the roll-out of the new

E X H I B I T   12–3

Illustration of Preselected Mixes

Asset Class	A	B	C	D	E
Money market	50%	30%	10%	0%	0%
Bond	30%	30%	30%	20%	0%
Large company domestic equities	12%	24%	36%	48%	60%
Intermediate and small company domestic equities	4%	8%	12%	16%	20%
International equities	4%	8%	12%	16%	20%

investment program, approximately 60 percent of all employee dollars in the plan were invested in the fixed income asset class. Active employees had 48 percent of their assets in fixed income while retirees had 77 percent of their assets in fixed income. After the new investment options were introduced, total employee dollars in fixed income investments dropped to 45 percent, with the corresponding numbers for active employees and retirees dropping to 35 percent and 64 percent, respectively. Fully 75 percent of active employees invested in one of the predetermined asset mixes.

Implementation   Once the asset classes or portfolios to be offered have been determined, appropriate investment objectives for each asset class must be established. This is essential in order to ascertain that the right investment manager is selected for each assignment. The objectives should clearly articulate the plan sponsor's expectations as to risk and return, any investment style preferences, and the time horizon over which the assets will be managed. For example, a plan sponsor may wish to introduce an equity option intended to replicate the broad market averages without taking undue amounts of risk. Alternatively, another equity option may be offered with the objective of substantially outperforming the market averages, with a correspondingly higher degree of risk.

The relevant time horizon is also critical for guidance in hiring the appropriate managers. In a balanced fund targeted toward employees within five years of retirement, aggressive equity options are probably inappropriate. Where corporate circumstances are such that it is known that the plan will terminate within a certain time frame—as in the event of a merger or acquisition—it is equally inappropriate to offer investment options whose success is dependent on long investment horizons.

Within each asset class, the plan sponsor must also decide whether to pursue active or passive investment management styles. Passive styles are designed to replicate their respective markets. They have the advantage of being easy to communicate to employees and tend to be significantly less expensive than active investment management options. If, however, the plan sponsor believes they can be successful in choosing active managers who will outperform the markets in the long run, then the range of options broadens considerably. It may be appropriate to combine both active and passive management styles, either within or across asset classes.

The next major task in the implementation process is the selection of investment managers. Some plan sponsors have chosen the route of selecting a single provider of investment and administrative services in an attempt to simplify administration and communication. However, this results in considerably less flexibility in structuring investment options, sub-optimal manager selection, and may not necessarily result in lower fees. In addition, use of a single, brand-name provider may have the unintended result of identifying that provider, rather than the company, as the source of the benefits.

Selecting appropriate investment managers requires consideration of a number of factors, including the goals and objectives of the portfolio and the plan sponsor, past performance, and fees. In general, it is essential to develop an understanding of the factors which led to the historical investment performance, and some level of assurance that those same factors will be brought to bear on future investments. The following may provide a useful framework for evaluating prospective investment managers.

- History and ownership of the firm.
- Total assets and the number of accounts under management.
- Growth in assets and accounts under management.

- Number of employees and their backgrounds.
- Employee turnover.
- Investment style and decision-making processes.
- Research capabilities.
- Client turnover.
- Trading and operational capabilities.
- Compliance with applicable SEC rules and regulations.

Copies of sample portfolios and client reports can be helpful in understanding the manager's capabilities. It is often informative to follow a particular investment decision from germination of the idea to the ultimate implementation. Of course, thorough reference checks are indispensable to determine that the manager can, in fact, live up to its promises.

The bottom line for any investment management firm is how well it has performed in the asset class for which it is being considered. Performance evaluation is more than a simple comparison of the past one, three, or five years against a market index, however. Both long-term and short-term performance and trends in performance over these time frames and over market cycles need to be evaluated against a universe of other money managers with similar investment objectives as well as against an appropriate market benchmark. It is commonly recognized that certain investment styles go in and out of favor on an unpredictable basis. Thus, to compare a growth manager against the broad market indices over a period when growth has been out of favor does little to inform the observer as to how well the growth manager fulfilled its assignment. Instead, it is more appropriate to compare the firm's performance against both a passive portfolio of growth stocks (such as the Russell 1000 - Growth if it is a large-capitalization growth manager) and against a universe of managers with comparable investment styles and objectives.

In addition to evaluating the return characteristics of the firm, it is also important to understand the risks that manager assumed in generating the historical performance record. It is the risk-adjusted return which truly distinguishes a good manager.[4]

---

4. There are a number of statistical measures that can be applied for this purpose; a detailed discussion of these measures, however, is beyond the scope of this text.

Once the universe of potential managers has been narrowed to a few finalists, there is an important last step: the interview. The interview serves as a qualitative assessment of the investment firm's capabilities and its "fit" with the plan and the plan sponsor. As much science as has been applied to the process of selecting investment managers, only this final hands-on assessment can truly develop a feel for whether the investment manager can fulfill the role assigned by the plan sponsor.

Monitoring   Both the structure of plan investments and the performance of the investment managers must be monitored on an ongoing basis. Performance must be monitored in the context of the objectives which were established at the outset. Key questions to ask in the review process include:

- What were the returns for the last quarter? Year? Two years?
- How do they compare to the agreed-upon benchmarks?
- Are there any disturbing trends of consistent underperformance surfacing?
- How do the returns compare to the results achieved by other managers with similar objectives?
- Are the returns meeting expectations over the long run?
- Is the firm's investment policy still sound in light of changing capital market conditions?
- Have there been any substantive changes to investment policies, procedures or personnel?

Replacement of an investment manager can be expected periodically, either due to changes in the plan itself or due to unsatisfactory investment performance.

Questions to be asked periodically in evaluating the overall structure of plan investments include:

- Have the original goals and objectives changed?
- Is the number and type of investment options offered sufficient?
- Is employee usage of the available options appropriate given the demographics?
- Are investment and administrative expenses in line?

An Investment Management Checklist

The following checklist summarizes key questions plan sponsors should address in structuring and managing their defined contribution investment programs.

Design

- Do the investment choices span the appropriate spectrum of risk and reward choices, given plan objectives and the participant profile?
- Are employer contributions and undirected employee contributions invested in appropriate asset classes?
- Is the ability to change investment mix decisions appropriate, given the choices available, plan objectives, and participant profile?
- Is each investment option prudently diversified?
- Is useful investment information communicated to the participants for each investment option, including accurate, meaningful descriptions; qualified risk and return expectations; investment objectives; and frequent, consistent and understandable investment reports?
- Are the participants provided with sufficient information to enable them to make informed allocations among the investment options offered?

Implementation

- Has an explicit active/passive investment decision been made for each investment alternative?
- Has a prudent manager selection process been documented and applied to each manager hired?
- Is there a written statement of investment policies and objectives for each investment manager?

Monitoring

- Is a review of manager performance undertaken quarterly, with a more formal, in-depth review conducted at least annually?

- Have clear criteria been established for use in determining whether to retain and/or replace an investment manager?
- Are plan investment policies, procedures, and objectives formally reviewed and verified at least annually?
- Are the investment options offered evaluated at least annually?

CHAPTER 13

Plan Administration

Employers want their CODAs to operate efficiently, at the lowest possible cost, and in compliance with all legal requirements. These issues are of no consequence to the average plan participant, but participants *are* concerned about their rights under the plan, and they need a good deal of information. Thus, procedures and systems that will provide accurate, consistent, and timely responses to participants are also a key objective of plan administration.

This chapter begins with a review of administrative roles and responsibilities, followed by a discussion of the three major categories of administrative tasks—compliance, accounting, and reporting.

ROLES AND RESPONSIBILITIES

When employees elect to contribute to a savings plan CODA, contributions are deducted from their paychecks. Thus, the CODA and the *payroll system* must work in tandem. The *trustee* and the *plan recordkeeper* also play key roles.

The Trustee

In most plans (except those that are fully insured), employee and employer contributions are deposited in a trust. The primary function of the trustee is to receive, hold, and distribute plan assets in accordance with the plan provisions and at the direction of the plan committee. The plan may give the trustee exclusive authority to manage and control the plan assets, require the trustee to take direction from someone else with regard to asset management or delegate investment responsibility to one or more investment managers. Thus, the role the trustee plays with respect to plan assets may range from that of mere custodian to that of an investment manager with complete discretion and control over the assets. Specific duties may include the following:

- Maintaining custody of plan assets.
- Receiving all cash contributions and loan repayments.
- Issuing loan and distribution checks.
- Monitoring the prudence of investment policies and strategies.
- Voting shares of employer stock as directed by participants; voting shares of other stock held by the plan.
- Withholding taxes on plan distributions and submitting them to the IRS or the appropriate states.
- Filing Form 1099R with the IRS.
- Valuing trust portfolios.
- Controlling tenders of company stock.
- Preparing the annual trust accounting for the Form 5500 filing.
- Preparing trust valuation and transaction statements on a periodic basis (e.g., monthly or quarterly).

A trust fund in which the assets of several unrelated plans are invested is called a "common trust fund" or a "commingled fund." Banks, insurance companies, and mutual funds offer commingled funds as a way for plans to achieve broader diversification, greater investment opportunities, and more efficient administration. An individual plan sponsor's participation in a commingled fund is generally described in terms of the number of units (shares) it holds. Commingled funds are valued periodically, and the unit value is adjusted accordingly.

The Recordkeeper

The trustee maintains records and reports on CODA assets as a whole but does not maintain records and reports on funds attributable to each employee's participation. Thus, the plan sponsor must establish or arrange for a recordkeeping system to maintain and update the accounts of each participant. Such a system must recognize all deposits to participants' accounts, distributions from these accounts, and investment income earned.

Banks, mutual funds, insurance companies, stockbrokers, consulting firms, and software houses offer a range of recordkeeping services. Selection of an external recordkeeper requires careful consideration of the services that will best complement the employer's internal administration capabilities. Employers can also handle the entire function in-house. A computerized recordkeeping system is usually necessary to maintain accurate records.

Recordkeepers typically:

- Set up the administration system in accordance with plan provisions.
- Update participant accounts to reflect transactions.
- Determine how much income to allocate among participants by analyzing trust fund statements.
- Perform the accounting and reconciliation functions.
- Edit and reconcile employer payroll information.
- Process participant payment requests.
- Process participant investment change requests.
- Calculate available withdrawal and loan amounts.
- Calculate taxes on distributions.
- Calculate vested amounts and forfeitures.
- Perform compliance testing (e.g., coverage tests, ADP/ACP tests, Section 415 limits).
- Create reports for the employer, trustee, stock transfer agent, and participants.
- Prepare employee communications.
- Communicate with the employer, trustee, stock transfer agent, and payroll service.

- Provide consulting advice on technical issues and plan interpretation.

Certain recordkeepers may perform other administrative functions such as managing investments or acting as trustee. A bank or mutual fund will sometimes act as trustee, investment manager, and recordkeeper, for example.

Exhibit 13–1 illustrates the interaction among the payroll, trust, and recordkeeping functions. Payroll provides gross contribution deduction dollars to the trust for deposit and reports contributions to participant accounts to the recordkeeper.[1] Trust activities may precede or follow the updating of participant records. For example, the employer may deposit contributions and loan repayments to the trust with each payroll in which contributions are deducted. The recordkeeper may update participant records on a less frequent basis when the employer provides contribution data.

Other activities—such as distributions and fund balance transfers—are initiated by the recordkeeper, who maintains and values individual participant accounts. The valuation process, in which trust fund earnings are recognized in the participants' accounts, results in directions to the trustee to issue checks or

E X H I B I T   13–1

Interaction of Administrative Functions

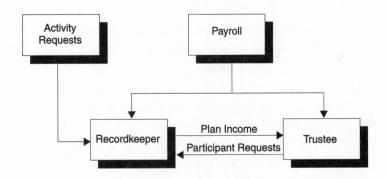

---

1. See page 159 for a discussion of deposit requirements.

transfer assets among the plan's funds. In these instances, record-keeping activities *precede* the corresponding activities in the trust.

Any timing differences between activities in the participant records and the trust fund must be reconciled. Only through this process can the employer be certain that all transactions in the participant records are properly accounted for in the trust fund.

Because the trustee is the focal point for all investment activity in the plan, close coordination among the employer, the trustee, and the recordkeeper is vital. The employer and the trustee must establish a procedure for depositing contributions and loan repayments in the trust. The employer and recordkeeper must establish procedures for instructing the trustee to issue disbursements from the plan and transfer plan balances in accordance with participant investment selections.

COMPLIANCE

The term *compliance* encompasses two important activities. The first is establishing and maintaining procedures to ensure that the plan is being administered in accordance with its terms. The second is establishing and maintaining procedures to monitor the plan's compliance with ADP/ACP testing requirements. These activities are discussed below.

Basic Administrative Procedures

Different plan designs have different administrative implications; a plan that permits account balances to be distributed in installments will require more administrative effort than a plan that permits only lump sum distributions, for example. The administrative consequences of various plan design decisions have been discussed earlier in Part Three; what follows is a brief summary of major plan events and related administrative procedures.

This list is by no means all-inclusive, but it does suggest the issues that must be considered in establishing administrative procedures to support specific plan provisions.

Event	Administrative Steps
Employment	Obtain and verify accuracy of employee data.
	Determine if employee was previously employed by the employer or a member of the controlled group to determine any need to reinstate prior service credits and forfeitures.
	Determine whether employment status is eligible under the plan.
	Provide employee with application for rollover contribution of any prior plan distribution.
	Initiate maintenance of records to determine when employee will be eligible to join the plan.
Plan Eligibility	Distribute SPD.
	Distribute enrollment form, beneficiary designation, and, if applicable, plan prospectus or equivalent information.
	Coordinate start of payroll deductions with payroll periods.
Employee Contributions	Start, stop, or reinstate contributions in accordance with plan provisions.
	Monitor elective deferral limit, Section 415 limits, and Section 401(a)(17) compensation limit; define action to be taken when limits are reached.
	Monitor changes to ensure that combined plan contributions and forfeitures do not exceed Section 415 limits.
	Consolidate payroll data for recordkeeping.
	Validate eligibility of rollover contributions.
	Determine timing of rollover and employee contribution deposits to trust.
	Monitor plan restrictions as to timing and frequency of rate changes.
	Define means for reducing rates for HCEs in the event of projected ADP/ACP problems.
	Develop employee communication material on excess contributions.
Employer Contributions	Determine who calculates employer match, on what basis, and with what frequency.
	Determine eligibility and allocation basis for annual employer contributions.
	Determine timing of contribution deposits to trust.
Investment Directions	Fulfill investment change requests for future contributions and prior plan balances.
	Monitor plan restrictions as to timing, frequency, and investment fund eligibility.
	Coordinate timing of asset transfers in the trust with effective date for requests.

Event	Administrative Steps
In-Service Withdrawals	Develop application and approval process for hardship withdrawals. Define order for debiting participant accounts and funds. Implement federal and state tax withholding elections. Develop required distribution procedures: notification of tax consequences and direct rollover eligibility; preparation of Form 1099-R. Establish payroll procedures to monitor plan withdrawal suspension restrictions.
Loans	Document loan administration procedures. Establish steps and timing for issuing a loan, including: application, promissory note, security agreement, truth-in-lending statement, repayments by payroll deduction. Define handling of payroll status changes (e.g., monthly to weekly salary frequency) and employment status changes (e.g., leave of absence, ineligible plan status, termination) with respect to loan repayment deductions. Define order for debiting participant accounts and funds. Coordinate hardship withdrawal and loans issues.
Leaves of Absence; Change to Ineligible Status	Determine ongoing rights under the plan. Develop procedure for repaying outstanding loans. Develop procedure for maintaining employee status (e.g., address changes).
QDROs	Establish written administration procedures, including determining qualified status of a domestic relations order and notifying participant and alternate payee. Identify plan provisions directing handling of QDROs. Establish steps for segregating participant's account in the recordkeeping system, including debiting of investment funds and subaccounts (e.g., pretax contributions and company contributions) and tax handling.
Termination Distributions	Define "termination date" and "reason" for vesting calculation and eligibility for plan contributions. Determine participant's balance for $3,500 cashout provisions. Develop required distribution procedures: notification of tax consequences and direct rollover eligibility, preparation of Form 1099-R. Obtain federal and state tax withholding elections. Determine when minimum required distributions are necessary. Develop procedures for handling multiple beneficiaries and tax forms. Define procedures for handling forfeitures. Determine handling of loans outstanding at termination.

ADP/ACP Testing

The ADP and ACP tests are discussed at length in Chapter 4.[2] The following summary of key administrative considerations—including steps that may help avert testing problems—assumes the reader is familiar with the information presented earlier.

Safe Harbor Matching Contributions   ADP/ACP testing may be avoided (except for aftertax employee contributions) if the employer makes the safe harbor matching contributions described on page 100.

Prior Year Percentages   By using actual deferral percentages of NHCEs for the prior year, the employer will be able to determine maximum HCE contribution levels at the beginning of the year.

Prospective Testing   If the plan sponsor does not wish to make safe harbor matching contributions and does not choose to use the ADP percentages of the NHCEs for the prior year, it is advisable to utilize prospective testing so as to ensure that a plan is in compliance at year end. This requires a system that projects year-to-date deferrals, contributions, and compensation data so as to determine plan year-end results. Responsibility for compliance testing generally rests with the recordkeeper, since the participant year-to-date deferral and contribution data is usually maintained on its system.[3]

Ideally, the testing system will enable the plan sponsor to model different cut-back scenarios to quantify reductions in HCE contributions sufficient to keep the plan in compliance and to evaluate how such cutbacks can best be made. In deciding how to make cutbacks to avert year-end problems, the plan sponsor is *not* required to use the leveling method.[4] For example, the plan

---

2. See discussion beginning on page 91.
3. If the recordkeeper is not responsible for calculating any of the contributions that must be included in the tests, the employer may decide to test on an in-house basis. Where this is the case, the recordkeeper need not be given compensation and demographic data for eligible employees who choose not to participate in the plan because there may be no other need to maintain this information in the recordkeeping system.
4. As discussed in Chapter 4, a plan that fails the ADP, ACP, or multiple use tests must refund excess contributions if the sponsor does not cure excesses with QNECs or QMACs.

document might permit the exercise of discretion to apply cutbacks only to certain HCEs (e.g., those in a business division with very low NHCE participation or those covered by a nonqualified supplemental executive deferred compensation program).[5]

Limiting Contributions   Plan sponsors may want to limit HCE contribution rates at the beginning of the plan year to help manage the compliance process, determining the limit on the basis of the prior year's test results. Note that, for a calendar year plan, it may not be possible to specify exactly who will be in the HCE group as of January 1; that determination depends, in part, on the prior year's compensation, which may not be established until payroll completes the annual Form W-2 reporting on the January 31 following the end of the year.[6] Thus, the plan sponsor may have to define an HCE group that differs slightly from the IRC testing definition in order to safely identify which employees will be affected by contribution limits at the start of the year. The plan can also use the prior year's HCE group and modify it as soon as final compensation information is available.

Any limit on HCE contributions should not apply to NHCEs; they should be permitted to contribute at the maximum.

Plans that match both elective and aftertax contributions may need to set combined rate limits. Otherwise, HCEs whose elective contributions are limited may switch to aftertax contributions, thereby affecting the results of the ACP test.

If, despite all efforts, the plan fails to meet the ADP/ACP tests at the end of the plan year, the plan will have to: (1) refund contributions from the accounts of HCEs; (2) recharacterize elective deferrals as aftertax contributions; and/or (3) make QNECs and/or QMACs. As noted in Chapter 4, when refunds are required on the ADP side, the plan should return unmatched elective deferrals before it returns elective deferrals that have attracted a matching employer contribution if it all possible. The same is true of the ACP test; unmatched aftertax contributions should be refunded first.

---

5. IRS Reg. 1.401(k)-1(f)(1)(ii) and 1.401(m)-1(e)(1)(i) state that a plan may limit contributions to avoid excesses but give no guidance—nor impose any restrictions—on how that is to be done.
6. The employer may be able to determine the HCE group based on the employee population as of a single day during the plan year, with certain adjustments. Generally, determining the HCE group in this manner will not improve the results.

PART 3   Plan Design and Operational Issues

The recordkeeping system will have to separately account for—or be able to distinguish—matched contributions and unmatched contributions in order to administer the refund.

Making QNECs and QMACs   As pointed out in Chapter 4, failure of the ADP test, the ACP test, and/or the multiple use test can be cured by contributing QNECs and /or QMACs to the plan (typically for NHCEs only).[7]

Before turning to the details, it is important to note that a cure can be costly, particularly if the plan has failed a test by a large margin. In addition, extra contributions are subject to various restrictions. Recall, for example, that QNECs and QMACs are fully vested at all times and are subject to restrictions on in-service withdrawals. Further, the same contributions cannot be used in more than one test. Thus, if QNECs for NHCEs are used to help the plan pass the ADP test, these QNECs cannot also be used for ACP purposes. Similarly, any QMACs made to the plan and used in the ADP test are not subject to the ACP test and, in fact, cannot be used to help pass the ACP test. Finally, a QNEC or a QMAC used to help the plan pass the ADP test cannot be used for any other nondiscrimination test such as the "amount" test of Section 401(a)(4).

To illustrate, consider a plan that fails the multiple use test. As the following example illustrates, the financial consequences of solving an ADP problem with QNECs or QMACs can differ. In this example, all eligible employees will share in a QNEC, whether or not they have authorized elective deferrals; only those employees who have actually made elective deferrals for the year in question—typically a small group—will share in a QMAC.

The plan in this example provides for a 50 percent employer match on elective deferrals only; aftertax employee contributions are permitted with no employer match. Thus, the total NHCE population can be divided into four groups: (1) employees who make elective deferrals but no aftertax contributions and who receive matching employer contributions; (2) those who make both elective deferrals and aftertax contributions and receive matching employer contributions; (3) those who make aftertax contributions only and do not receive matching contributions; and (4) those who make or receive no contributions at all.

---

7. Deadlines for making these contributions are described in Chapter 4.

The example assumes that the four employee groups participate as follows:

Group	Number	Compensation	Avg. Rate of Elective Deferrals	Avg. Rate of Matching Contribution	Avg. Aftertax Rate of Contribution	Avg. Def. Percentage Points	Avg. Cont. Percentage Points
1	660	$19,800,000	.057143	.028571	0	3,771.438	1,885.686
2	40	1,200,000	.057143	.028571	.02	228.572	194.284
3	10	200,000	0	0	.02	0	20.000
4	290	5,800,000	0	0	0	0	0
	1,000	$27,000,000				4,000.010	2,099.970

The 4,000.010 average deferral percentage points, divided by 1,000, produce an NHCE ADP of 4 percent; the 2,099.970 average contribution percentage points, also divided by 1,000, produced an NHCE ACP of 2.1 percent. Assume the HCE ADP is 6 percent and the HCE ACP is 3.5 percent.

The plan passes both the ADP and the ACP tests using the alternative limitation, but it fails the aggregate limit test. (The total percentage for HCEs is 9.5 percent, but only 9.1 percent is allowed under the aggregate limit test—[.04 times 1.25] plus [.021 plus .02] = .091.)

There are several ways to solve this problem using QNECs and QMACs. Three basic ways are described below. Combinations of these approaches are of course possible. These illustrations assume that a QNEC, if made, will be a uniform percentage of the compensation of the eligible employees for whom it is made. Other QNEC and QMAC contributions could be made—a flat dollar amount for each employee, for example.

- **Using the ADP Test:** Assume the employer decides to increase the ADP for the NHCEs from 4.0 percent to 4.8 percent so the plan will pass the basic or 1.25 ADP test. A QNEC of .8 percent for all 1,000 NHCEs will cost $216,000, based on this group's $27,000,000 payroll. By contrast, a QMAC for the 700 NHCEs who made elective deferrals will be based on a smaller payroll of $21,000,000. The required QMAC contribution will be 1.1428 percent, however, and this larger percentage contribution yields a cost of $239,988.

- **Using the ACP Test:** Assume the employer decides to increase the ACP for NHCEs to 2.8 percent from 2.1 percent so the plan will pass the basic or 1.25 ACP test. A uniform percentage QNEC contribution for all 1,000 employees would be .7 percent, for an employer cost of $189,000. The QMAC contribution rate of 1.0286 percent, applied to the smaller payroll, would yield an employer cost of $216,006.

- **Using the Aggregate Limit Test:** Here the employer can increase either the ADP or ACP of the NHCEs, using either QNECs or QMACs. The uniform percentage QNEC contribution rate to adjust the ADP would be .32 percent, or $86,400 on a $27,000,000 payroll. The QMAC contribution for the 700 eligibles would be .4571 percent, yielding a contribution of $95,991 on the lower payroll. A QNEC contribution of .4 percent would be necessary to adjust the ACP, resulting in a dollar contribution of $108,000; the QMAC contribution to adjust the ACP would be .6 percent and would cost $126,000.

As Exhibit 13–2 illustrates, the costs of the solutions described above range between a low of $86,400 and a high of $239,988. But

E X H I B I T   13–2

Illustration: Solving ADP/ACP Test Problems With QNECs and QMACs

Solution	Dollar Cost
Passing the ADP Test	
QNEC	$216,000
QMAC	239,988
Passing the ACP Test	
QNEC	189,000
QMAC	216,006
Passing the Aggregate Limit Test	
Increasing ADP	
QNEC	86,400
QMAC	95,991
Increasing ACP	
QNEC	108,000
QMAC	126,000

the appropriate solution is not solely a function of cost. For example, the employer must decide, in terms of its overall objectives, whether it wants to make supplemental contributions only for those who are participating (QMACs) or for all eligible employees (QNECs). The employer should also consider the administrative costs and complexities associated with establishing accounts for employees who do not participate but will still share in a QNEC.

PLAN ACCOUNTING

At any point in time, an employee's benefit under a defined contribution plan equals his or her account balance. In general, the account balance will consist of amounts that have been contributed by the employer and the employee, adjusted for investment gains and losses, less prior distributions. Thus, the employer will have to maintain appropriate records for all of these transactions.[8]

The recordkeeper is responsible for maintaining participant account balances. The employer's payroll department notifies the recordkeeper of contributions that have been deducted from participants' compensation on an employee-by-employee basis. These contributions, along with employer contributions, are invested in the funds offered by the plan. Trust funds are valued on a periodic basis—anywhere from daily to annually—to reflect investment gains and losses for the period. The recordkeeper must reflect these market value changes to participant accounts on a periodic basis, but no more frequently than the valuation of the funds by the trustee.

Returns on plan investments—realized income, unrealized appreciation (depreciation) and realized gains and losses—can be reflected in participant accounts using one of three methods: (1) cash (market value) accounting; (2) unit value accounting; and (3) share accounting. The accounting method will generally depend on the type of investment fund. An employer stock fund can be maintained under any of the three methods, because a participant's balance can be distributed in kind (i.e., in the form of shares). Other funds must be accounted for on a cash or unit basis. The choice of an accounting method will also depend on how the

---

8. If employer stock is involved, the original cost basis of the stock must also be included in the employee's records. This information will be necessary for tax purposes when the stock is distributed.

employer wants employees to view participation in the plan, for example, as individual ownership (share accounting) or joint ownership (cash or unit value accounting).

The key characteristic of *cash* accounting is that participant account balances are expressed as cash amounts; contributions, loans, withdrawals, and other transactions are reported as dollars and cents. Earnings are also reported as positive (or negative) cash entries in the participant records. All earnings, both realized and unrealized, are allocated.

Unit accounting expresses participant balances as units of participation. Cash contributions to the account (including loan repayments) are used to purchase units, and the value of an employee's units depends on the net asset value of the fund as of a given valuation date. If an employee has 100 units credited to his or her account in a fund with 10,000 units outstanding, the employee owns 1 percent of that fund. If the fund's net asset value is $15,000, the value of the employee's participation is 1 percent of $15,000, or $150.

The net asset value of the fund ($15,000) divided by the number of units outstanding (10,000) yields a unit value of $1.50. Earnings for the period will equal the change in the unit value multiplied by the number of units in the employee's account. If the market value of the fund in the above example rises to $16,000, the unit value will increase to $1.60 and the value of the employee's units will increase to $160.

Share accounting expresses participant balances as cash and shares (whole and fractional). The market value of the stock on a given valuation date multiplied by the number of shares in a participant's account determines the current value of the participant's share balance. Thus, as with unit value accounting, unrealized gains and losses are reflected in the change in market value. A change in unit value reflects realized income as well, but a change in share market value reflects *only* unrealized gains and losses; realized income is allocated in the participant records on a cash basis.

It is important to remember that trust funds and participant records may be valued at different times. Thus, the value of the trust funds will equal the value shown in the participant records on any given valuation date only if: (1) records are updated as frequently as the trust is valued, and (2) participant records are maintained on a cash (and not accrual) basis; that is, no contributions, loan repayments, distributions, transfers, and so forth are recorded in participant records the same day they actually affect the trust funds. This is the necessary process in the case of daily valuation recordkeeping.

Records are often kept on an accrual basis, however, so recordkeeping and trust fund valuations must be reconciled. Assume, for example, that participant records and trust funds are valued on a monthly basis, and the employer deposits contributions to the trust fund following each semimonthly payroll. In this situation, the second deposit to the trust each month may not be actually deposited by month end; thus, the trust fund value at month end may not include the second payroll. But the participant records will be updated for the month to reflect all contributions attributable to that month's payroll based on data furnished by payroll. This difference is a reconciling item between the trust fund and the recordkeeper.

Other reconciling items involve recordkeeping activities that have not yet been recognized by the trust fund. For example, requests for loans processed as part of a month-end recordkeeping valuation may not be reflected in the trust fund until a few weeks past month end (due to the time required to value funds). In other words, the participant records will show a reduction in the account balance in the amount of the loan, but the month-end trust fund value will not.

PLAN REPORTING

Plan administrators must disclose and report the terms and conditions of their plans in accordance with reporting requirements established by the IRS and DOL. Most of these requirements were described in detail in Chapter 7.[9] In general, they fall into two categories: reporting to participants and reporting to government agencies. In some cases, the same reports must be provided to both. The table (page 278-280) summarizes the reporting requirements described in Chapter 7 as well as additional items that must be reported for tax purposes, for example, Forms 1099-R and the 1096 transmittal.

---

9. See discussion beginning on page 145.

Item	Description	When Due	To Whom
Summary Plan Description (SPD)	Summary of plan in easily understandable language.	New plans—within 120 days of effective date or date of adoption if later. SPDs must be updated every 5 years to incorporate plan amendments; and every 10 years if no amendments.	All participants/ beneficiaries receiving benefits/ DOL.
Summary of Material Modification (SMM)	Summary of any change to SPD information.	Within 210 days after end of plan year in which change is adopted.	All participants/ beneficiaries receiving benefits/ DOL.
Form 5500	Annual report.	Within seven months after plan year end, plus extensions.	IRS/to participants on written request.
Schedule A	Insurance information.		
Schedule C	Service provider and trustee information—reports payments to service providers.		
Schedule E	ESOP annual information.		
Schedule P	Annual return of fiduciary—starts the running of the statute of limitations on any tax-exempt trust that loses its exemption at a future date. Optional, but important.		
Schedule SSA	Registration statement identifies terminated participants with deferred vested benefits.		
Form 5558	Annual report extension request—requests an extension up to two months. Not required if plan year corporate tax extension is granted.	Prior to 5500 deadline.	IRS.

Item	Description	When Due	To Whom
Summary Annual Report	Data on plan's financial activities, as reported on Form 5500.	Within nine months of plan year end or two months after 5500 is due, if later.	All participants/ beneficiaries.
Form 1099-R and 1096 transmittal	Report of plan distributions.	1/31 payees. 2/28 IRS.	Payees/IRS.
Form 5300 [Form 5307-ESOP]	Application for determination or plan qualification.	Usually filed by due date of tax return for year determination is desired.	IRS.
Form 5308	Request for change in plan/trust year.	By last day of short plan year or trust's short tax year.	IRS.
Form 5310	Application for determination of plan qualification on termination.	None, but advisable to file as soon as possible before plan termination date.	IRS.
Form 5310-A	Notice of merger, consolidation or transfer of plan assets or liabilities, or plan termination.	At least 30 days prior to the event; requirement has been waived for most defined contribution plans.	IRS.
Rollover Notice (402 g Notice)	Explanation of rollover opportunities, tax withholding, and tax consequences of distributions.	Not less than 10 and not more than 90 days before the annuity starting date; 30 days may be waived by recipient under certain circumstances.	Recipients of distributions.
Optional Forms Explanation	Written explanation of payment forms.	Same as above.	Recipients of distributions.

Item	Description	When Due	To Whom
Form S-8	Registration statement for offering of company stock—required only when employee contributions are invested in company stock; immediately effective upon filing.	Must precede or accompany enrollment materials.	SEC.
Prospectus	Disclosure of pertinent plan information—must be kept current. 1990 SEC regulations eliminate requirement for separate disclosure via a prospectus (e.g., an SPD timely distributed and containing required disclosures may be used).	Must precede or accompany enrollment materials.	All participants and beneficiaries.
Form 11-K	Annual report required where employee contributions invested in company stock; 1990 SEC regulations permit use of Form 5500 financial statements to meet 11-K requirements.	Within 180 days of plan year end.	SEC.
Insider Reporting	Insider reporting requirements, where contributions may be invested in company stock.		SEC/Plan Sponsor.
Form 3	Initial statement of ownership.	Within 10 days of becoming an insider.	
Form 4	Reporting for nonexempt transactions.	Within 10 days of month end.	
Form 5	Annual reporting for exempt purchases and sales of stock.	Within 45 days of fiscal year end.	

As noted in Chapter 7, Form 5500 requires comprehensive financial and participant statistical data; plan sponsors must file this annual report with the IRS, which forwards the information to the DOL. Failure to file a Form 5500 can result in penalties payable to both the IRS and the DOL.

An audit of the plan by an independent qualified public accountant is required as part of the Form 5500 filing, unless plan assets consist solely of allocated insurance contracts or unless the plan covers less than 100 participants. Documentation needed to prepare the Form 5500 includes the trustee's annual (plan year) report, the year-end reconciliation between participant balances and trust fund assets, and plan eligibility and participation statistics.

If a plan allows employees to contribute to an employer stock fund, the plan sponsor must file financial records with the SEC each year. The deadline for filing the SEC Form 11-K is 180 days after the end of the plan year.

Completion of the 11-K will generally provide everything necessary for the subsequent Form 5500 filing.

Participants receiving distributions from the plan during the current calendar year must be provided with detailed tax information on amounts paid on Form 1099-R.[10] The employer is responsible for preparing this tax form by January 31 of the year following the year of distribution, although it usually delegates this responsibility to the recordkeeper or trustee. The same tax information must be provided to the IRS by February 28, on paper or via magnetic tape, if the number of forms exceeds 250.

Plan administrators must withhold taxes from distributions eligible for rollover treatment unless these amounts are directly transferred to an IRA or to another employer's qualified plan; otherwise, withholding must take place unless the recipient elects not to have withholding apply. The recordkeeper or trustee generally calculates the amount of taxes to be withheld. Submission of withheld taxes, via Form 945, is usually the responsibility of the trustee, as is reconciliation of annual withholding. If the recordkeeper is calculating the amounts to be withheld and actually generating and submitting the Form 1099-R tax filings for participants and the

---

10. Separate reporting is required for distributions of excess deferrals and contributions so as to avoid the possible inclusion of these amounts with other distributions that could qualify for rollover treatment.

IRS, it will have to provide the trustee with annual reconciliation information.

While participant statements need be generated only once a year (and then only if requested by the participant), most employers issue them more frequently such as quarterly. Frequent reporting assures that participants are aware of the growth in their account balances and gives them the information they need to manage their plan assets. In addition, a participant statement is an effective audit tool. Given the number and variety of transactions that can occur, it is important that participants monitor their account balances; an informative, timely participant statement is an effective way to support this objective.

CHAPTER 14

Effective Communication

Defined contribution plans—and CODAs in particular—pose special communication challenges. Many of these plans require employees to make decisions that will have an impact on their financial futures. As a result, communications must move beyond the facts to provide information that will help employees evaluate the choices available to them.

The nondiscrimination requirements and other legislative and regulatory changes have further complicated the communication process. In addition, defined contribution plans—once viewed as stand-alone savings accounts—now play an increasingly important role in providing retirement income and must be communicated as part of the *total* retirement picture.

This chapter begins with a discussion of the fundamental elements of a successful benefit communication program: assessing communication needs, setting communication objectives, defining key messages, selecting appropriate media, and evaluating communication effectiveness. It concludes with a discussion of these special communication issues:

- Providing investment information.
- Evaluating retirement income needs.
- Making use of communication technology.

ASSESSING COMMUNICATION NEEDS

Talking to employees to assess their understanding of a topic before the communication process begins gives employers an opportunity to target specific communication needs. Employees may be fully aware of the tax advantages of making pretax contributions to a defined contribution plan, for example, but they may not know how different investment strategies could affect the ultimate value of their plan accounts. Assessing needs in advance allows the plan sponsor to determine which areas should be emphasized during the communication process.

An assessment of the communication environment—whether through a written survey, employee focus groups, or interviews—should be designed to:

- Measure current understanding of benefit plan provisions.
- Measure perception of the advantages and disadvantages of investing in a plan.
- Uncover information gaps and areas of special communication needs.
- Evaluate the effectiveness of past communication and determine preferred communication approaches.

Information gathered during the assessment phase will be critical in guiding the development of a communication plan that will respond appropriately to employees' information needs.

The advantages of assessment often go beyond mere fact-finding and the resulting refinement of the communication approach, however. The process also:

- Gives employees an opportunity to express their opinions on issues of importance to them.
- Focuses employee attention on benefits, making them more interested, knowledgeable, and receptive to messages on the subject.
- Identifies existing barriers—in perceptions or attitudes—that will require special attention in communication planning and implementation.
- Gives management an opportunity to respond to key concerns about plan design—through revision or a more complete explanation of the rationale behind plan provisions.

Even modest revisions in plan design or communication made as a result of employee input can translate into increased acceptance of a benefit plan or provision.

SETTING COMMUNICATION OBJECTIVES

Once the assessment phase is complete, the plan sponsor can develop specific communication objectives and strategies to guide the communication process. Stated objectives for a communication plan to introduce a new CODA might include the following, for example:

- Maximizing employee appreciation and enthusiasm for the new plan.
- Building the understanding and motivation employees need to make informed enrollment decisions.
- Producing skilled, effective meeting leaders who can deliver benefit messages.
- Providing opportunities for employees to ask questions— and get answers.
- Making it easy for employees to enroll.

These objectives are broad but measurable—particularly during the evaluation phase of the communication process described below.

When possible, more specific communication objectives should be expressed quantitatively. Examples include:

- Increasing participation of employees earning up to $25,000 by 10 percent.
- Increasing overall contribution levels by 1 percent.
- Decreasing questions about loan provisions by 50 percent.

A comprehensive communication plan will encompass both short-term objectives (relating to the enrollment period, for example) and long-term objectives designed to support the continuing reinforcement of employer messages.

DEFINING KEY MESSAGES

The key messages of any communication will be defined by the needs of employees—an increasingly diverse group in most companies. Communication will typically emphasize the topics discussed below.

Plan Design Rationale

Plan design is often grounded in corporate and competitive strategies, and today's employees recognize—and expect—this link. Straightforward, clear, and concise messages conveying the rationale behind a plan or a specific plan provision are essential in creating initial acceptance. Failure to convey these messages may raise questions among employees and detract from their understanding and appreciation of a plan.

The overall rationale behind a plan is often best communicated by management in introductory letters to employees, announcement flyers, and the like. Exhibit 14–1 provides an example of a management letter introducing an ESOP and a profit-sharing plan.

Key messages should be reinforced on an ongoing basis. Reinforcement is particularly important in the case of a profit-sharing plan or ESOP, where employee performance and productivity often have a significant impact on the value of contributions and account balances on a year-by-year basis.

E X H I B I T   14–1

Excerpt From an ESOP/Profit-Sharing Announcement Letter From Management

As an employee of XYZ Company, you contribute to our growth and success. In return, the Company provides two retirement plans through which you share in our growth financially, both now and over the long term. The basic philosophy behind both plans is shared rewards for shared performance. XYZ is investing in your future because the better we do together, the more we can benefit individually. The Employee Stock Ownership Plan (ESOP) gives you a stake in XYZ's long-term success by making you a stockholder—through annual contributions of stock to your ESOP account, which will be paid out when you leave the Company.

The Profit-Sharing Plan reflects each year's performance results through annual contributions based on profits. Part of your share is automatically deferred for payment when you leave the Company; the remainder you can generally defer or take as cash.

The plans represent an opportunity to build your financial assets, but they also represent a challenge. Your efforts, along with those of your fellow employees, will help determine the long-term success of the Company and the benefits that these plans will provide.

How the Plan Works

The mechanics of any benefit plan need to be communicated in basic terms. A summary of any defined contribution plan should cover the following topics:

- Eligibility.
- Enrollment and beneficiary designations.
- How employee contributions are made and how they can be changed or stopped.
- How employer matching contributions, if any, are determined.
- How investment elections are made and how they can be changed.
- How money can be accessed—including withdrawals or loans during employment and plan payments when employment ends.
- The tax consequences of plan investments and payments.

When the employer contributes to the plan, some explanation of vesting and vesting schedules will be necessary as well. In addition, a summary of plan provisions should make some reference to IRS contribution limits, even though few employees may be affected.

Employers who offer company stock as an investment fund may need to provide additional information—explaining investment alternatives for ESOP participants who are near retirement age and who must be permitted to diversify, for example.[1] In the special case of a leveraged ESOP, information about the plan's loan—how it was made and how it will be repaid—helps employees understand their stake in the business. The value and mechanics of preferred stock versus common stock issues may also aid in understanding the workings of an ESOP.

Reporting and disclosure requirements under Title I of ERISA and subsequent DOL regulations have expanded the information employers must communicate about their defined contribution plans. The detail of required communication is often best reserved for the summary plan description, where it will serve as resource material. (Required disclosures to employees are described in Chapter 7.)

---

1. See Chapter 5.

Highlighting Advantages

The advantages of employer-sponsored defined contribution plans are often the subject of newspaper and magazine articles and are publicized by financial advisors and retirement planners as well. However, a well-designed and company-specific communication campaign is much more likely to generate enthusiasm for these plans among employees. Examples of approaches plan sponsors can use to illustrate the advantages of investing in a savings plan, profit-sharing plan, or ESOP follow:

The Pretax Advantage   Exhibit 14–2 shows one method of communicating the advantages associated with the ability to contribute pretax dollars to an employer-sponsored plan.

E X H I B I T   14–2
_____

Excerpt From 401(k) Savings Plan Communication Materials
Illustrating the Advantage of Pretax Savings

Here's an Example... More Take-Home Pay

Suppose you're earning $30,000 a year and contributing 5 percent of your pay to the plan. You are married and file a joint return for federal income tax withholding purposes. Here's a comparison of what can happen to your take-home pay when you save aftertax versus pretax dollars:

	5 Percent Aftertax	5 Percent Pretax
Pay	$30,000	$30,000
Before-tax savings	0	minus 1,500
Taxable pay	$30,000	$28,500
Federal income tax (15%)	minus 2,800	minus 2,575
Aftertax savings	minus 1,500	0
Net pay	$25,700	$25,925
Difference in take-home pay	—	plus · $225

You save the same amount—$1,500—but by making pretax contributions, you take home $225 more in pay. And because of the tax savings, the $1,500 you contribute reduces your take-home pay by only $1,275.

In addition, the Company will match your savings at the rate of 50 cents on each dollar you save—that's $750. So in one year's time, you will save a total of $2,250 in the plan ($1,500 plus $750), but the net effect on your pay is only $1,275.

Worksheets can also be personalized to show individual employees how various contribution levels will affect their take-home pay and total savings. In addition, employers can take advantage of interactive telephone or personal computer (PC) technologies to reinforce their messages or to provide employees with help in making decisions involving their personal financial situations.

Exhibit 14–3 shows another approach: a table enabling employees to estimate their own tax savings at various contribution levels.

The Value of Employer Contributions The value of matching employer contributions can also be demonstrated through the use of examples, worksheets, and personalized or interactive communication as described above. Exhibit 14–4 (page 290) shows a sample worksheet.

E X H I B I T   14–3

Excerpt From 401(k) Savings Plan Communication Materials
Estimating Tax Savings

Use the following chart to estimate the tax advantages of contributing to the plan by locating the annual pay, savings percentage, and filing status closest to your own.

		Your Estimated Annual Reduction in Federal Income Tax Withholding Could Be:	
If Your Annual Pay Is:	And Your Annual Contribution Is:	Single/One Exemption	Married/Three Exemptions
$16,000	3% 480	$65	$65
	5 800	105	105
	7 1,120	145	145
20,000	3 600	70	70
	5 1,000	120	120
	7 1,400	170	170
25,000	3 750	210	115
	5 1,250	350	190
	7 1,750	490	265

(Table continues in $5,000 salary increments)

Excerpt From 401(k) Savings Plan Communication Materials
Worksheet Showing Value of Employer Matching Contributions

XYZ Company Helps You Save

Another advantage of saving money in the Savings Plus Plan is that the Company will help you build your savings. XYZ will match the first 5 percent of pay you contribute at the rate of 50 cents for each dollar.

To find out how much the Company will add to your account each year, simply calculate the annual dollar amount you plan to save. Then multiply 50 percent (.50) times your annual contribution—up to 5 percent of your pay—to find out the Company match:

$ _____   X   .50   = $ _____

Your annual contribution   XYZ matching   Annual XYZ matching
up to 5 percent of pay   percentage   to contribution

The Power of Compound Interest Illustrations of the effect of interest compounding can strongly influence employees' perceptions of the value of the defined contribution plan. Exhibit 14–5 (page 291) provides an example. Such an illustration can be made even more powerful by incorporating pay increase projections.

The Convenience of Payroll Deductions The ease of making contributions to an employer- sponsored savings plan may be a key to participation for employees. Illustrations of the net effect of contributing on a regular basis may be helpful in demonstrating how easy it is to participate in the plan.

The Advantages of Dollar Cost Averaging Investors aspire to buy low and sell high, but correct market timing has proven to be an elusive skill. A basic concept called dollar cost averaging may help employees resolve the question of when to buy. By investing a predetermined amount of money in a plan investment option on a regular basis, an employee will buy fewer shares or units when the price is high and more when it is low; thus, over time, the average price he pays will be somewhere in the middle of the investment option's price range. While the employee will miss some opportunities to buy at the lowest price, he won't commit all of his funds at the highest price, either.

E X H I B I T   14–5

Excerpt From 401(k) Savings Plan Communication Materials
The Power of Compound Interest

The Power of Compound Interest: If you invest $2,000 a year for the first 9 years of a 40-year period with annual compounding at 10 percent, you will earn more than someone who invests $2,000 a year from Year 10 through 40. The total contribution in the latter case would be 3.5 times greater, yet would earn 27 percent less.

	Early Funding			*Late Funding*	
Year	Contribution	Year-End Value	Year	Contribution	Year-End Value
1	$2,000	$2,160	1	$0	$0
2	2,000	4,493	2	0	0
3	2,000	7,012	3	0	0
4	2,000	9,733	4	0	0
5	2,000	12,672	5	0	0
6	2,000	15,846	6	0	0
7	2,000	19,273	7	0	0
8	2,000	22,975	8	0	0
9	2,000	26,973	9	0	0
10	0	29,131	10	2,000	2,160
11	0	31,461	11	2,000	4,493
12	0	33,978	12	2,000	7,012
13	0	36,697	13	2,000	9,733
14	0	39,632	14	2,000	12,672
15	0	42,803	15	2,000	15,846
16	0	46,227	16	2,000	19,273
17	0	49,925	17	2,000	22,975
18	0	53,919	18	2,000	26,973
19	0	58,233	19	2,000	31,291
20	0	62,892	20	2,000	35,954
21	0	67,923	21	2,000	40,991
22	0	73,357	22	2,000	46,430
23	0	79,225	23	2,000	52,304
24	0	85,563	24	2,000	58,649
25	0	92,408	25	2,000	65,500
26	0	99,801	26	2,000	72,900
27	0	107,785	27	2,000	80,893
28	0	116,408	28	2,000	89,524
29	0	125,721	29	2,000	98,846

E X H I B I T   14–5 (continued)

	Early Funding			Late Funding	
Year	Contribution	Year-End Value	Year	Contribution	Year-End Value
30	0	135,778	30	2,000	108,914
31	0	146,640	31	2,000	119,787
32	0	158,372	32	2,000	131,530
33	0	171,041	33	2,000	144,212
34	0	184,725	34	2,000	157,909
35	0	199,503	35	2,000	172,702
36	0	215,463	36	2,000	188,678
37	0	232,700	37	2,000	205,932
38	0	251,316	38	2,000	224,566
39	0	271,421	39	2,000	244,692
40	0	293,135	40	2,000	266,427
Investment:		$ 18,000			$ 62,000
Earnings:		$275,135			$204,427
Total:		$293,135			$266,427

Understanding the Limits

In addition to understanding the advantages of contributing to their CODAs and other defined contribution plans, employees need to know the circumstances in which they can and cannot have access to their funds, particularly when they are permitted to make pretax contributions or to elect to defer company contributions that might otherwise be paid as cash. Communication materials should include a summary of withdrawal and loan provisions, if any, and the tax consequences of plan payments.

Communication Activities and Media

The communication process includes these essential elements:

- Creating initial awareness and building understanding of basic plan provisions.

- Educating and informing employees so they are able to evaluate the alternatives available to them.
- Reinforcing key messages on an ongoing basis.

Specific communication activities within this framework can be categorized as basic or optional.

Basic Activities   Basic communication activities include announcing and describing the plan and educating employees about the range of choices available to them.

Examples of basic activities to create initial awareness include:

- A supervisor's or manager's memo to alert employees to any plan changes and outline the upcoming communication program.
- A letter to employees from management to reinforce communication objectives and convey the rationale behind plan design.
- Newsletters, bulletins, articles in an employee publication, posters, and payroll stuffers to build anticipation and enthusiasm for the program.

Basic activities during the *awareness phase* should typically cover broad concepts and philosophies, with modest details about plan provisions. In developing initial communication materials, however, plan sponsors can be guided by preferences expressed by employees during the *assessment phase*. Employees may have indicated a preference for small, digestible doses of information, for example, or they may prefer to hear all of the details at once.

Basic activities during the *educational phase*—often designed to support an enrollment or election process—should be structured to deliver detailed information to employees. Face-to-face communication is consistently ranked as a preferred source of information by employees, and employee meetings can provide an excellent forum for trained meeting leaders to deliver benefit information, supported by an audiovisual presentation (videotape, slides, or overhead transparencies). Such meetings give employees the opportunity to ask questions, learn about enrollment procedures, and receive communication materials.

Employee information packages typically contain a summary of the plan and a description of the plan's election options, providing the details necessary for employees and their families to make informed decisions. An information package might also contain supporting workbooks or worksheets and enrollment materials.

Additional Activities   Additional communication activities can be designed to address the special communication needs of specific employee groups, support the enrollment process, or generally promote and enhance the overall communication of a plan. Examples of such activities include:

- A telephone hotline employees can call for answers to questions. Trained meeting leaders or benefit administrators can act as hotline operators. As an alternative, some plan sponsors train retired employees—valuable and experienced resources—to operate benefit hotlines during the course of a plan communication.
- Question and answer sheets, special benefit bulletins, or newsletters to address the questions employees ask most frequently.
- Paycheck stuffers, desk drops, posters, and bulletin board notices—electronic or posted—to remind employees of deadlines and maintain awareness and enthusiasm.
- Optional family meetings, giving family members the opportunity to learn about a benefit plan firsthand. As an alternative, video or audio cassettes can be used to generate interest and to share information about a plan outside of meetings. A lending library check-out system allows employees to educate themselves and family members at home.
- Novelties—including hats, pens, T-shirts, mugs, paperweights, rulers, key chains, or tote bags—serve as ongoing, tangible reminders of a benefit plan.

These are just a few examples of communication materials and activities plan sponsors can use to build awareness and educate employees.

Ongoing Activities An effective communication plan will also include follow-up activities to reinforce key messages and maintain momentum. Possibilities include:

- Response cards in the enrollment package to elicit employees' reactions to a benefit plan and its communication.
- Articles in internal publications reporting general information about a plan and enrollment.
- Regular, personalized statements to maintain the visibility of the plan.
- Summary plan descriptions prepared in a format that allows easy access to information.

Evaluating Communication Effectiveness

Evaluation is the first step to refining and improving the effectiveness of communication processes. The success of a program can be measured against the objectives set during the communication planning stage. Evaluation might take the form of a response card, as noted above, or a telephone survey to measure employee reaction to the plan and the communication effort.

Plan sponsors can also obtain quantitative and qualitative information about employee communication needs by measuring meeting attendance, counting and analyzing errors on enrollment forms, and recording the number and type of questions received during the communication period.

SPECIAL ISSUES

Most employees recognize that they cannot rely on social security and employer-provided benefits to meet all their financial needs during retirement. Nonetheless, many have done little financial planning. In a 1994 Towers Perrin survey of 1,000 employees, most of the working Americans acknowledged that they are largely responsible for providing for their own retirement. And half said that they had already done "a lot" or "a fair amount" of financial planning, while another 31 percent said they had done at least "some"planning. By contrast, in a similar survey conducted by

Towers Perrin in 1991, only one-quarter of the respondents indicated that they had done at least some planning. Today, moreover, 79 percent now say they are saving for retirement—compared with just 66 percent in 1991.

Regrettably, the conventional wisdom—that employees understand how CODAs and other defined contribution plans work—does not withstand close scrutiny. These plans are certainly visible, and employees appreciate seeing their money accumulate. But the Towers Perrin survey revealed some real gaps in understanding—gaps that may keep employees from accumulating enough money for their retirement.

Fully three-quarters of savings plan participants said that they are either "very comfortable" or "somewhat comfortable" about making savings plan investment decisions (83 percent of men versus 67 percent of women). Nonetheless, the survey findings revealed a fairly widespread lack of knowledge about investment basics. For example:

- 39 percent of respondents who participate in CODAs or savings plans did not know how their dollars were allocated among asset classes.
- 17 percent of savings plan participants did not know whether stocks or "guaranteed" investments will produce higher returns over a 20-year period; half of the remaining respondents thought that guaranteed investments will perform better (35 percent) or the same (15 percent) as stocks.
- 32 percent of plan participants believed there is no risk at all associated with an investment in bonds; 14 percent believed there is no risk at all associated with an investment in a "mutual" or "balanced" fund.

These results underscore changing benefit communication needs. As CODAs and other defined contribution plans begin to play a larger role in providing total retirement income, employees need to know more than the basic facts about how their plans work. They need to know what their income needs are likely to be during retirement, what they can expect in the way of retirement income, and what they can do to reduce any gap between needs and revenues.

Evaluating Savings Needs

If employees are to make informed decisions about their financial futures, they need to know what income they can expect from social security and from employer-sponsored defined benefit, defined contribution, and postretirement health care and life insurance plans. By comparing this information to the expenses they are likely to face during retirement, they will be in a position to estimate personal savings needs and design savings programs to meet those needs.

Traditional approaches to providing this information include printed materials, preretirement counseling, and training sessions. Communication materials like those excerpted in Exhibits 14–2 through 14–5, for example, reinforce the financial advantages of participating in a CODA or other defined contribution plan to the fullest extent possible.

By taking advantage of communication technology, employers can personalize this information and make it possible for employees to model the impact of various financial decisions. Exhibit 14–6 shows a screen from an interactive planning program that runs on a personal computer. The screen compares retirement

E X H I B I T   14–6

Retirement Income Versus Retirement Expenses

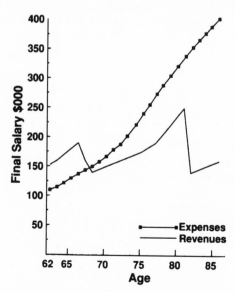

income needs[2] to the revenue stream generated by social security and all employer-provided plans (pension, CODA, and postretirement medical) for a hypothetical employee.

By changing various assumptions—the annual percentage of pay contributed to the CODA, for example, or the expected rate of return on plan assets—employees can test the financial impact of decisions that are within their control.

Providing Meaningful Investment Information

As was pointed out in Chapter 7, the DOL has released an interpretive bulletin distinguishing between investment advice and investment education in participant-directed investment plans. By summarizing the types of information that would not be considered to be investment advice, the DOL has defined four safe harbors for plan sponsors and 401(k) professionals. These safe harbors were briefly identified in Chapter 7 and are described in greater detail in the following. It should be noted that the form of the information—whether oral, in writing, video or software—and who provides it—plan sponsor, fiduciary or service provider—are not relevant in determining whether the information is investment education or investment advice.

The safe harbors are:

- General Plan Information. Plan information is considered to include the benefits of participating and increasing plan contributions, the effect of preretirement withdrawals on retirement income, and other general features of the plan. Descriptions of plan investment choices, including descriptions of investment objectives, risk and return characteristics, and historical return information are included in this safe harbor. As long as the information does not refer to the appropriateness of a specific investment option for an individual, it will not be considered to be investment advice under ERISA.

---

2. Projected expenditures are based on Bureau of Labor Statistics data, adjusted to reflect pay levels and take inflation and taxes into account throughout the retirement years. Expense items include daily living expenses; income and property taxes; medical and long-term care expenses, including Medicare premiums; entertainment/vacation expenses; and auto/transportation expenses.

- General Financial and Investment Information. Under this safe harbor, general financial and investment concepts—including historic differences in rates of return associated with different asset classes, the effect of inflation, estimates of future retirement income needs, determining investment time horizons and assessing risk tolerance—are all considered appropriate educational topics. Examples of the types of investment concepts that might be explained without being considered investment advice include risk and return, diversification, dollar cost averaging and the advantages of tax deferral.

- Asset Allocation Models. Asset allocation model portfolios for hypothetical individuals with different time horizons and risk profiles may be used under this safe harbor, as long as the models are based on generally accepted investment theories and all material facts and assumptions are included. If the asset allocation model identifies a specific asset classification and the investment alternative under the plan that matches that classification, the model should identify all investment alternatives available under the plan which match that classification. These models must include a statement that individuals should consider their other income, assets, and investments in addition to plan investments when applying a particular asset allocation model to their own situations. Since the model allows a participant to apply the investment concepts underlying the model to his or her individual situation, the model itself will not be considered to be investment advice under ERISA.

- Interactive Investment Materials. Questionnaires, worksheets, interactive software and other materials which a participant can use to estimate future retirement needs and the impact of various investment allocation strategies on meeting those needs would not be considered to be investment advice under this safe harbor. As with the asset allocation model, these materials must be based on generally accepted investment principles, disclose underlying assumptions, and identify all similar investment alternatives if a particular plan investment alternative is identified with a particular asset classification. And, just as with the

asset allocation model, a statement must accompany these
materials which explains that when applying these materials to an individual situation, other income, assets and
investments should be considered in addition to plan
investments.

In short, the DOL interpretive bulletin has cleared the way for
plan sponsors and service providers to educate participants to
assess their own situations and make informed investment decisions. And while these safe harbors are not the exclusive means of
providing investment education, they provide guidance to help
shape an educational program that is both useful and informative
for participants.

Employees also need information about the way other choices
can affect their financial futures. Different distribution options[3]
have different financial consequences, for example, as do different
retirement ages. Exhibit 14–7 illustrates this point. The graph on
the left compares revenues and expenses for an employee who
retires at age 60 and takes her 401(k) account balance as an installment distribution paid over a five-year period. The graph on the

EXHIBIT   14–7

Retirement Income Versus Retirement Expenses

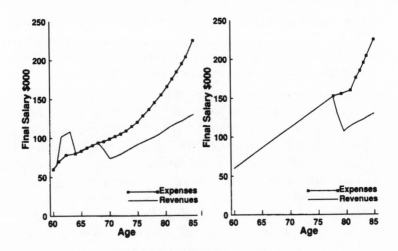

---

3. See Chapter 6.

right shows what happens if she delays retirement by two years and draws down her account balance as needed, subject to the minimum distribution rules.

An informed choice among investment and distribution options may enable employees to achieve a better match between retirement revenues and expenditures—at no additional cost to the plan sponsor.

As CODAs and other defined contribution plans assume a larger role in providing retirement income, it is important that employees play an active role in retirement planning and decision-making. A thoughtful communication and education program will provide them with the information they need to make the most of the resources available to them.

Appendices

Benefit and Contribution Limits

Indexed Employee Benefit Limits

	1987	1988	1989	1990	1991	1992	1993	1994	1995	1996
Section 415 Defined Benefit Dollar Limit	$ 90,000	$ 94,023	$ 98,064	$102,582	$108,963	$112,221	$115,641	$118,800	$120,000	$120,000
Section 415 Defined Contribution Dollar Limit	$ 30,000	$ 30,000	$ 30,000	$ 30,000	$ 30,000	$ 30,000	$ 30,000	$ 30,000	$ 30,000	$ 30,000
Elective Deferral Limit	$ 7,000	$ 7,313	$ 7,627	$ 7,979	$ 8,475	$ 8,728	$ 8,994	$ 9,240	$ 9,240	$ 9,500
Maximum Compensation Limit	$200,000	$200,000	$200,000	$209,200	$222,200	$228,860	$235,840	$150,000	$150,000	$150,000
Excess Distribution Limit/Excess Accumulation Limit	$112,500	$117,529	$122,580	$128,228	$136,204	$140,276	$144,551	$148,500	$150,000	$155,000
Highly Compensated Employee Definition Limits	$ 50,000 $ 75,000	$ 52,235 $ 78,353	$ 54,480 $ 81,720	$ 56,990 $ 85,485	$ 60,535 $ 90,803	$ 62,345 $ 93,518	$ 64,245 $ 96,368	$ 66,000 $ 99,000	$ 66,000 $100,000	$ 66,000 $100,000
ESOP Payout Limits	$100,000 $500,000	$104,470 $522,350	$108,960 $544,800	$113,980 $569,900	$121,070 $605,350	$124,690 $623,450	$128,490 $642,450	$132,000 $660,000	$132,000 $670,000	$135,000 $690,000

Section 415 Limits on Contribution and Benefits

Limitation Years Ending In	Maximum Annual Benefit Under Defined Benefit Plans	Maximum Annual Additions Under Defined Contribution Plans
1976	$ 80,475	$26,825
1977	$ 84,525	$28,175
1978	$ 90,150	$30,050
1979	$ 98,100	$32,700
1980	$110,625	$36,875
1981	$124,500	$41,500
1982*	$136,425	$45,475
1983–1987*	**	**

*In the case of a plan established after July 1, 1982, the maximum annual benefit is $90,000 and the maximum annual addition is $30,000.

**For limitation years *beginning* after December 31, 1982, and before 1988, the maximum annual benefit is $90,000 and the maximum annual addition is $30,000. Transition rules may alter these limits.

Sample 401(k) Savings Plan Document[1]

For Review By Legal Counsel

_____

(Date)

_____

Name of Plan

Effective _____

The _____ (the "Plan") as stated herein is an amendment and restatement of the _____ Plan as in effect on _____.

The provisions of the Plan are subject to a determination by the Internal Revenue Service that the Plan is qualified under Section 401(a) of the Internal Revenue Code of 1986, as amended. It is further intended that the Plan also conform to the requirements of Title I of the Employee Retirement Income Security Act of 1974, as amended from time to time.

PLAN DOCUMENT—TABLE OF CONTENTS

ARTICLE 1 DEFINITIONS

---

1. Important note: This sample plan document does not reflect the provisions of the Small Business Job Protection Act of 1996 that are summarized throughout this book. As we go to press, many interpretive issues involving the Act remain unresolved. No use should be made of this sample document without consulting legal counsel.

ARTICLE 2 SERVICE COUNTING RULES

ARTICLE 3 ELIGIBILITY

ARTICLE 4 PRETAX, AFTERTAX, AND ROLLOVER CONTRIBUTIONS

ARTICLE 13 PLAN ADMINISTRATION

ARTICLE 14 ESTABLISHMENT OF FUND

ARTICLE 15 AMENDMENT, TERMINATION, AND MERGER OF THE PLAN

ARTICLE 16 TOP-HEAVY PLAN REQUIREMENTS

ARTICLE 17 MISCELLANEOUS

ARTICLE 1: DEFINITIONS

1.1   "Accounts" shall mean, with respect to any Participant, his Pretax Account, Aftertax Account, Rollover Account, Employer Account, and Loan Account and shall, as to each such Account, include any subaccount established thereunder. "Account" shall mean any one (1) or more of the foregoing "Accounts."

1.2   "Affiliated Employer" shall mean _____ and any of its subsidiaries or affiliates, whether or not such entities have adopted the Plan, and any other entity which is a member of a "controlled group of corporations," a group under "common control," or an "affiliated service group," all as determined under Code Sections 414(b), (c), (m), (o), or solely for purposes of Section 6.11, the rules set forth in Code Section 415(h), which includes _____.

1.3   "Aftertax Account" shall mean the Account established for a Participant in accordance with Section 7.1.

1.4   "Aftertax Contribution" shall mean the contributions that a Participant elects to make to the Plan in accordance with Section 4.2.

1.5   "Average Contribution Percentage" shall mean, for any
       Plan Year, the average of the ratios determined under Sec-
       tion 1.14 for (i) the group of Eligible Employees who are
       Highly Compensated Employees and (ii) the group of Eli-
       gible Employees who are Nonhighly Compensated
       Employees.

1.6   "Average Deferral Percentage" shall mean, for any Plan
       Year, the average of the ratios determined under Section
       1.15 for (i) the group of Eligible Employees who are Highly
       Compensated Employees and (ii) the group of Eligible
       Employees who are Nonhighly Compensated Employees.

1.7   "Beneficiary" shall mean the person or persons, entity or
       entities (including a trust(s)), or estate that shall be entitled
       to receive benefits payable pursuant to the provisions of
       this Plan by virtue of a Participant's death.

1.8   "Board" shall mean the Board of Directors of _____,
       except that any action taken by the Board may also be taken
       by a duly authorized committee of the Board.

1.9   "Break in Service" shall mean a Termination followed by
       the completion of a One Year Break in Service.

1.10   "Code" shall mean the Internal Revenue Code of 1986, as
       amended from time to time.

1.11   "Committee" shall mean the committee of individuals
       appointed by the Board to be responsible for the operation
       and administration of the Plan in accordance with the pro-
       visions of Article 13.

1.12   "Compensation" shall mean [base pay] [all remuneration
       received by an Employee from the Employer during a Plan
       Year that is considered as wages reportable under Code
       Section 6051(a)(3), prior to reductions for Pretax Contribu-
       tions made to the Plan or salary reduction contributions to
       a plan excludable from income under Code Section 125].
       For Plan Years beginning on and after January 1, 1989 and
       before January 1, 1994, "Compensation" shall not include
       amounts over two hundred thousand dollars ($200,000), as
       indexed under Section 401(a)(17) of the Code, determined
       on an annual basis. For Plan Years beginning on and after
       January 1, 1994, "Compensation" shall not include
       amounts over one hundred fifty thousand dollars

($150,000), as indexed under Section 401(a)(17) of the Code; determined on an annual basis. Under the family aggregation rules of Section 414(q)(6) of the Code, an Eligible Employee who is a highly Compensated Employee and a five (5) percent owner or one of the ten (10) most Highly Compensated Employees and his Family Members shall be treated as one Employee for purposes of this Section 1.12.

1.13 "Computation Period" shall mean the Plan Year, except for purposes of determining eligibility, in which case, it shall mean the twelve (12) month period commencing with the Employee's Employment Commencement Date or most recent date of rehire following a Break in Service. If the Eligible Employee fails to satisfy the requirements for eligibility in that twelve (12) month period, the Computation Period for determining eligibility for that Eligible Employee shall thereafter be the Plan Year that begins within such twelve (12) month period and each Plan Year thereafter.

1.14 "Contribution Percentage" shall mean, for any Plan Year, for each Eligible Employee, whose Entry Date on which he first became entitled to participate in accordance with Section 3.3 has occurred, the ratio for each such Eligible Employee of the amount of Aftertax Contributions made by such Eligible Employee, if any, and Employer Matching Contributions, if any, made to the Plan and allocated to such Eligible Employee for such Plan Year in accordance with Articles 4 and 5, to such Eligible Employee's compensation within the meaning of Code Section 414(s) [for] [while eligible during] such Plan Year. In determining the Contribution Percentage of a Highly Compensated Employee, all Aftertax Contributions and Employer Matching Contributions made on behalf of such Highly Compensated Employee to any plan maintained by an Affiliated Employer shall be aggregated.

1.15 "Deferral Percentage" shall mean, for any Plan Year, for each Eligible Employee, whose Entry Date on which he first became entitled to participate in accordance with Section 3.3 has occurred, the ratio for each such Eligible Employee of Pretax Contributions, if any, made to the Plan by the

Employer on behalf of such Eligible Employee for such Plan Year to such Eligible Employee's compensation (within the meaning of Code Section 414(s)) [for] [while eligible during] such Plan Year. In determining the Deferral Percentage of a Highly Compensated Employee, all Pretax Contributions made on behalf of such Highly Compensated Employee to any plan maintained by an Affiliated Employer shall be aggregated.

1.16 "Disability" shall mean a physical or mental condition of such severity and duration as to entitle the Participant to disability benefits under the Federal Social Security Act. "Disabled Participant" shall mean a Participant who is in receipt of disability benefits under the Federal Social Security Act.

1.17 "Effective Date of this Restatement" shall mean _____.

1.18 "Eligible Employee" shall mean an Employee of an Employer, who is entitled to participate in the Plan upon meeting the requirements in accordance with Section 3.1, other than (a) an Employee whose terms and conditions of employment are the subject of a collective bargaining agreement between an Employer and a collective bargaining agent unless and until participation in the Plan shall have been negotiated for and agreed to in writing by the representatives of such Employer and the collective bargaining agent, or (b) a Leased Employee.

1.19 "Eligibility Service" shall mean Service as counted for determining an Employee's right to become a Participant in the Plan, as determined in accordance with Article 2.

1.20 "Employee" shall mean any person who is a common-law employee or a Leased Employee of an Affiliated Employer.

1.21 "Employer" shall mean _____ and any other Affiliated Employer which, with the consent of the Board, shall adopt this Plan for some or all of its Eligible Employees. "Employer" when used in this Plan shall refer to such adopting entities either individually or collectively, as the context may require.

1.22 "Employer Account" shall mean the account established for a Participant in accordance with Section 7.1.

1.23 "Employer Matching Contribution" shall mean the contributions made by the Employer to the Plan in accordance with Section 5.1(a).

1.24 "Employment Commencement Date" shall mean the date on which an Employee is first credited with an Hour of Service.

1.25 "Entry Date" shall mean the first day of the payroll period coincident with or immediately following January 1, April 1, July 1, and September 1 in every calendar year during which the Plan is in effect.

1.26 "ERISA" shall mean the Employee Retirement Income Security Act of 1974 (Public Law #93-406), as amended from time to time.

1.27 "Family Member" shall mean an individual described in Section 414(q)(6)(B) of the Code, except that in determining whether Compensation paid to Family Members exceeds the limit on Compensation under Section 401(a)(17) of the Code, as described in Section 1.12, the term "Family Member" shall include only the Spouse of the Eligible Employee and any lineal descendants who have not attained age 19 before the close of the Plan Year.

1.28 "Fund" shall mean any fund provided for in a trust arrangement, or a combination of a trust arrangement and one or more insurance company contracts, which is held by a Funding Agent, to which contributions under the Plan on and after the Effective Date will be made, and out of which benefits are paid to Participants or otherwise provided for.

1.29 "Funding Agent" shall mean a trustee or insurance company or any duly appointed successor or successors selected to hold a Fund.

1.30 "Highly Compensated Employee" shall mean an Employee who performs service during the Determination Year and is described in one or more of the following groups in accordance with IRS regulations:

(a) An Employee who is a five percent (5%) owner as defined in Section 416(i)(1)(iii) of the Code, at any time during the Determination Year or the Look-back Year.

(b)   An Employee who receives Compensation in excess of $75,000 during the Look-back Year. (The $75,000 limitation will be adjusted annually for increases in the cost of living in accordance with Section 415(d) of the Code).

(c)   An Employee who receives Compensation in excess of $50,000 during the Look-back Year and is a member of the top-paid group for the Look-back Year. (The $50,000 limitation will be adjusted annually for increases in the cost of living in accordance with Section 415(d) of the Code).

(d)   An Employee who is an officer within the meaning of Section 416(i) of the Code during the Look-back Year and who receives Compensation in the Look-back Year greater than fifty percent (50%) of the dollar limitation in effect under Section 415(b)(1)(A) of the Code, for the calendar year in which the Look-back Year begins. Notwithstanding the foregoing, no more than 50 or, if lesser, the greater of three (3) employees or ten percent (10%) of the Employees shall be treated as officers; provided, however, if no officer is described in this subparagraph (d), then the highest-paid officer for such year shall be treated as herein described.

(e)   An Employee who is (i) described in paragraph (b), (c) or (d) above, and (ii) one of the 100 Employees who receives the most Compensation from the Employer during the Determination Year, when the Determination Year is substituted for the Look-back Year in paragraphs (b), (c), or (d).

A former Employee shall be treated as a Highly Compensated Employee if such former Employee had a separation year prior to the Determination Year and was a Highly Compensated active Employee for either (1) such Employee's separation year or (2) any Determination Year ending on or after the Employee's 55th birthday.

A separation year is the Determination Year in which the Employee separates from service. Notwithstanding the foregoing, an Employee who separated from service before January 1, 1987, is a Highly Compensated Employee only if he was a five percent (5%) owner or received Compensation in excess of $50,000 during (i) the Employee's separation year (or the year preceding such separation year), or (ii) any year ending on or after such Employee's 55th birthday (or the last year ending before such Employee's 55th birthday).

Notwithstanding anything to the contrary in this Plan, Sections 414(b), (c), (m), (n) and (o) of the Code are applied prior to determining whether an Employee is a Highly Compensated Employee.

For purposes of this section,

(a) "Compensation" shall mean compensation as defined in Section 414(q)(7) and the regulations thereunder.

(b) "Determination Year" shall mean the Plan Year for which the determination of who is Highly Compensated is being made.

(c) "Look-back Year" shall mean the twelve (12) month period preceding the Determination Year.

(d) "Top-paid Group" shall mean the top twenty percent (20%) of Employees when rated on the basis of Compensation paid during the year. The number of Employees in the group will be determined in accordance with Section 414(q)(8) of the Code.

The Employer shall have the right to elect to determine Highly Compensated Employees by reference to calendar year Compensation, in accordance with IRS regulations. If the Employer so elects, the Employer must make such election with respect to all other qualified plans it maintains.

1.31 "Hour of Service" shall mean an hour of service calculated in accordance with the provisions of Article 2.

1.32 "Leased Employee" shall mean any person who renders personal services to an Affiliated Employer and who is described in Section 414(n)(2) of the Code by reason of providing such services, other than a person described in Section 414(n)(5) of the Code.

1.33   "Limitation Year" shall mean the twelve (12) month period ending on each _____.

1.34   "Loan Account" shall mean the account established for a Participant in accordance with Section 7.1.

1.35   "Named Fiduciary" shall mean a fiduciary designated as such under the provisions of Article 13.

1.36   "Nonhighly Compensated Employee" shall mean an Eligible Employee other than a Highly Compensated Employee.

1.37   "Normal Retirement Age" shall mean the later of:

   (a)   The time a Participant attains age 65, or

   (b)   The fifth (5th) anniversary of the time the Participant commences participation in the Plan.

1.38   "One-Year Break in Service" shall mean a Plan Year computation period in which an Employee is credited with 500 Hours of Service or less. An Employee shall not be deemed to have incurred a One-Year Break in Service if the Employee is absent from Service because of an authorized leave of absence granted in writing for medical, disability, vacation, education or such other circumstances approved by the Committee in a uniform and nondiscriminatory manner.

   In the case of an Employee who is absent from work for any period on or after the first day of the first Plan Year beginning after December 31, 1984, by reason of:

   (a)   The pregnancy of the Employee,

   (b)   The birth of a child of the Employee,

   (c)   The placement of a child with the Employee in connection with the adoption of such child by the Employee, or

   (d)   The care of a child for a period beginning immediately following such birth or placement, the Plan shall include, solely for purposes of determining whether the Employee has incurred a One-Year Break in Service, the Hours of Service which would normally have been credited to the Employee but for such absence, or in any case in which the Committee is unable to determine the Hours of Service which would normally have been credited to the Employee, eight (8) Hours of

Service per day of absence, provided, however, that the total number of hours treated in this manner as Hours of Service shall not exceed 501 Hours of Service. The hours described in the preceding sentence shall be credited in the Plan Year in which the absence from work begins if the Employee would be prevented from incurring a One-Year Break in Service in such period solely because the period of absence is treated as Hours of Service as provided above. Otherwise, the Hours of Service shall be credited on behalf of the Employee in the immediately following Plan Year.

In the case of an Employee who is absent from work for any period beginning on or after August 5, 1993 because of a leave under the Family and Medical Leave Act of 1993, the Plan shall include, to the extent not otherwise credited to the Employee under the terms hereof and solely for the purpose of determining whether the Employee has incurred a One-Year Break in Service, the Hours of Service which would normally have been credited to the Employee under the terms hereof but for such absence.

1.39   "Participant" shall mean an Eligible Employee who meets the requirements for participation under Section 3.3 or an Employee or former Employee for whom a Pretax Account, an Aftertax Account, a Rollover Account and/or an Employer Account is maintained. For purposes of Sections 3.1, 4.1, 4.2 and 5.1, the term "Participant" shall not include an Employee who is a Participant solely because a Rollover Account is being maintained on his behalf.

1.40   "Plan" shall mean the _____ Plan, as embodied herein, and any amendments thereto, and shall also refer to any predecessor plan for which this document is a restatement, and any predecessor plan that has been merged into this Plan.

1.41   "Plan Sponsor" shall mean _____.

1.42   "Plan Year" shall mean the period beginning on _____and ending on _____.

1.43   "Predecessor Employer" shall mean, with respect to an Employee, one or more of the following organizations or units, if the Employee was previously employed by them: _____.

1.44 "Predecessor to this Plan" shall mean any plan for which this Plan is a restatement, any plan which has been merged into this Plan or any Predecessor to this Plan, or any other plan sponsored by an entity which became an Affiliated Employer by acquisition or merger, and which adopted this Plan or a Predecessor to this Plan for any of its employees who had been participants in such other plan.

1.45 "Pretax Account" shall mean the account established for a Participant in accordance with Section 7.1.

1.46 "Pretax Contribution" shall mean the contributions that an Employer makes to the Plan on behalf of a Participant in accordance with Section 4.1.

1.47 "Qualified Nonelective Contributions" shall mean the additional contributions, if any, that an Employer may make to the Plan pursuant to Sections 6.1 and 6.4 to satisfy the nondiscrimination requirements on Pretax and/or Aftertax and Employer Matching Contributions.

1.48 "Rollover Account" shall mean the account established for a Participant in accordance with Section 7.1.

1.49 "Rollover Contribution" shall mean the contribution made to this Plan of a distribution from a qualified plan of a former employer, in accordance with Section 4.7.

1.50 "Service" shall mean an Employee's period of employment with an Employer or an Affiliated Employer that is counted as "Service" in accordance with Article 2. [Service shall include employment with a Predecessor Employer for certain purposes, as provided under Article 2.]

1.51 "Spouse" shall mean the wife of a male Participant or the husband of a female Participant as determined under applicable State law.

1.52 "Termination" shall mean the cessation of active employment with the Employer or an Affiliated Employer.

1.53 "Termination Date" shall mean the first date on which an Employee ceases active employment with the Employer or any Affiliated Employer.

1.54 "Valuation Date" shall mean the last business day of each calendar month.

1.55 "Vesting Service" shall mean Service as counted for determining a Participant's right to vest in his Employer Account under Article 7, as determined under the rules of Article 2.

1.56 "Year of Eligibility or Vesting Service" shall mean a Year of Service as determined under the appropriate Computation Period for calculating Eligibility or Vesting Service under the rules of Article 2.

1.57 "Year of Service" shall mean a twelve (12) month Computation Period during which the Employee is credited with 1,000 or more Hours of Service, under the rules of Article 2.

ARTICLE 2: SERVICE COUNTING RULES

2.1 *Hours of Service—General Rule* An Employee shall be credited with an Hour of Service for:

(a) Each hour for which a person is directly or indirectly paid, or entitled to payment, by an Affiliated Employer or a Predecessor Employer for the performance of duties. These hours shall be credited to the person during the appropriate Computation Period in which the duties are performed;

(b) Each hour for which a person is directly or indirectly paid, or entitled to payment, by an Affiliated Employer or a Predecessor Employer for reasons other than for the performance of duties (such as vacation, holiday, illness, incapacity including disability, jury duty, military duty, leave of absence or layoff). These hours shall be credited to the Employee during the Computation Period in which the nonperformance of duties occurs, but the total credit for any single continuous period during which the employee performs no duties (whether or not in a single Computation Period) of such hours shall not exceed 501 hours. The computation of non-work hours described in this subsection will be computed in accordance with the provisions of the Department of Labor Regulation Section 2530.200b-2; and

(c) Each hour for which back pay, irrespective of mitigation of damages, has been either awarded or agreed to by an Affiliated Employer or Predecessor Employer. These hours will be credited to the person for the Plan Year to which the award or agreement pertains.

(d) Each hour for which an Employee is not paid or entitled to payment but during which he normally would have performed duties for an Affiliated Employer during any period for which he is eligible to receive benefits under the long-term disability plan of an Affiliated Employer.

2.2 *Hours of Service—Equivalencies* In calculating Hours of Service the Committee may, in lieu of actual hour counting, use any of the following equivalencies for classifications of employees for whom exact hour counting would be administratively burdensome, provided that, if the Committee decides to calculate Hours of Service based upon any of the following equivalencies for any classification of employees, the equivalencies shall be reasonable and nondiscriminatory, and shall be consistently applied. The equivalencies which may be used are:

(a) *Hours Worked* 870 hours worked shall be treated as equivalent to 1000 Hours of Service and 435 hours worked shall be treated as equivalent to 500 Hours of Service.

(b) *Regular Time Hours* 750 regular time hours shall be treated as equivalent to 1000 Hours of Service and 375 regular time hours shall be treated as equivalent to 500 Hours of Service.

(c) *Days of Employment* One day of employment for which the Employee would have been credited under the general rules with at least one Hour of Service shall be equivalent to 10 Hours of Service.

(d) *Weeks of Employment* One week of employment for which the Employee would have been credited under the general rules with at least one Hour of Service shall be treated as 45 Hours of Service.

(e) *Semimonthly Payroll Periods* One semimonthly payroll period for which the Employee would have been credited under the general rules with at least one Hour of Service shall be treated as 95 Hours of Service.

(f) *Months of Employment* One month of employment for which the Employee would have been credited under the general rules with at least one Hour of Service shall be treated as 190 Hours of Service.

In interpreting the foregoing equivalencies the Committee shall rely on Department of Labor Regulations Section 2530.200b-3.

2.3 *Eligibility Service* An Eligible Employee shall be credited with a Year of Eligibility Service if he is credited with 1,000 or more Hours of Service during the applicable Computation Period or, if he fails to be credited with 1,000 or more Hours of Service in that Computation Period, he shall be credited with a Year of Eligibility Service if he is credited with 1,000 hours in any Computation Period commencing after his Employment Commencement Date or rehire date.

2.4 *Vesting Service* An Employee shall be credited with a Year of Vesting Service for each Year of Service except that Vesting Service shall not include:

(a) *Pre-18 Service* Any Year of Service completed prior to the date on which the Employee has attained age eighteen (18).

(b) *Pre-Plan Service* Any Year of Service completed prior to the date of establishment of the Plan and any Predecessor to this Plan.

(c) *Pre-ERISA Service* Any Year of Service completed prior to January 1, 1975, if such Year of Service would have been disregarded under the rules of the Plan and any Predecessor to this Plan as in effect on January 1, 1975.

(d) *Rule of Parity* In the case of an Employee who had never made Pretax Contributions to the Plan and was not vested in his Employer Account at his Termination Date and who has incurred a number of consecutive One-Year Breaks in Service equal to the greater of five (5) or the number of Years of Service credited to him prior to the first of such consecutive five (5) One-Year Breaks in Service, Years of Service during Plan Years prior to such Break in Service.

ARTICLE 3: ELIGIBILITY

3.1   *Eligibility* An Eligible Employee who was a Participant in the Plan on the Effective Date of this Restatement shall continue to be eligible to participate in the Plan. Each other Eligible Employee shall become eligible to participate in the Plan upon the attainment of age 21 and completion of one (1) Year of Eligibility Service.

3.2   *Eligibility Upon Reemployment* A former Participant or a former Eligible Employee who had met the eligibility requirements of Section 3.1 who is reemployed by the Employer as an Eligible Employee shall be eligible to participate in the Plan as of his reemployment date. An Eligible Employee who had not met the eligibility requirements of Section 3.1 before his Termination Date shall be eligible to participate in the Plan upon satisfaction of the requirements in Section 3.1.

3.3   *Notification of Eligibility to Participate and Entry into Plan* The Committee shall notify each Eligible Employee of the eligibility requirements and benefits under the Plan prior to the Entry Date he first becomes entitled to participate. An Eligible Employee (including a former Participant who is reemployed) who has satisfied the eligibility requirements specified in this Article 3 may become a Participant by filing an election to have Pretax Contributions made on his behalf, in accordance with Section 4.1, or to make Aftertax Contributions in accordance with Section 4.2. Such Eligible Employee's participation shall become effective on the Entry Date coincident with or next following the date on which such Eligible Employee files his election with the Committee or as soon as practicable thereafter. In order to become a Participant, an Eligible Employee shall also be required to make investment elections pursuant to Section 8.2 and to designate a Beneficiary pursuant to Section 10.7.

ARTICLE 4: PRETAX, AFTERTAX, AND ROLLOVER CONTRIBUTIONS

4.1   *Pretax Contributions* Subject to the provisions of Sections 6.1, 6.7, 6.10 and 9.2(b), a Participant may direct the Employer, on forms prescribed by the Committee, to make contributions to the Plan on his behalf of a stated whole percentage of his Compensation. A Participant's Pretax Contributions to this Plan and any other plan qualified under Code Section 401(k) maintained by an Affiliated Employer shall not exceed seven thousand dollars ($7,000) or such higher amount as may be permitted under Code Section 402(g)(5) for any taxable year.

If, on or before March 1 of any year, a Participant notifies the Plan Administrator in writing, that all or a portion of the Pretax Contributions made on his behalf is in excess of the dollar limit under Section 402(g)(5) for the preceding taxable year of the Participant, the Plan Administrator shall make a reasonable effort to distribute such excess Pretax Contributions and income allocable to the Participant, but in no event may such distribution be made later than the April 15 following such notification. In the case where the excess Pretax Contributions arose taking into account only Pretax Contributions made to this Plan and other plans of an Affiliated Employer, a Participant shall be deemed to have notified the Committee. The income allocable to such excess Pretax Contributions shall include income for the Plan Year for which the excess Pretax Contributions was made and for the period between the end of such Plan Year and the date of the distribution. The income allocable to excess Pretax Contributions shall be determined under the alternative method set forth in Reg. Section 1.402(g)-1(e)(5)(iii) and the income for the period between the end of the Plan Year and the date of distribution shall be determined in accordance with the safe harbor method set forth in Reg. Section 1.402(g)-1(e)(5)(iv). Any amount distributed under this Section 4.1 shall be included in the Participant's Deferral Percentage unless such a Participant is a Nonhighly Compensated Employee and such excess arose solely because of excess Pretax

Contributions made to this Plan and other plans of an Affiliated Employer.

4.2   *Aftertax Contributions* Subject to the provisions of Sections 6.4, 6.10 and 9.2(b), a Participant may, on forms prescribed by the Committee, elect to make contributions to the Plan of a stated whole percentage of his Compensation.

4.3   *Change of Contribution Level* A Participant may, on forms prescribed by the Committee, direct the Employer to change the rate of Pretax Contributions made on his behalf. A Participant may also, on forms prescribed by the Committee, change his rate of Aftertax Contributions. Changes may be made at any time during the Plan Year, but in no event more than four (4) times in any Plan Year, and shall become effective on the Entry Date coincident with or next following the filing of the forms or as soon as practicable thereafter.

4.4   *Suspension of Contributions* A Participant may, on forms prescribed by the Committee, direct the Employer to suspend the Pretax Contributions made on his behalf. A Participant may also, on forms prescribed by the Committee, elect to suspend his Aftertax Contributions. Suspensions may be made at any time during the Plan Year and shall become effective on the Entry Date coincident with or next following the filing of the forms or as soon as practicable thereafter. A Participant who directs the Employer to suspend the Pretax Contributions made on his behalf and/or who elects to suspend his Aftertax Contributions may resume such contributions by filing a form prescribed by the Committee. Resumption of contributions shall commence on the Entry Date coincident with or next following the filing of the form or as soon as practicable thereafter.

4.5   *Manner of Contributions* All Pretax and Aftertax Contributions shall be in the form of Employee-authorized payroll deductions. Such deductions shall be made in whole percentages each payroll period, subject to the change and suspension of contribution provisions of Sections 4.3 and 4.4.

4.6   *Remittance and Allocation of Pretax and Aftertax Contributions* Pretax Contributions and Aftertax Contributions shall be remitted to the Funding Agent by the Employer as soon as practicable, but in no event more than ninety (90) days after the end of the payroll period during which such Contributions are made, and shall be allocated to each Participant's Pretax and/or Aftertax Account as of the next Valuation Date coincident with or next following the end of the payroll period during which such Contributions are made.

4.7   *Rollover Contributions* An Employee of an Employer may, subject to such uniform and nondiscriminatory terms and conditions as may be established from time to time by the Committee, request the Committee to authorize the Funding Agent to accept a rollover of a distribution of the value of the Employee's account or benefit from the qualified plan of a former employer. A Rollover Contribution shall be accepted provided the following conditions are met:

(a)   The Rollover Contribution to this Plan is in cash;

(b)   The Rollover Contribution does not include any Employee Contributions;

(c)   The Committee receives a letter from the Employee's former employer stating that the distribution to the Employee is from a plan qualified under Section 401(a) of the Code and that the distribution is being made on account of the Employee's severance of employment;

(d)   The Employee makes a written statement that the Rollover Contribution shall be made to this Plan within sixty (60) days of his receipt of the distribution from the other qualified plan and that the proposed Rollover Contribution, to the best of his knowledge, meets all of the Code requirements for rollover treatment.

The amount of the Rollover Contribution shall be held in the Participant's Rollover Account. Such Account shall be invested in accordance with Article 8 and shall be adjusted for debits and credits in accordance with Section 7.2.

ARTICLE 5: EMPLOYER CONTRIBUTIONS

5.1   Employer Contributions

(a)   The Employer shall contribute for each Participant an amount equal to fifty percent (50%) of the Participant's

Pretax Contributions up to ten percent (10%) of the Participant's Compensation.

(b) The Employer shall also make any contributions required by Section 10.5.

(c) The Employer may make additional contributions to the Plan in order to satisfy the limitations on Pretax Contributions under Section 6.1 and on Aftertax and Employer Matching Contributions under Section 6.4, as provided for under Section 6.1 and 6.4, respectively.

5.2 *Remittance and Allocation of Employer Contributions* All Employer contributions pursuant to Section 5.1 shall be transmitted to the Funding Agent as soon as practicable after each payroll period during which such contributions are made and shall be allocated as of the next Valuation Date to each Participant's Employer Account.

5.3 *Forfeitures of Employer Contributions* Any amounts forfeited by Participants in accordance with Section 10.5 or any forfeitable excess amounts resulting from the limitations in Sections 6.2, 6.5 and 6.7 shall be used by the Employer to reduce its contributions made pursuant to Section 5.1.

ARTICLE 6: NONDISCRIMINATION REQUIREMENTS AND MAXIMUM ANNUAL ADDITIONS

6.1 *Nondiscrimination Requirements for Pretax Contributions* For any Plan Year, the amount of Pretax Contributions must satisfy either subsection (a) or (b) as set forth below:

(a) The Average Deferral Percentage for Highly Compensated Employees may not exceed one and twenty-five one-hundredths (1.25) times the Average Deferral Percentage for Nonhighly Compensated Employees.

(b) The Average Deferral Percentage for Highly Compensated Employees

(1) may not exceed two (2) times the Average Deferral Percentage for Nonhighly Compensated Employees, and

(2)   may not exceed the Average Deferral Percentage for Nonhighly Compensated Employees by more than two (2) percentage points.

The Committee is empowered to monitor the Plan throughout the Plan Year and decrease or suspend the amount of Pretax Contributions by Highly Compensated Employees or any group of Highly Compensated Employees made pursuant to Section 4.1. Any such decrease or suspension shall also be effective for purposes of determining Employer Matching Contributions to be made pursuant to Section 5.1.

The Employer may also, in its sole discretion, make Qualified Nonelective Contributions on behalf of Eligible Employees who are Nonhighly Compensated Employees in an amount sufficient to satisfy the nondiscrimination requirements of this Section. Such contributions shall be allocated based on the ratio which each such Eligible Employee's Compensation bears to the total Compensation of all such Eligible Employees for the Plan Year. Such additional contributions, if any, shall be fully vested.

6.2   *Excess Pretax Contributions* If for any Plan Year it is determined that the nondiscrimination requirements under Section 6.1 are not satisfied:

(a)   Certain Highly Compensated Employees shall have the Pretax Contributions made on their behalf reduced retroactively in accordance with the leveling method described in Section 6.8;

(b)   At the Committee's sole discretion, a Highly Compensated Employee who has had the Pretax Contributions made on his behalf reduced under Subsection (a) shall have the amount of such reduction treated in one (1) or both of the following manners:

(1)   All or a portion of the amount of such reduction plus any investment earnings allocable to such reduction shall be added to the Highly Compensated Employee's Aftertax Account and the amount of the reduction shall be treated as an Aftertax Contribution. Recharacterization shall

only be made within two and one-half (2-1/2) months following the last day of the Plan Year for which the reduction was necessary.

(2) All or a portion of the amount of such reduction plus any investment earnings allocable to such Pretax Contributions shall be paid in cash to the Highly Compensated Employee. Payment shall be made within two and one-half (2-1/2) months following the last day of the Plan Year for which the reduction was necessary, if practicable, but in no event later than the last day of the Plan Year following such Plan Year. For any Plan Year, the amount of excess Pretax Contributions to be distributed to any Participant shall be reduced by the amount of excess deferrals distributed to such Participant in accordance with Section 4.1 for the Participant's taxable year ending with or within the Plan Year. The income allocable to such excess Pretax Contributions shall include income for the Plan Year for which the Pretax Contributions were made, determined in accordance with the alternative method set forth in Reg. Section 1.401(k)-1(f)(4)(ii)(C) and will include income for the period between the end of such Plan Year and the date of the distribution, determined in accordance with the safe harbor method set forth in Reg. Section 1.401(k)-1(f)(4)(ii)(D). Any Employer Matching Contributions attributable to excess Pretax Contributions or excess deferrals (and income allocable to such Employer Matching Contributions determined using the same method for determining income on excess Pretax Contributions) shall be forfeited within the period specified immediately above and shall be used to reduce future Employer Contributions under Section 5.1.

6.3   *Family Aggregation Rules for Pretax Contributions* The family aggregation rules of Section 414(q)(6) of the Code shall apply to any Eligible Employee who is Highly Compensated and a five (5) percent owner or one of the ten (10) most Highly Compensated Employees. The Average Deferral Percentage for the Family Members, which are treated as one Eligible Employee who is Highly Compensated, shall be the Average Deferral Percentage determined by combining the Pretax Contributions and Compensation of all eligible Family Members.

If the Average Deferral Percentage of a Highly Compensated Employee is determined under the family aggregation rules, excess Pretax Contributions shall be allocated among the Family Members in proportion to the Pretax Contributions of each Family Member that were combined to determine the Average Deferral Percentage rates.

6.4 *Nondiscrimination Requirements for Aftertax and Employer Matching Contributions* For any Plan Year, the amount of Aftertax and Employer Matching Contributions must satisfy either Subsection (a) or (b) as set forth below:

(a) The Average Contribution Percentage for Highly Compensated Employees may not exceed one and twenty-five one-hundredths (1.25) times the Average Contribution Percentage for Nonhighly Compensated Employees.

(b) The Average Contribution Percentage for Highly Compensated Employees

(1) May not exceed two (2) times the Average Contribution Percentage for Nonhighly Compensated Employees, and

(2) May not exceed the Average Contribution Percentage for Nonhighly Compensated Employees by more than two (2) percentage points.

The Committee is empowered to monitor the Plan throughout the Plan Year and to decrease or suspend the amount of Aftertax Contributions made by Highly-Compensated Employees pursuant to an election made pursuant to Section 4.2.

The Employer may also, in its sole discretion, make Qualified Nonelective Contributions on behalf of Eligible Employees who are Nonhighly Compensated Employees in an amount sufficient to satisfy the nondiscrimination requirements of this Section. Such contributions shall be allocated based on the ratio which each such Eligible Employee's Compensation bears to the total Compensation of all such Eligible Employees for the Plan Year. Such additional contributions shall be fully vested.

6.5   *Excess Aftertax and Employer Matching Contributions* If for any Plan Year it is determined that the nondiscrimination requirements under Section 6.4 are not satisfied:

(a)   Certain Highly Compensated Employees shall have the total of their Aftertax and Employer Matching Contributions reduced retroactively in accordance with the leveling method described in Section 6.8.

(b)   A Highly Compensated Employee who has had the total of his Aftertax and Employer Matching Contributions reduced in accordance with this Section 6.5 shall have the amount of such reduction taken first from his Aftertax Contributions for the Plan Year. If a further reduction is necessary, it shall be made from the Highly Compensated Employee's Employer Matching Contributions for the Plan Year.

(c)   Reduced Aftertax Contributions and nonforfeitable Employer Matching Contributions plus any investment earnings allocable to such Contributions shall be paid in cash to the Highly Compensated Employee. Payment shall be made within two and one-half (2-1/2) months following the last day of the Plan Year for which the reduction was necessary, if practicable, but in no event later than the last day of the Plan Year following such Plan Year.

The income allocable to such reduced Aftertax Contributions and nonforfeitable Employer Matching Contributions shall be determined in accordance with the alternative method set forth in Reg. Section 1.401(m)-1(e)(3)(ii)(C) and will include income for the Plan Year for which the Aftertax Contributions and Employer Matching Contributions were made and for the period between the end of such Plan Year and the date of distribution, determined in accordance with the safe harbor method set forth in Reg. Section 1.401(m)-1(e)(3)(ii)(D). Forfeitable Employer Matching Contributions (and income attributable to such matching contributions determined in the same manner as for determining income on reduced Aftertax Contributions and Employer Matching Contributions) shall be forfeited within the period specified immediately above and shall be used to reduce future Employer contributions under Section 5.1.

6.6   *Family Aggregation Rules for Aftertax and Employer Matching Contributions* The family aggregation rules of Section 414(q)(6) of the Code shall apply to any Eligible Employee who is Highly Compensated and a five (5) percent owner or one of the ten (10) most Highly Compensated Employees. The Average Contribution Percentage for the family group, which is treated as one Eligible Employee who is Highly Compensated, shall be the Average Contribution Percentage determined by combining Aftertax and Employer Matching Contributions and Compensation of all eligible Family Members. Excess Aftertax and Employer Matching Contributions shall be allocated among such Family Members in proportion to the Aftertax and Matching Contributions of each Family Member that were combined to determine the Average Contribution Percentage.

6.7   *Additional Nondiscrimination Limitation* If the nondiscrimination requirements in Sections 6.1 and 6.4 are satisfied solely by using the limit set forth in Subsection (b) in both Sections, then the requirements in either Subsections (a) or (b) must be satisfied:

(a)   The sum of the Average Deferral Percentage and the Average Contri bution Percentage for Highly Compensated Employees may not exceed the sum of

    (1)   One and twenty-five one-hundredths (1.25) times the greater of

        (A)   The Average Deferral Percentage of the Nonhighly Compensated Employees, and

        (B)   The Average Contribution Percentage of the Nonhighly Compensated Employees; and

    (2)   The lesser of

    (A) Two (2) times the lesser of the Average Deferral Percentage and the Average Contribution Percentage of the Nonhighly Compensated Employees, and

    (B) Two percentage points (2%) plus the lesser of the Average Deferral Percentage and the Average Contribution Percentage of the Nonhighly Compensated Employees.

(b) The sum of the Average Deferral Percentage and Average Contribution Percentage for Highly Compensated Employees may not exceed the sum of

    (1) One and twenty-five one-hundredths (1.25) times the lesser of

        (A) The Average Deferral Percentage of the Nonhighly Compensated Employees, and

        (B) The Average Contribution Percentage of the Nonhighly Compensated Employees; and

    (2) The greater of

        (A) Two (2) times the greater of the Average Deferral Percentage and Average Contribution Percentage of the Nonhighly Compensated Employees, and

        (B) Two percentage points (2%) plus the greater of the Average Deferral Percentage and the Average Contribution Percentage of the Nonhighly Compensated Employee.

(c) If the nondiscrimination requirements under Subsections (a) and (b) are not satisfied, amounts in excess of that required to meet the nondiscrimination requirements shall be treated as an Excess Pretax Contribution and/or Excess Aftertax and Employer Matching Contribution in the same manner as provided in Sections 6.2 and 6.5, respectively.

6.8   *Leveling Method* If the nondiscrimination requirements of Section 6.1 or 6.4 are not met, Pretax Contributions (or Aftertax and Employer Matching Contributions) shall be reduced retroactively under the leveling method as follows:

(a) The Highly Compensated Employee with the highest Deferral Percentage (or Contribution Percentage) shall have his total Pretax Contributions (or Aftertax and Employer Matching Contributions) reduced to the extent required to satisfy the nondiscrimination requirements of Section 6.1 (or Section 6.4) or to cause such Highly Compensated Employee's Deferral Percentage (or Contribution Percentage) to equal that of the Highly Compensated Employee with the next highest Deferral Percentage (or Contribution Percentage).

(b) If the nondiscrimination requirements set forth in Section 6.1 (or Section 6.4) are still not satisfied after the reduction in subsection (a) is made, the Highly Compensated Employee with the highest Deferral Percentage (or Contribution Percentage) shall have their total Pretax Contributions (or Aftertax and Employer Matching Contributions) reduced to the extent required to meet the nondiscrimination requirements of Section 6.1 (or Section 6.4) or to cause such Highly Compensated Employees Deferral Percentage (or Contribution Percentage) to equal that of the Highly Compensated Employee with the next highest Deferral Percentage (or Contribution Percentage).

(c) If the nondiscrimination requirements set forth in Section 6.1 (or Section 6.4) are still not satisfied after the reduction in subsection (b) is made, the process shall be repeated until the nondiscrimination requirements of Section 6.1 (or Section 6.4) are satisfied.

6.9 *Aggregation of Plans* In the event this Plan is aggregated with any other plan maintained by an Affiliated Employer and treated as a single plan for purposes of Code Section 401(a)(4) and 410(b) (other than Section 410(b)(2)(A)(ii)), all Pretax Contributions, Aftertax Contributions and Employer Matching Contributions made under the two plans shall be treated as made under a single plan, and if two or more of such plans are permissively aggregated for purposes of Sections 401(k) and 401(m) of the Code, such plans shall be treated as a single plan for purposes of satisfying Section 401(a)(4) and 410(b) of the Code.

6.10   *Disaggregation of Plan* Notwithstanding anything contained
        in the Plan to the contrary, in the event the mandatory dis-
        aggregation rules of Reg. Section 1.401(k)-1(g)(11)(iii) and/
        or 1.401(m)-1(b)(3)(ii) require that this Plan be treated as
        two (2) or more separate plans, the provisions of the Plan
        shall be applied separately with respect to each deemed
        separate plan, as necessary and appropriate.

        In the case of a deemed separate plan that covers Eligible
        Employees employed within a classification with respect to
        which retirement benefits have been the subject of collec-
        tive bargaining, the provisions of Sections 6.1, 6.2 and 6.3
        shall apply to such deemed separate plan effective for Plan
        Years beginning on or after January 1, 1993 and the provi-
        sions of Sections 6.4, 6.5, 6.6 and 6.7 shall be deemed satis-
        fied by such deemed separate plan.

6.11   *Code Section 415 Limits* The annual additions made on
        behalf of a Participant hereunder shall be limited to the
        extent required by Section 415 of the Code and rulings,
        notices, and regulations issued thereunder. To the extent
        applicable, Section 415 of the Code and rulings, notices and
        regulations issued thereunder are hereby incorporated by
        reference into this Plan. In calculating these limits, the fol-
        lowing rules shall apply:

        (a)   In the event the Committee determines that the annual
               additions made on behalf of a Participant during any
               Limitation Year are in excess of the limitations of this
               Section 6.11 as the result of a mistake in estimating a
               Participant's compensation, a reasonable error in
               determining the amount of Pretax Contributions that
               may be made with respect to any Participant or under
               other limited facts and circumstances which the Com-
               missioner of Internal Revenue finds justify the use of
               these rules, such annual additions shall be reduced by
               returning the Participant's Aftertax Contributions
               and/or unmatched Pretax contributions, as appropri-
               ate, plus any gains or losses, for such Limitation Year
               in such amount so that the limitations of this Section
               6.11 are not exceeded. Any Aftertax Contributions
               and Pretax Contributions thus distributed shall be

disregarded for purposes of Sections 1.14, 1.15 and 4.1, as appropriate.

If, following the return of all the Participant's Aftertax Contributions and/or unmatched Pretax Contributions that may be refunded, the annual additions made on behalf of a Participant during the Limitation Year are still exceeded, such annual additions shall be reduced to the extent necessary, proportionally from matched Pretax Contributions, and from Employer Matching Contributions for such Limitation Year, so that the limitations of this Section 6.11 are not exceeded. The amount of such reduction attributable to matched Pretax Contributions shall be refunded to the Participant and the amount attributable to Employer Matching Contributions shall be credited to an unallocated Employer Contribution account. The unallocated Employer Contribution account shall not be subject to adjustment in accordance with Section 7.2 and shall be deemed to be an Employer Matching Contribution for the Participant for the next succeeding Limitation Year (and succeeding Limitation Years as necessary) and used to fulfill the Employer's obligations in such following Limitation Year (or Years). However, if the Participant is not covered under the Plan as of the end of the Limitation Year, the excess amounts shall be held in the unallocated Employer Contribution account and reallocated in the next Limitation Year to all the remaining Participants in the Plan. Any Pretax Distributions distributed and any Employer Matching Contributions forfeited shall be disregarded for purposes of Sections 1.14, 1.15 and 4.1, as appropriate.

(b)   If the Participant is, or ever has been, covered under one or more qualified defined benefit plans maintained by the Employer or Affiliated Employer, the combined plan limits of Code Section 415(e) shall be calculated by reducing the limits applicable to the defined benefit plans first, prior to restricting annual additions to this Plan.

ARTICLE 7: PARTICIPANT ACCOUNTS

7.1   *Participant Accounts* The Committee shall establish the following accounts for each Participant, as appropriate:

(a)   *Pretax Account* The value of Pretax Contributions made on behalf of each Participant shall be accounted for in his Pretax Account.

(b)   *Aftertax Account* The value of each Participant's Aftertax Contributions shall be accounted for in his Aftertax Account. A Participant's Aftertax Contributions made before January 1, 1987 and Aftertax Contributions made after December 31, 1986 shall be separately accounted for in subaccounts established for such contributions within the Participant's Aftertax Account.

(c)   *Rollover Account* The value of a Participant's Rollover Contribution under Section 4.7 shall be accounted for in his Rollover Account.

(d)   *Employer Account* The value of Employer Matching Contributions made on behalf of each Participant shall be accounted for in his Employer Account. In addition, the value of any Qualified Non-Elective Contributions made pursuant to Sections 6.1 and 6.4 shall be accounted for in a subaccount established within the Employer Account for this type of contribution.

(e)   *Loan Account* If a Participant takes a loan from the Plan pursuant to Section 9.4, the promissory note shall be accounted for in his Loan Account.

The maintenance of such Accounts is for accounting purposes only and segregation of the Fund's assets shall not be required. Contributions shall be allocated to Participants' Accounts as soon as practicable after they are made.

7.2   *Allocations to Accounts* As of each Valuation Date, the Funding Agent shall determine the fair market value of the Fund and the Committee shall determine the fair market value of each Participant Account. The Account balances of each Participant shall be adjusted on a reasonable and consistent basis to reflect the following events since the preceding Valuation Date:

(a)   Forfeitures and distributions from his Accounts;

(b) Investment elections and his pro rata share of gains/ losses and expenses of the investment funds in which his Account balances are invested;

(c) His Pretax and Aftertax Contributions, and Rollover Contributions, if any;

(d) His allocations of Employer contributions made pursuant to Section 5.1; and

(e) Other credits and charges properly allocable.

In determining the value of the Fund and each individual Account, the Funding Agent and the Committee shall exercise their best judgment, and all determinations of value shall be binding upon all Participants and their Beneficiaries. All allocations shall be deemed to have been made as of the Valuation Date, regardless of when allocations are actually made.

The Committee shall also have the right to authorize the Funding Agent to determine the fair market value of the Fund on a date other than a Valuation Date when it deems necessary to preserve the assets of the Plan.

7.3 *Separate Contracts Maintained* The Plan shall maintain as a separate contract for purposes of Code Section 72(e)(8) the subaccount for Participant's Aftertax Contributions made after December 31, 1986 and earnings thereon. The Plan shall maintain as a separate contract the Participant's subaccount for his Aftertax Contributions made before January 1, 1987 and earnings thereon, the Participant's Pretax Account, and the Participant's Employer Account. Any withdrawal or distribution hereunder shall be charged against the separate contracts in the following order:

(a) From the contract containing the Participant's subaccount for his Aftertax Contributions made before January 1, 1987, up to the amount of such contributions,

(b) From the contract containing the Participant's subaccount for Aftertax Contributions made after December 31, 1986, up to the full value of such subaccount, including earnings, and

(c) From the contract containing the Participant's Pretax Account, Employer Account and Rollover Account

and the contract containing the subaccount for Aftertax Contributions made before 1987.

ARTICLE 8: INVESTMENT OF CONTRIBUTIONS

8.1   *Investment Funds* The agreement entered into between the
       Employer and the Funding Agent pursuant to Section 14.1
       to invest and retain the assets of the Plan shall provide at
       least [four (4)] investment fund options in which Partici-
       pants can invest their Pretax, Aftertax and Employer
       Matching Contributions, Qualified Nonelective Contribu-
       tions and Rollover Contributions. Those funds shall
       include:

       (a)   The Fixed Income Fund—a fund consisting primarily
             of one or more fixed income investments.

       (b)   The Balanced Fund—a fund primarily invested in a
             blend of common stocks and fixed income securities
             that can reasonably be expected to provide a high
             level of current income consistent with the preserva-
             tion of capital and high degree of liquidity.

       (c)   The Equity Growth Fund—a fund primarily invested
             in securities and/or other property that can reason-
             ably be expected to result in capital appreciation.

       (d)   The Employer Common Stock Fund—a fund invested
             in the common stock of the Employer.

       Pending investment and disbursement, the Fund may be
       invested in investments of a short-term nature.

8.2   *Election of Investment Fund for Contributions* A Participant
       shall direct, at the time he becomes a Participant in the
       Plan, on forms prescribed by the Committee, the manner in
       which his Pretax, Aftertax and Employer Matching Contri-
       butions and Rollover Contributions are to be invested.
       Qualified Nonelective Contributions shall be invested in
       the same manner as a Participant's Employer Matching
       Contributions are to be invested, provided, however, that
       Qualified Nonelective Contributions made on behalf of Eli-
       gible Employees who are not otherwise Participants shall
       be invested in [the Balanced Fund]. Investments shall be

made in one (1) or more of the investment funds available
under Section 8.1.

8.3   *Change in Election of Investment Fund for Future Contributions*
Subject to any limitations imposed by the Funding Agent
and the Committee, a Participant may, on forms prescribed
by the Committee, change his investment election for
future Pretax, Aftertax and Employer Matching Contributions. Qualified Nonelective Contributions shall be
invested in the same manner as a Participant's Employer
Matching Contributions are to be invested, provided, however, that Qualified Nonelective Contributions made on
behalf of Eligible Employees who are not otherwise Participants shall be invested in [the Balanced Fund]. Changes
may be made at any time during the Plan Year and shall
become effective on the Valuation Date coincident with or
next following the filing of the forms or as soon as practicable thereafter.

8.4   *Change in Election of Investment Fund for Past Contributions*
Subject to any limitations imposed by the Funding Agent
and the Committee, a Participant may, on forms prescribed
by the Committee, transfer all or a portion of the value of
his Accounts from one fund to another fund. Transfers may
be made at anytime during the Plan Year and shall become
effective on the Valuation Date coincident with or next following the filing of the forms or as soon as practicable
thereafter.

ARTICLE 9: WITHDRAWALS AND LOANS

9.1   Withdrawals of Pretax, Aftertax and Employer
Contributions

(a)   A Participant who is an Employee shall have no right
to withdraw any portion of his Qualified Nonelective
Contribution subaccount of his Employer Account. A
Participant who is an Employee shall have no right to
withdraw any portion of his Pretax Account or his
Employer Account or Rollover Account except as provided in Section 9.2.

(b) A Participant who is an Employee may, as of any Entry Date, make a withdrawal of all or a portion of the value of his Aftertax Account as of the Valuation Date coincident with or next following such Entry Date. Such withdrawals shall not be made more frequently than twice in any Plan Year.

(c) A request for a withdrawal under this Section 9.1 shall be made on forms and in accordance with procedures prescribed by the Committee. The minimum amount of a withdrawal shall be the lesser of two hundred dollars ($200) or the total amount available for withdrawal.

9.2   Hardship Withdrawals

(a) A Participant who is an Employee may, in the event of Hardship, be permitted to make a withdrawal from his Accounts. For purposes of this Section 9.2, the term "Hardship" shall mean:

   (1) Medical expenses as defined in Code Section 213(d) incurred by the Participant, the Participant's Spouse or any of his dependents or necessary for these persons to obtain such medical care;

   (2) Purchase (excluding mortgage payments) of a principal residence for the Participant;

   (3) Payment of tuition and related educational fees for the next twelve (12) months of post-secondary education for the Participant, his Spouse, or any of his dependents;

   (4) The need to prevent the eviction of the Participant from his principal residence or foreclosure on the mortgage of the Participant's principal residence;

   (5) Expenses arising from circumstances of sufficient severity that a Participant is confronted by present or impending financial ruin or his family is clearly endangered by present or impending want or deprivation; and

(6) Any other expenses that the Internal Revenue Service announces as qualifying as a "hardship" under Code Section 401(k).

(b) For a Hardship withdrawal to be granted, the following requirements must be met:

(1) The amount of the withdrawal must not be in excess of the amount necessary to alleviate the Hardship, including amounts necessary to pay any Federal, State and local income taxes or penalties reasonably expected to result from the distribution.

(2) The Participant must have made all withdrawals, other than hardship withdrawals, and take all nontaxable loans currently available to him under this Plan and any other plan maintained by an Affiliated Employer.

(3) Notwithstanding Sections 4.1 and 4.2, such Participant shall not be permitted to have elective contributions made on his behalf or to make employee contributions to this Plan or any other plan maintained by an Affiliated Employer during the twelve (12) month period following his receipt of such withdrawal. For this purpose, the phrase "any other plan maintained by an Affiliated Employer" means all qualified and nonqualified plans of deferred compensation maintained by an Affiliated Employer. The phrase includes a stock option, stock purchase, or similar plan, or a cash or deferred arrangement under a cafeteria plan, within the meaning of Code Section 125, but does not include a health or welfare benefit plan, including one that is part of such a cafeteria plan.

(4) The maximum Pretax contribution such Participant is permitted to have made on his behalf under Code Section 402(g) to this Plan and any other plan maintained by an Affiliated Employer for the calendar year following the

calendar year of the Hardship withdrawal shall be reduced by the amount of such elective contributions made on behalf of the Participant in the calendar year of the Hardship withdrawal to this Plan and all other plans maintained by an Affiliated Employer in which the Participant participated.

(c) The amount necessary to fund the withdrawal shall be taken first from the value of the Participant's Rollover Account, if any, and then from the value of the Participant's Employer Account, excluding the value of the Participant's Qualified Nonelective Contributions subaccount. Any further amounts necessary to alleviate the Hardship shall be taken from the Participant's Pretax Account up to an amount not in excess of the value of the Pretax Account as of December 31, 1988 and the total of the Participant's Pretax Contributions made after December 31, 1988.

(d) A request for a withdrawal under this Section 9.2 shall be made on forms prescribed by the Committee. The Committee shall establish a uniform and nondiscriminatory policy for reviewing withdrawal applications and any determination made by the Committee shall be final but subject to appeal under Section 13.8.

9.3 *Valuation and Payment of Withdrawals* In the event of a withdrawal under this Article 9, the value of a Participant's Accounts shall be determined by the Trustee as of the Valuation Date coincident with or next following the date on which the Trustee receives instructions from the Committee to make the Hardship withdrawal. Withdrawals shall be paid to the Participant in cash on the earliest practicable date following the aforementioned Valuation Date.

9.4 *Loans* A Participant who is an Employee or a former Employee who is a party-in-interest (as defined in Section 3(14) of ERISA) of the Employer may, on forms and in accordance with procedures prescribed by the Committee, apply to borrow from the value of the nonforfeitable portion of his Accounts. Any loan made under this Section 9.4 shall be subject to the following provisions:

(a) Only two (2) loans shall be made to a Participant in any given Plan Year and no Participant shall have more than two (2) loans outstanding at any given time.

(b) The amount of a loan shall not be less than one thousand dollars ($1,000). At the time a loan is made, the amount of such loan shall not exceed the lesser of (i) fifty thousand dollars ($50,000) reduced by the Participant's highest outstanding loan balance during the one (1) year period ending on the day before the date on which a loan is made, and (ii) fifty percent (50%) of the value of the nonforfeitable portion of the Participant's Accounts as of the last Valuation Date. The amount of the loan shall be a multiple of one hundred dollars ($100).

(c) The rate of interest that will be charged on a loan for its duration shall be the prevailing rate charged by commercial lenders for loans made under similar circumstances, as of the first day of the calendar quarter in which the loan is made, provided the rate does not violate applicable usury laws. Such rate shall be determined by the Committee, in its sole discretion.

(d) The term of the loan shall not be less than six (6) months nor exceed five (5) years, unless the loan is used to acquire a dwelling unit which, within a reasonable period of time (determined at the time the loan is made), is to be used as the principal residence of the Participant, and except as provided by the Secretary of the Treasury, shall require substantially level amortization of the loan (with payments not less frequently than quarterly) over its term. All loans shall be repaid by payroll deductions. Any loan may be repaid in whole or in part without penalty subject to such rules as the Committee may determine, provided the amount of any pre-payment is made through certified check.

(e) An amount having a value equal to the principal amount of the loan shall be deducted from the Account of a Participant to whom a loan is made. Such amount shall be deducted on a pro-rata basis from the investment funds in which the Participant's Account is invested, pursuant to Article 8, at the time the loan is made. Payroll deductions made to repay the loan shall be invested in accordance with the Participant's investment election under Article 8, which is in effect at the time such payment is made.

(f)   As evidence of a loan, a Participant shall provide an interest-bearing promissory note to the Committee in such form as shall be prescribed by the Committee and bearing the rate of interest determined pursuant to Section 9.4(c). A Participant's note shall be secured by the vested portion of his Account. The promissory note shall be an asset of the Fund which is allocated to the Loan Account of the Participant. For purposes of the Plan, such note shall have a fair market value at any given time equal to the unpaid balance of the note, plus the amount of any accrued but unpaid interest.

(g)   Notwithstanding any provision herein to the contrary, if any unpaid balance remains on a loan when a Participant terminates his employment with the Employer, the Committee shall deduct the unpaid amount of the loan plus accrued interest, if any, from the benefits which become payable to or on behalf of the Participant under the Plan.

(h)   Loans shall be available to all Participants who are parties-in-interest (as defined in Section 3(14) of ERISA) on a reasonably equivalent basis. The terms of all Participant loans are subject to the review and approval of the Committee and the denial of a loan to a Participant is subject to appeal by the Participant under Section 13.8.

(i)   Notwithstanding the foregoing, no loan shall be made to a Participant during the period in which the Committee is making a determination of whether a domestic relations order affecting the Participant's Account is a qualified domestic relations order, within the meaning of Code Section 414(p). Further, if the Committee is in receipt of a qualified domestic relations order with respect to any Participant's Account, it may prohibit such Participant from obtaining a loan until the alternate payee's rights under the order are satisfied.

(j) The Committee shall establish such rules and regulations as may be necessary to administer loans hereunder. Specifically, such rules and regulations shall specify the procedure for applying for Plan loans, the basis on which loans shall be approved or denied, the events constituting default and the steps that will be taken to preserve Plan assets in the event of default.

ARTICLE 10: ENTITLEMENT TO BENEFITS

10.1 *Retirement* A Participant who retires from employment with the Employer or an Affiliated Employer on or after his Normal Retirement Age shall be entitled to receive a retirement benefit equal to one hundred percent (100%) of the value of his Account.

10.2 *Disability* A Disabled Participant shall be entitled to receive a disability benefit equal to one hundred percent (100%) of the value of his Accounts.

10.3 *Termination of Employment* A Participant whose employment with the Employer and an Affiliated Employer is terminated for any reason other than retirement in accordance with Section 10.1, Disability in accordance with Section 10.2, or death in accordance with Section 10.7 shall be entitled to receive:

(a) One hundred percent (100%) of the value of his Pretax Account;

(b) One hundred percent (100%) of the value of his After-tax Account;

(c) One hundred percent (100%) of the value of his Rollover Account; and

(d) One hundred percent (100%) of the value of the Qualified Nonelective Contribution subaccount of his Employer Account; and

(e) A percentage of the value of his Employer Account based on his Years of Vesting Service in accordance with the following schedule:

[If the Participant's Years of Vesting Service Are:	The Vested Portion Is:
Less than 5	0%
5 or more	100%]

[If the Participant's Years of Vesting Service Are:	The Vested Portion Is:
Less than 3	0%
At least 3 but less than 4	20%
At least 4 but less than 5	40%
At least 5 but less than 6	60%
At least 6 but less than 7	80%
7 or more	100%]

10.4 *Vesting on Plan Termination* In the event of termination or partial termination of the Plan, each affected Participant shall be one hundred percent (100%) vested in his Account. The foregoing sentence shall not apply to a former participant who has been cashed-out (including those deemed cashed out under Section 10.5) or who has incurred five (5) consecutive One Year Breaks in Service.
[FOR PLANS WITH 5-YEAR CLIFF VESTING SCHEDULE]

10.5 *Forfeitures* A Participant who does not have a one hundred percent (100%) nonforfeitable interest in his Employer Account and whose employment with the Employer or an Affiliated Employer is terminated under Section 10.3 shall be deemed to be cashed out and shall forfeit that portion of his Employer Account in which he does not have a nonforfeitable interest. Such forfeiture shall be effective on the Valuation Date coincident with or next following the Participant's Termination Date. Forfeited amounts shall be applied to reduce subsequent Employer contributions made under Section 5.1.

A Participant or former Participant who is subsequently reemployed by the Employer or an Affiliated Employer prior to incurring five (5) consecutive One-Year Breaks in Service shall have the forfeited part of his Employer Account restored. Upon reemployment, the Employer shall make a contribution on behalf of such Participant equal to the amount forfeited, unadjusted for any gains or losses that may have resulted had the amounts not been forfeited.

[FOR PLANS WITH 7-YEAR GRADED SCHEDULE]

10.5 *Forfeitures, Reinstatement and Separate Accounts*

(a) A Participant who has less than a one hundred percent (100%) nonforfeitable interest in his Employer Account, whose employment with the Employer or an Affiliated Employer is terminated under Section 10.3 and who receives a distribution from his Employer Account, shall forfeit that portion of his Employer Account in which he does not have a nonforfeitable interest. Such forfeiture shall be effective on the Valuation Date coincident with or next following the Participant's Termination. Forfeited amounts shall be applied to reduce subsequent Employer contributions made under Section 5.1.

A Participant or former Participant who is subsequently reemployed by the Employer or an Affiliated Employer prior to incurring five (5) consecutive One Year Breaks in Service shall have the forfeited part of his Employer Account restored if the Participant repays the amount previously distributed no later than five (5) years from the Participant's reemployment commencement date. Upon repayment, the Employer shall make a contribution on behalf of such Participant equal to the amount forfeited, unadjusted for any gains or losses that may have resulted had the amounts not been forfeited.

In the case of a Participant who has less than a one hundred percent (100%) nonforfeitable interest in his Employer Account, whose employment with the Employer or an Affiliated Employer is terminated under Section 10.3 and who defers receipt of the distribution from his Employer Account, the Plan shall maintain the Participant's Employer Account until the Participant has incurred five (5) consecutive One Year Breaks in Service or receives a distribution, if earlier. The portion of the Employer Account in which the Participant does not have a nonforfeitable interest shall be forfeited on the Valuation Date coincident with or next following such event.

(b) If a distribution or withdrawal has been made to a Participant from his Employer Account at a time when he has less than a one hundred percent (100%) nonforfeitable interest in his Employer Account, the vesting schedule in Section 10.3(e) will thereafter apply only to the portion of the Employer Account attributable to Employer Matching Contributions allocated after such distribution or withdrawal. The balance in the Account immediately after such distribution or withdrawal shall be maintained in a separate account for the purpose of determining the Participant's nonforfeitable interest therein at any later time. The Participant's nonforfeitable percentage in the portion of his Employer Account held in such separate account at any later time shall be the (a) Participant's nonforfeitable percentage of the sums of such separate account at such later time plus all prior distributions from such account, minus (b) all prior distributions from such account.

10.6   Death

(a) A death benefit shall be payable to the Beneficiary of a Participant who dies while actively employed by the Employer or an Affiliated Employer. The death benefit shall be equal to one hundred percent (100%) of the value of the Participant's Account.

(b) A death benefit shall be payable to the Beneficiary of a Participant who dies after his Termination Date but prior to receiving the full value of the nonforfeitable portion of his Account to which he was entitled under Section 10.1, 10.2 or 10.3, as the case may be. The death benefit shall be equal to the value of the undistributed portion of such Account.

(c)   The value of a Participant's Account shall be determined as of the Valuation Date coincident with or next following the date of the Participant's death and distributed in accordance with Sections 11.1 and 11.2.

10.7   *Beneficiary* Each Participant shall have the right to designate, on forms provided by the Committee, one or more Beneficiaries to receive any amount that may be payable under the Plan because of such Participant's death.

A Participant shall have the right to revoke or change his Beneficiary designations at any time. If no Beneficiary is designated, the Beneficiary cannot be found, or if the designated Beneficiary is deceased, any amount payable under the Plan shall be paid to the Spouse, if any, of the Participant. If the Participant has no Spouse, or if the Spouse is deceased, any amount payable under the Plan shall be paid to the children of the Participant per capita. If the Participant has no children, or if the children are deceased, any amount payable under the Plan shall be paid to the estate of the Participant.

Notwithstanding the foregoing, the Beneficiary of a Participant who is legally married at the time of death shall be the Participant's surviving Spouse unless the surviving Spouse has consented in writing to the Participant's designation of another Beneficiary, the consent acknowledges the effect of the designation, names the specific Beneficiary or class of Beneficiaries (if applicable), and the designation is witnessed by [a Plan representative or] a notary public. Notwithstanding the foregoing, if the Participant establishes to the satisfaction of the Committee that such consent cannot be obtained because there is no Spouse or the Spouse cannot be located, the Spouse will be deemed to have consented to the designation of such other Beneficiary.

10.8   *Small Payments* Notwithstanding Sections 10.1, 10.2, 10.3, 10.6 and 11.2, the Committee shall direct that the value of the nonforfeitable Account of a Participant be immediately distributed if such value is less than three thousand five hundred dollars ($3,500). The value of the Account shall be determined as of the Valuation Date coincident with or next following the date on which the Participant becomes a

Disabled Participant, the Participant's Termination Date or the date of the Participant's death, as the case may be, and shall be distributed as soon as practicable following such Valuation Date.

ARTICLE 11: DISTRIBUTION OF BENEFITS

11.1 *Form of Benefit Payment* A Participant may elect to receive the value of his Account to which he is entitled under the Plan pursuant to Article 10 in any one of the following forms:

(a) Payment to him, in a single sum, of cash equal to the value of his Account.

(b) Delivery to him of the number of full shares of stock attributable to his Account in the Employer Common Stock Fund and payment to him, in a single sum, of the cash value of any fractional share of such stock together with cash equal to the value of his Account in the other investment funds under the Plan. For the purpose of determining the value of a share of Common Stock, shares will be valued based on the average of the high and low prices reported on the Composite Transactions listing for the New York Stock Exchange for the relevant Valuation Date.

(c) Substantially equal cash installments payable monthly over a period of up to fifteen (15) years. The amount of each periodic payment shall be determined by dividing the value of the Participant's Account in the Fund by the number of months remaining in the payment period which was selected by the Participant. A Participant's election of this option is irrevocable. Notwithstanding the foregoing, a Participant may request in writing to the Committee that the Plan pay all or any part of any remaining credit to him on account of financial hardship. For this purpose, financial hardship shall be deemed to exist when the former Participant has large financial commitments by reason of illness or other unusual family conditions and is having difficulty meeting his financial obligations.

The Beneficiary of a Participant who is entitled to a death benefit under Section 10.7 may elect to receive the value of the Participant's Account paid to him solely in the manner provided in Section 11.1(a) or 11.1(b).

A Participant or Beneficiary shall elect the form of payment on forms and in the manner prescribed by the Committee.

11.2 *Benefit Commencement* The Plan shall make distributions to Participants and Beneficiaries as soon as practicable after the Valuation Date coincident with or next following the Participant's retirement, becoming a Disabled Participant, Termination Date or death, and the completion of all required consents for such distribution. No distribution shall be made without the Participant's consent before the latest date set forth under the last paragraph of this Section 11.2, except as provided for small payments under Section 10.8. The Committee shall furnish to each Participant a general description of the material features of the optional forms of benefit payment available under Section 11.1, and each Participant shall affirmatively consent to such benefit payment, no more than 90 days and no less than 30 days before the date of benefit distribution to the Participant. [In accordance with IRS regulations, distributions may commence less than 30 days after the explanation described above is provided to the Participant, provided that the Committee informs the Participant that the Participant has a right to a period of at least 30 days after receiving the explanation to consider the decision of whether or not to elect a distribution (and a particular form of benefit payment), and the Participant, after receiving the explanation, affirmatively elects a distribution.]

Any amounts that may be credited to a Participant's Employer Account after the payment of the value of such Account shall be paid as soon as practicable after the Valuation Date coincident with such amounts being credited to the Participant's Employer Account. The Participant may elect to delay the distribution of his Account payable pursuant to Section 10.1, 10.2 or 10.3, subject to the requirements of this Section and Section 11.3.

Notwithstanding the foregoing, if a Participant who is a former Employee fails to elect a form of benefit payment, a distribution from the Plan, payable in a single sum of cash pursuant to Section 11.1(a), shall not commence later than sixty (60) days after the end of the Plan Year in which the latest of the following occurs:

(a) The Participant attains or would have attained age sixty-five (65);

(b) The Participant terminates employment with the Employer and any Affiliated Employer; or

(c) The Participant's fifth (5th) anniversary of commencement of participation in the Plan.

11.3 *Minimum Required Distributions* Notwithstanding any provision in the Plan to the contrary, all distributions under the Plan shall be made in accordance with the requirements of Section 401(a)(9) of the Code and the regulations thereunder, including the incidental death benefit requirement of IRS Proposed Regulations Section 1.401(a)(9)-2. The provisions in this section override any distribution options under the Plan if inconsistent with the requirements of Section 401(a)(9).

(a) *Pre-Death Distribution* Distributions to a Participant shall commence no later than the April 1st of the calendar year following the calendar year in which a Participant attains age seventy and one-half (70-1/2). However, if a Participant attained age 70-1/2 before January 1, 1988, distributions to such Participant shall commence no later than the April 1 following the calendar year in which such Participant retires. [Distributions shall be made in the form specified under Section 11.1(a).] [Distributions shall be made in one of the forms specified under Section 11.1. In no event shall distributions be made for a period greater than the life expectancy of the Participant or joint life expectancy of the Participant and his Spouse, determined as of April 1st of the calendar year in which the Participant attains age 70-1/2 or retires, as the case may be.]

(b) *Post-Death Distributions* In the event of the death of the Participant, any payments due following the death of the Participant shall be made in accordance with Section 10.6. In the case of a Participant who had begun to receive distributions under Section 11.3(a), distributions shall be made after such Participant's death at least as rapidly as before his death. In the case of other Participants, in no event shall distributions be made later than the end of the calendar year which contains the fifth (5th) anniversary of the date of the Participant's death.

11.4   *Eligible Rollover Distributions*

(a) This Section applies to distributions made on or after January 1, 1993. Notwithstanding any provision of the Plan to the contrary that would otherwise limit a distributee's election under this Section, a distributee may elect, at the time and in the manner prescribed by the Committee, to have any portion of an eligible rollover distribution paid directly to an eligible retirement plan specified by the distributee in a direct rollover.

(b) Definitions:

(1) *Eligible rollover distribution* An eligible rollover distribution is any distribution of all or any portion of the balance to the credit of the distributee, except that an eligible rollover distribution does not include: any distribution that is one of a series of substantially equal periodic payments (not less frequently than annually) made for the life (or life expectancy) of the distributee or the joint lives (or joint life expectancies) of the distributee and the distributee's designated beneficiary, or for a specified period of ten years or more; any distribution to the extent such distribution is required under Section 401(a)(9) of the Code; and the portion of any distribution that is not includible in gross income (determined without regard to the exclusion for net unrealized appreciation with respect to employer securities).

(2) *Eligible retirement plan* An eligible retirement plan is an individual retirement account described in Section 408(a) of the Code, an individual retirement annuity described in Section 408(b) of the Code, an annuity plan described in Section 403(a) of the Code, or a qualified trust described in Section 401(a) of the Code, that accepts the distributee's eligible rollover distribution. However, in the case of an eligible rollover distribution to the surviving spouse, an eligible retirement plan is an individual retirement account or individual retirement annuity.

(3) *Distributee* A distributee includes an Employee or former Employee. In addition, the Employee's or former Employee's surviving Spouse and the Employee's or former Employee's Spouse or former Spouse who is the alternate payee under a qualified domestic relations order, as defined in Section 414(p) of the Code, are distributees with regard to the interest of the spouse or former spouse.

(4) *Direct rollover* A direct rollover is a payment by the Plan to the eligible retirement plan specified by the distributee.

ARTICLE 12: VOTING OF STOCK AND TENDER OFFERS

12.1 *Voting of Shares* Each Participant shall have the right and shall be afforded the opportunity to direct the manner in which whole shares of the common stock of the Company held in the Employer Common Stock Fund and attributable to his Account as of the Valuation Date coincident with or preceding the record date shall be voted at all stockholders' meetings. The Company shall appoint an independent third-party ("Agent") for the purpose of confidentially receiving and tallying the instructions from Participants. The Agent shall transmit such instructions solely to the Funding Agent. Neither the Funding Agent nor the third-party shall disclose such instructions to the Company or the Committee or any officer, director or affiliate. Any stock for which a signed voting-direction instrument is not received from the Participant, or is not subject to being received, shall be voted by the Funding Agent in the same proportion as the stock for which signed voting-direction instruments are received as to the matter to be voted upon.

12.2   *Ownership of Shares* Participants do not acquire ownership of common stock held by the Funding Agent in their Accounts until the Funding Agent delivers to them on termination stock certificates which have been registered in their names on the stock books of the Company.

12.3   *Tender Offers* A Participant may direct the Funding Agent in writing how to respond to a tender or exchange offer for any or all whole shares of Company stock held in the Employer Common Stock Fund and attributable to his Account as of the Valuation Date preceding, or coincident with, the offer. A Participant's instructions hereunder shall be confidential and shall not be disclosed to the Company or the Committee. The Committee shall notify each Participant and timely distribute or cause to be distributed to him such information as will be distributed to stockholders of the Company in connection with any such tender or exchange offer. The Committee shall engage an independent third-party ("Agent") to confidentially receive instructions from Participants and transmit them to the Funding Agent. The Agent shall transmit solely to the Funding Agent instructions of Participants and shall not disclose such instructions to the Company or the Committee. Upon receipt of such instructions, the Funding Agent shall tender such shares of Company stock as and to the extent so instructed. If the Funding Agent shall not receive instructions with respect to a Participant regarding any such tender or exchange offer for such shares of Company stock (or shall receive instructions not to tender or exchange such shares), the Funding Agent shall have no discretion in such matter and shall take no action with respect thereto. Any shares for which instructions are not subject to being received shall be tendered by the Funding Agent only in the same proportion as the stock for which instructions to tender are received. Any securities received by the Funding Agent as a result of a tender of shares of Company stock shall be held, and any cash so received, shall be invested in short-term investments for the Account of the Participant with respect to whom shares were tendered pending any reinvestment by the Funding Agent consistent with the purpose of the Plan.

ARTICLE 13: PLAN ADMINISTRATION

13.1 *Appointment of Committee* A Committee consisting of at least three (3) members shall be appointed by the Board to administer the Plan on behalf of the Board. Vacancies in the Committee shall be filled from time to time by appointment of a new Committee member by the Board. A member of the Committee shall hold office until he gives written notice of his resignation to the Board, until death, or until removal by the Board.

13.2 *Powers and Duties of the Committee*

(a) The Committee shall have full power, discretion, and authority to administer the Plan and to construe and apply all of its provisions on behalf of the Employer. The Committee is the Named Fiduciary within the meaning of Section 402(a) of ERISA for purposes of Plan administration. The Committee's powers and duties, unless properly delegated, shall include, but shall not be limited to:

(1) Designating agents to carry out responsibilities relating to the Plan, other than fiduciary responsibilities.

(2) Deciding questions relating to eligibility, continuity of employment, and amounts of benefits.

(3) Deciding disputes that may arise with regard to the rights of Employees, Participants or Beneficiaries and their legal representatives, under the terms of the Plan. Decisions by the Committee will be deemed final in each case.

binding upon all Participants in the Plan and upon all persons claiming any rights, including Beneficiaries.

13.7   *Payment of Expenses* The members of the Committee will serve without compensation for their services. The compensation or fees of consultants, actuaries, accountants, counsel and other specialists and any other costs of administering the Plan or Fund, will be paid by the Fund unless at the discretion of the Employer paid by the Employer.

13.8   *Claim Procedure* Any Participant or Beneficiary may submit a written application to the Committee for payment of any benefit that may be due him under the Plan. Such application shall set forth the nature of the claim and any information as the Committee may reasonably request. Upon receipt of any such application, the Committee shall determine whether or not the Participant or Beneficiary is entitled to the benefit hereunder.

If a claim is denied, in whole or in part, the Committee shall give written notice to any Participant or Beneficiary of the denial of a claim for the commencement, continuation or calculation of amount of retirement benefits under the Plan. The notice shall be given within ninety (90) days after receipt of the Participant's or Beneficiary application unless special circumstances require an extension for processing the claim. In no event shall such extension exceed a period of ninety (90) days from the end of such initial review period. The notice will be delivered to the claimant or sent to the claimant's last known address, and will include the specific reason or reasons for the denial, a specific reference or references to pertinent Plan provisions on which the denial is based, a description of any additional material or information for the claimant to perfect the claim, which will indicate why such material or information is needed, and an explanation of the Plan's claims review procedure.

If the claimant wishes to appeal the claim's denial, the claimant or a duly authorized representative will file a written request with the Committee for a review. This request must be made by the claimant within sixty (60) days after receiving notice of the claim's denial. The claimant or representative may review pertinent documents relating to the claim and its denial, may submit issues and comments in writing to the Committee and may request a hearing. Within sixty (60) days after receipt of such a request for review, the Committee shall reconsider the claim, and if the claimant shall have so requested, shall afford the claimant or his representative a hearing before the Committee and make a decision on the merits of the claim. If circumstances require an extension of time for processing the claim, the sixty (60) day period may be extended but in no event more than one hundred and twenty (120) days after the receipt of a request for review. The decision on review will be in writing and include specific reasons and references to the pertinent Plan provisions on which the decision is based.

ARTICLE 14: ESTABLISHMENT OF FUND

14.1   *Funding Agreement* Contributions made by the Employer and Participants pursuant to Articles 4 and 5 hereof shall be held in a Fund or Funds. The Employer shall enter into a trust arrangement, or a combination of a trust arrangement and insurance company contract(s), with one or more Funding Agents providing for the administration of the Fund or Funds in which the assets of this Plan are held.

ARTICLE 15: AMENDMENT, TERMINATION AND MERGER OF THE PLAN

15.1   *Right to Amend the Plan* The Employer reserves the right to modify, alter or amend this Plan from time to time to any extent that it may deem advisable including, but without limiting the generality of the foregoing, any amendment deemed necessary to ensure the continued qualification of the Plan under Section 401 of the Code or the appropriate provisions of any subsequent revenue law. No such amendment shall increase the duties or responsibilities of a Funding Agent without its consent thereto in writing. No such amendment(s) shall have the effect of reinvesting in the Employer the whole or any part of the principal or income to purposes other than for the exclusive benefit of

Participants or Beneficiaries at any time prior to the satisfaction of all the liabilities under the Plan with respect to such persons. No amendment shall reduce a Participant's Account balance on the effective date of the Plan amendment or eliminate an optional form of benefit under the Plan with respect to the Participant's Account balance on the date of the amendment. [In the case of any person who is subject to Section 16 of the Securities and Exchange Act of 1934, the Employer shall not amend the Plan regarding the amount, price and timing, within the meaning of the Securities and Exchange Commission's Rule 16(b)-3(c)(2)(ii)(A), of any contribution under the Plan more than once every six months.]

15.2   *Right to Terminate the Plan* The Employer shall have the right to terminate this Plan at any time. In the event of such termination all affected Participants shall be vested as provided in Section 10.4.

15.3   *Plan Mergers, Consolidations and Transfers* The Plan shall not be automatically terminated by the Employer's acquisition by or merger into any other company, trade or business, but the Plan shall be continued after such merger provided the successor employer agrees to continue the Plan with respect to affected Participants herein. All rights to amend, modify, suspend or terminate the Plan with respect to Participants of the Employer shall be transferred to the successor employer, effective as of the date of the merger or acquisition. The merger or consolidation with, or transfer of the allocable portion of the assets and liabilities of the Fund to any other qualified retirement plan trust shall be permitted only if the benefit each Plan Participant would receive, if the Plan were terminated immediately after such merger or consolidation, or transfer of the allocable portion of the assets and liabilities, would be at least as great as the benefit he would have received had this Plan been terminated immediately before the date of merger, consolidation or transfer.

15.4   *Amendment of Vesting Schedule* If the vesting provisions of this Plan are amended, including an amendment caused by the expiration of top-heavy status under the terms of

Article 16, Participants with three (3) or more Years of Service, or three (3) or more years of employment, whether or not consecutive, at the later of the date the amendment is adopted or becomes effective, shall automatically be vested, from that point forward, in the greater of the amount vested under the vesting schedule as amended or the amount vested under the vesting schedule prior to amendment.

ARTICLE 16: TOP-HEAVY PLAN REQUIREMENTS

16.1 *General Rule* For any Plan Year for which the Plan is a Top-Heavy Plan as defined in Section 16.5, any other provisions of the Plan to the contrary notwithstanding, the Plan shall be subject to the provisions of this Article 16.

16.2 *Vesting Provision* Each Participant who has completed an Hour of Service during the Plan Year in which the Plan is a Top-Heavy Plan and has completed the number of Years of Vesting Service specified in the following table, shall have a nonforfeitable right to the percentage of his Employer Account (other than the Qualified Nonelective Contribution subaccount) under this Plan, in accordance with the following table:

[Years of Vesting Service	The Vested Portion Is
Less than 3	0%
3 or more	100%]

[Years of Vesting Service	The Vested Portion Is
Less than 2	0%
2	20%
3	40%
4	60%
5	80%
6 or more	100%]

Each Participant's vested portion of his Employer Account shall not be less than his vested Employer Account determined as of the last day of the last Plan Year in which the Plan was not a Top-Heavy Plan. If the Plan ceases to be a

Top-Heavy Plan, an Employee with three or more years of employment, whether or not consecutive, shall have the vested portion of his Employer Account determined either in accordance with this Section 16.2 or Section 10.3, as provided in Section 15.4.

16.3 *Minimum Contribution Provisions* Each Eligible Employee who (i) is a non-key employee, as defined in Section 16.7, and (ii) is employed on the last day of the Plan Year, even if such Participant has failed to complete one thousand (1,000) Hours of Service during such Plan Year, shall be entitled to have an Employer contribution of not less than three percent (3%) of the Participant's compensation, as defined for purposes of Section 415 of the Code, allocated to his Employer Account.

The minimum contribution percentage set forth above shall be reduced for any Plan Year to the percentage at which contributions are made under the Plan for the Plan Year for the key employee, as defined in Section 16.7, for whom such percentage is the highest for such Plan Year. For this purpose, the percentage with respect to a key employee shall be determined by dividing the contributions for such key employee by his compensation, as defined for purposes of Section 415 of the Code.

Contributions taken into account under the immediately preceding sentence shall include contributions under the Plan, including Pretax Contributions, and under all other defined contribution and defined benefit plans required to be included in an aggregation group, as defined in Subsection 16.5(c), but shall not include any plan required to be included in such aggregation group if such plan enables a defined benefit plan required to be included in such group to meet the requirements of Sections 401(a)(4) and 410 of the Code.

Contributions taken into account under this Section 16.3 shall not include any contributions under Social Security or any other federal or state law.

16.4 *Coordination with Other Plans* In the event that another defined contribution plan or defined benefit plan maintained by the Employer or any Affiliated Employer provides contributions or benefits on behalf of Participants in the Plan, such other plan shall be treated as part of this Plan pursuant to applicable principles (such as Rev. Rul. 81-202 or any successor ruling) in determining whether this Plan satisfies the requirements of Sections 16.2 and 16.3.

16.5 *Top-Heavy Plan Definition* The Plan shall be a Top-Heavy Plan for any Plan Year if, as of the determination date, as defined in Subsection (a), the aggregate of the Accounts under the Plan for Participants who are key employees, as defined in Section 16.7, exceeds sixty percent (60%) of the present value of the aggregate of the Accounts for all Participants, or if this Plan is required to be in an aggregation group, as defined in Subsection (c), which for such Plan Year is a top-heavy group, as defined in Subsection (d). For purposes of making this determination, the Accounts of a Participant (i) who is not a key employee but who was a key employee in a prior Plan Year or (ii) who has not performed any service for the Employer at any time during the five (5) year period ending on the determination date, shall be disregarded.

(a) "Determination date" means for any Plan Year the last day of the immediately preceding Plan Year.

(b) The present value shall be determined as of the most recent Valuation Date that is within the twelve (12) month period ending on the determination date, and as described in the regulations prescribed under the Code. Present values for purposes of determining whether this Plan is a Top Heavy Plan shall be based on the following interest and mortality rates:

    (i) Interest Rate: _____

    (ii) Mortality Rate: _____

(c) "Aggregation group" means the group of plans, if any, that includes both the group of plans that are required to be aggregated and the group of plans that are permitted to be aggregated.

    (1) The group of plans that are required to be aggregated, the "required aggregation group," includes

        (i)   each plan of an Affiliated Employer, in which a key employee is a participant, including collectively bargained plans, and

        (ii)   each other plan of an Affiliated Employer, including collectively bargained plans, which enables a plan in which a key employee is a participant to meet the requirements of Sections 401(a)(4) and 410 of the Code.

    (2)   The group of plans that are permitted to be aggregated, the "permissive aggregation group," includes the required aggregation group plus one (1) or more plans of an Affiliated Employer, that is not part of the required aggregation group and that the Committee certifies as constituting a plan within the permissive aggregation group. Such plan or plans may be added to the permissive aggregation group only if benefits are comparable to those provided by the plans in the required aggregation group and, if after the addition, the aggregation group as a whole continues to meet the requirements of Sections 401(a)(4) and 410 of the Code.

(d)   "Top-heavy group" means the aggregation group, if, as of the applicable determination date, the sum of the present value of the cumulative accrued benefits for key employees under all defined benefit plans included in the aggregation group plus the aggregate of the accounts of key employees under all defined contribution plans included in the aggregation group exceeds sixty percent (60%) of the aggregate accrued benefits and accounts for all employees under such defined benefit and defined contribution plans. If the aggregation group that is a top-heavy group is a required aggregation group, each plan in the group will be top heavy. If the aggregation group that is a top-heavy group is a permissive aggregation group, only those plans that are part of the required aggregation group will be treated as top heavy. If the aggregation group is not a top-heavy group, no plan within such group will be top heavy.

(e)   In determining whether the Plan constitutes a Top-Heavy Plan, the Committee shall make the following adjustments in connection therewith:

(1)   When more than one (1) plan is aggregated, the Committee shall determine separately for each plan as of each plan's determination date the present value of the accrued benefits and account balances. The results shall then be aggregated by adding the results of each plan as of the determination dates for such plans that fall within the same calendar year.

(2)   In determining the present value of the cumulative accrued benefits or the value of the account of any Employee, such present value or account shall include the amount in dollar value of the aggregate distributions made to such Employee under the applicable plan during the five (5) year period ending on the determination date, unless reflected in the value of the accrued benefit or account balances as of the most recent Valuation Date. Such amounts shall include distributions to employees which represented the entire amount credited to their accounts under the applicable plan, and distributions made on account of the death of an employee to the extent such death benefits do not exceed the present value of the account.

(3)   Further, in making such determination, such present value or account shall include any Rollover Contribution, or similar transfer, as follows:

(i)   If the Rollover Contribution, or similar transfer, is initiated by the Employee and made to or from a plan maintained by another employer, the plan providing the distribution shall include such distribution in the present value or account; the plan accepting the distribution shall not include such distribution in the present value or account unless the plan accepted it before December 31, 1983.

(ii)   If the Rollover Contribution, or similar transfer, is not initiated by the Employee or made from a plan maintained by an Affiliated Employer, the plan accepting the distribution shall include such distribution in the present value or account whether the plan accepted the distribution before or after December 31, 1983; the plan making the distribution shall not include the distribution in the present value or such account.

16.6   *Change in 415(e) Limits* In the event the Employer also maintains a defined benefit plan that provides benefits to Participants in this Plan, and if the Plan is a Top-Heavy Plan, the combined plan limit of Section 415(e) of the Code shall be applied by substituting "1.0" for "1.25" in Code Sections 415(3)(2)(B) and 415(e)(3)(b). However, this provision does not apply if the Plan would not be a Top-Heavy Plan if "ninety percent (90%)" were substituted for "sixty percent (60%)" in Section 16.5 or if the Plan provides an Employer Contribution under Section 16.3 of not less than four percent (4%) of the Participant's compensation, as defined for purposes of Section 415 of the Code.

16.7   *Key Employee* The term "key employee" means any Employee, including former Employees under the Plan who, at any time during the Plan Year containing the determination date or during any of the four (4) preceding Plan Years, is or was one of the following:

(a)   An officer of an Affiliated Employer, having annual compensation from the Affiliated Employer greater than fifty percent (50%) of the dollar amount in effect under Code Section 415(b)(1)(A). Whether an individual is an officer shall be determined by the Committee on the basis of all the facts and circumstances, such as an individual's authority, duties and term of office, not on the mere fact that the individual has the title of an officer. For any such Plan Year, there shall be treated as officers no more than the lesser of (i) fifty (50) Employees, or (ii) the greater of three (3) Employees or ten percent (10%) of the greatest number of Employees. For this purpose, the highest paid officers shall be selected.

(b) One of the ten (10) Employees having annual compensation greater than the dollar limitation in effect under Code Section 415(c)(1)(A) and owning (or considered as owning, within the meaning of the constructive ownership rules of the Code) more than one-half percent (.5%) interest in the value and the largest percentage interests in an Affiliated Employer. An Employee who has such an ownership interest is considered to have one (1) of the largest interests in the Affiliated Employer unless at least ten (10) other Employees own a greater interest than that Employee during any year in the testing period and such other employees have annual compensation during such Plan Year of ownership greater than the dollar limitation in effect under Code Section 415(c)(1)(A) for the Plan Year. Ownership shall be determined on the basis of percentage of ownership interest in total ownership value and not dollar amounts.

(c) Any person who owns (or is considered as owning within the meaning of the constructive ownership rules of the Code) more than five percent (5%) of the outstanding stock of an Affiliated Employer or possessing more than five percent (5%) of the combined total voting power of an Affiliated Employer.

(d) A one percent (1%) owner of the outstanding stock of an Affiliated Employer having an annual compensation from the Affiliated Employer of more than one hundred fifty thousand dollars ($150,000).

For purposes of this Section 16.7, compensation shall mean compensation as defined in Section 414(q)(7) of the Code.

For purposes of Subsections (a), (b), (c) and (d) of this definition, a Beneficiary of a key employee shall be treated as a key employee. For purposes of Subsections (c) and (d), each Affiliated Employer is treated separately in determining ownership percentages; but in determining the amount of compensation, each Affiliated Employer is taken into account.

16.8   *Non-Key Employee* The term "non-key employee" means any employee and any Beneficiary of an employee who is not a key employee.

16.9   *Collective Bargaining Rules* The provisions of Sections 16.2, 16.3 and 16.4 do not apply with respect to any Employee included in a unit of employees covered by a collective bargaining agreement unless the application of such Sections has been agreed upon with the collective bargaining agent.

ARTICLE 17: MISCELLANEOUS

17.1   *Limitation on Distributions* Notwithstanding any provision of this Plan regarding payment to Beneficiaries or Participants, or any other person, the Committee may withhold payment to any person if the Committee determines that such payment may expose the Plan to conflicting claims for payment. As a condition for any payments, the Committee may require such consent, representations, releases, waivers or other information as it deems appropriate. To the extent required by law, the Committee shall comply with the terms of any judgment or other judicial decree, order, settlement or agreement including, but not limited to, a Qualified Domestic Relations Order as defined in Code Section 414(p).

17.2   *Limitation on Reversion of Contributions* Except as provided in subsections (a) through (c) below, Employer contributions made under the Plan will be held for the exclusive benefit of Participants or Beneficiaries and may not revert to the Employer.

   (a)   A contribution made by the Employer under a mistake of fact may be returned to the Employer within one (1) year after it is contributed to the Plan.

   (b)   A contribution conditioned on the Plan's initial qualification under Sections 401(a) and 501(a) of the Code may be returned to the Employer, if the Plan does not qualify, within one (1) year after the date the Plan is denied qualification.

(c) A contribution conditioned upon its deductibility under Section 404 of the Code may be returned, to the extent the deduction is disallowed, to the Employer within one (1) year after the disallowance.

The maximum contribution that may be returned to the Employer will not exceed the amount actually contributed to the Plan, or the value of such contribution on the date it is returned to the Employer, if less.

17.3 *Voluntary Plan* The Plan is purely voluntary on the part of the Employer and neither the establishment of the Plan nor any Plan amendment nor the creation of any fund or account, nor the payment of any benefits will be construed as giving any Employee or any person legal or equitable right against the Employer, any trustee or other Funding Agent, or the Committee unless specifically provided for in this Plan or conferred by affirmative action of the Committee or the Employer according to the terms and provisions of this Plan. Such actions will not be construed as giving any Employee or Participant the right to be retained in the service of the Employer. All Employees and / or Participants will remain subject to discharge to the same extent as though this Plan had not been established.

17.4 *Nonalienation of Benefits* Participants and Beneficiaries are entitled to all the benefits specifically set out under the terms of the Plan, but neither those benefits nor any of the property rights in the Plan are assignable or distributable to any creditor or other claimant of a Participant or Beneficiary. A Participant will not have the right to anticipate, assign, pledge, accelerate, or in any way dispose of or encumber any of the monies or benefits or other property that may be payable or become payable to such Participant or his Beneficiary provided, however, the Committee shall recognize and comply with a valid Qualified Domestic Relations Order as defined in Code Section 414(p).

17.5 *Inability to Receive Benefits* If the Committee receives evidence that a person entitled to receive any payment under the Plan is physically or mentally incompetent to receive payment and to give a valid release, and another person or any institution is maintaining or has custody of such person, and no guardian, committee, or other representative of the estate of such person has been duly appointed by a court of competent jurisdiction, then any distribution made under the Plan may be made to such other person or institution. The release of such other person or institution will be a valid and complete discharge for the payment of such distribution.

17.6 *Missing Persons* If the Committee is unable, after reasonable and diligent effort, to locate a Participant or Beneficiary where no contingent beneficiary is provided under the Plan, who is entitled to a distribution under the Plan, the distribution due such person will be forfeited after five (5) years. If, however, such a person later files a claim for such benefit, it will be reinstated without any interest earned thereon. In the event that a distribution is due to a Beneficiary where a contingent beneficiary is provided under the Plan (including the situation on which the contingent beneficiary is the Participant's estate), and the Committee is unable, after reasonable and diligent effort, to locate the Beneficiary, the benefit shall be payable to the contingent beneficiary, and such non-locatable Beneficiary shall have no further claim or interest hereunder. Notification by certified or registered mail to the last known address of the Participant or Beneficiary will be deemed a reasonable and diligent effort to locate such person.

17.7 *Limitation of Third Party Rights* Nothing expressed or implied in the Plan is intended or will be construed to confer upon or give to any person, firm, or association other than the Employer, the Participants or Beneficiaries, and their successors in interest, any right, remedy, or claim under or by reason of this Plan except pursuant to a Qualified Domestic Relations Order as defined in Code Section 414(p).

17.8 *Invalid Provisions* In case any provision of this Plan is held illegal or invalid for any reason, the illegality or invalidity will not affect the remaining parts of the Plan. The Plan will be construed and enforced as if the illegal and invalid provisions had never been included.

17.9   *One Plan* This Plan may be executed in any number of
        counterparts, each of which will be deemed an original and
        the counterparts will constitute one and the same instru-
        ment and may be sufficiently evidenced by any one
        counterpart.

17.10   *Use and Form of Words* Whenever any words are used herein
        in the masculine gender, they will be construed as though
        they were also used in the feminine gender in all cases
        where that gender would apply, and vice versa. Whenever
        any words are used herein in the singular form, they will be
        construed as though they were also used in the plural form
        in all cases where the plural form would apply, and vice
        versa.

17.11   *Headings* Headings to Articles and Sections are inserted
        solely for convenience and reference, and in the case of any
        conflict, the text, rather than the headings, shall control.

17.12   *Governing Law* The Plan will be governed by and construed
        according to the federal laws governing employee benefit
        plans qualified under the Code and according to the laws
        of the state of _____ where such laws are not in con-
        flict with the federal laws.

        IN WITNESS WHEREOF, _____has
        adopted this Plan effective _____.

        _____

        ATTEST: By:_____
                  By:_____
                  Title:_____
                  Date:_____